10/03 $1—

D0953777

WILL THIS DO?

For my Grand-daughter
Constance Watson

WILL THIS DO?

The First Fifty Years of
AUBERON WAUGH

An Autobiography

CARROLL & GRAF PUBLISHERS, INC.
NEW YORK

First Carroll & Graf edition 1998
Second Printing June 1998

Carroll & Graf Publishers
19 West 21st Street
New York, NY 10010-6805

Library of Congress Cataloging-in-Publication Data is available.
ISBN: 0-7867-0519-1

Manufactured in the United States of America

CONTENTS

By the same author

Apologia

Various motives may be ascribed to an autobiographer, the least attractive of which is self-justification, whether in the sense of paying off old scores, answering critics or simply promoting a winsome self-portrait. I do not think this has been my intention, although it is true that the children of Evelyn Waugh did not come particularly well out of his published letters and diaries. Thus on 23 December, 1946, he complains:

> The presence of my children affects me with deep weariness and depression. I do not see them until luncheon, as I have my breakfast alone in the library, and they are in fact well trained to avoid my part of the house, but I am aware of them from the moment I wake. Luncheon is very painful. Teresa has a mincing habit of speech and a pert, humourless style of wit, Bron is clumsy and dishevelled, sly, without intellectual, aesthetic or spiritual interest. . . .

This stern criticism, applied to a boy who had only just celebrated his seventh birthday, obviously demands some sort of reply. It continues throughout the *Letters* and *Diaries* of Evelyn Waugh with only a few breaks until his death at the age of sixty-two on 10 April 1966. I can do no more than promise that the motive behind this book is most emphatically not to reinstate its author, or his brothers or sisters. I have always been rather proud of the monstrous child and even worse adolescent to be found at those painful luncheons. The descriptions of them in Chapter Two offer an alternative, but not a contradictory, perception. I had thought, at one stage, to cover the ground with a short memoir of Evelyn Waugh but could not decide what to call him: Evelyn? Unthinkable. Papa? Too sentimental. Waugh? I did not dare. The problem remains unresolved even in this volume.

If the question of motive is pressed, I suppose I will have to fall back, as my first position, on the simple explanation that a professional writer has only so many shots in his locker, and autobiography is one of them. Why otherwise, apart from vulgar exhibitionism, should anyone seek his merits to disclose, or draw his frailties from their dread abode? Perhaps this account of my first fifty years, written while the sap is still rising, if only in a sluggish and unattractive motion, will prompt important questions about the meaning and purpose of life – if such elevated thoughts can be inspired by a collection of half-remembered anecdotes, jokes and inaccurate gossip. But as I tried to assemble the salient events of my own absurd and chaotic progress, a thought did occur to me.

One of the reasons for writing the book might have been to offer a little anthem of thanks – some would call it a prayer – for the comfortable and agreeable life I enjoy now at fifty, and have enjoyed, with only one or two remissions, for most of my life. Nearly everybody who has lived in Britain in the period between 1939 and 1991 has been prodigiously lucky compared to those who lived in most other places at most other times. Some might call it a prayer. Others, a gloat.

Like many of those born into the English upper middle class, I have sometimes been tempted to think that life might have been even more agreeable for my maternal grandfather, Aubrey Herbert, for instance, who had not only a fine mansion in Somerset to live in, with five thousand acres, but also a large house in Bruton Street, Mayfair and a palatial villa and estate in Portofino, Italy.

But Herbert lived only a short life between 1880 and 1923 and was almost blind; medical knowledge at the time was insufficient to cure him. He experienced the horrors of the First World War at the retreat from Mons and Gallipoli; possibly as a form of self-punishment, he spent most of his adult life travelling rough in bandit-infested areas of the near East. As if this were not punishment enough, he held a seat in Parliament for the last twelve years of his life, even if he did not attend very often. His premature death, at the age of forty-three, was caused by the foolish advice of a friend that the best cure for blindness was having the teeth drawn. This resulted in blood poisoning. Few of us can suppose his life was more comfortable or agreeable than our own, for all its apparent privilege.

Perhaps all lives reduce, outside the imponderable perception of God, to a scrapbook of false or partial recollections, deliberate evasions and suppressions. But I should make it plain that this is only *an* autobiography. It has no claim to be definitive. My Uncle Alec Waugh wrote innumerable autobiographies, as the mood took him. It is quite possible that if I am still alive in ten years time, I shall have written half a dozen of them, each telling an entirely different story. Any change of mood or circumstance may produce a flood of new memories. Many who have lived more interesting lives than my own – Galahad Threepwood springs to mind – spend their later years composing endless memoirs which, through some awkward spirit of perfectionism, they never actually publish. That is not my failing. The only question left hanging in the air is the one which every journalist asks himself on submitting an article. It is also the one with which we may all eventually, in trembling hope, face our Maker: *Will this do?*

Combe Florey
16 November 1990

Part I
Youth

CHAPTER ONE

Pixton 1939-1945

I was born just before midnight on 17 November 1939 at Pixton Park, Dulverton, Somerset, the home of my maternal grandmother, Mary Herbert.

Two and a half months earlier, the Second World War had been declared. An elderly Austrian countess, Gretel Coudenhove-Kalergi, was staying at Pixton at the time with her maid, called Betty. They decided to remain at Pixton for the duration, occupying two of the best bedrooms on the first floor. Nobody, so far as I know, queried their right to stay, and there was never any question of their paying for their keep. In the afternoons they went for a walk in the park, and at mealtimes the countess was to be found at the dining-room table. She revealed Japanese blood by an impenetrable oriental smile. Nobody talked to her much because there was little to say. After she had stayed about a year, she started presenting my grandmother with little water-colours she painted, showing flowers, butterflies and occasionally Pekineses in a style which might be identified as central European mid-1930s rococo chinoiserie. They were terribly, terribly ugly, but my grandmother loyally had them all framed or made into place-mats or lampshades. After the war, it was thought the countess might have left, but it turned out that the Red Army was in occupation of her family estates so she stayed for a few more years, no doubt contributing the occasional extra lampshade of great ugliness.

I mention Countess Coudenhove-Kalergi at such length, and at such an early stage, because a description of Pixton has to start somewhere. The countess was not a particularly close friend of anyone's but had entertained my senior aunt, Gabriel, in Vienna at some time before the Anschluss. She just stayed on, joining a large population of retired nannies, housekeepers and maids who occupied different parts of the house, living their own lives and jealously protecting their own territory.

The house was the model for Boot Magna Hall, in *Scoop*, which Evelyn Waugh started writing on return from his honeymoon in 1937. In fact, some of it was written at Pixton. My mother was not pleased to see her family home held up to ridicule in this way, and always identified *Scoop* as her least favourite of the novels, although she never gave the reason for this, at any rate in my hearing.

I do not know if my grandmother ever made the connection between Pixton and Boot Magna Hall. Perhaps she never read the book. Her temper, in those days, was uncertain and her relations with her son-in-law were always a trifle strained, ever since their first meeting four years earlier when she had received him at the family home in Portofino as a friend of her eldest daughter, Gabriel – and ex-husband of her niece, Evelyn Gardner. On that occasion she drove him from the house by pelting him with hard Italian buns. I never saw my father look comfortable or happy at Pixton. Much grander houses made him welcome and part of themselves. At Pixton, there was the subtle suggestion that he did not belong.

All the fiercer, then, the pride and joy of those who felt they did belong. Although I spent only the first six years of my life at Pixton, along with the exotic countess and others who made up the extended household – aunts, cousins, retired nannies and household servants in various states of physical disarray – I returned there for several visits a year throughout my childhood and continued visiting it often until Uncle Auberon's death in 1974. As a result, and because it is such a large, grand and unusual place, it lived and continues to live in my imagination, although long since sold.

I have mentioned the various aged, retired nannies and servants living in different parts of the house. Also to be found from time to time were elderly relatives, who threatened to settle more or less permanently: Granny Grace was in fact my step-great-great-grandmother, widow of my great-great-grandfather, the tenth Lord Wemyss, whom she married in 1900 when his lordship was already eighty-two years old. Hers was the first naked female form I saw. In old age, she did not lock the bathroom door when she had a bath, for fear she should fall down or suffer a seizure. At the age of three I wandered into her bathroom on a general tour of inspection. Having studied her agitated form for a few minutes, I said to her – or so she afterwards claimed: 'How beautiful you are looking today, Granny Grace.'

It was exactly the right thing to say, of course. I would like to think that the experience helped me in later years in my relations with women.

Another very elderly relation who often threatened to settle was called Cousin Gerry Liddell. She was an aunt of Guy Liddell, the deputy head of M.I.5, an amiable man who recruited large sections of White's Club to protect us from spies and fifth columnists in the Second World War – among them my Uncle Eddie Grant, who also stayed at Pixton between important assignments watching fascist agents among the pheasant coverts of north Devon and Shropshire. But I do not think I ever saw Cousin Gerry without her clothes. She played the piano very loudly in a way which was thought quite creditable for someone who was stone-deaf. I do not suppose the piano had been tuned for many years, in any case.

Pixton, in the early 1940s when I started to become aware of things, was already several stages down the road of change and decay described at Boot Magna Hall in *Scoop*. My grandmother, who was born Mary Vesey, only child of the fourth Lord de Vesci, had spent part of her childhood at the de Vesci seat in Ireland, Abbeyleix – in many ways an even larger version of Pixton. The Irish side of her did not see anything odd in the decrepitude. My father had a story of going into the drawing-room at Pixton during the war and finding Hilaire Belloc pulling furiously at a bell. 'Ze footmen, zey sit in ze pantry and zey say: "Hold, it is a Poet who has rung. We shall not answer."'

Of course the bell had been disconnected for many years, probably since my grandfather's tragically premature death in 1923. Far from there being young footmen in the pantry to scoff at the poet's summons, there might have been one very old retainer, probably lame, almost certainly stone-deaf.

Belloc was a fairly frequent visitor to Pixton in the capacity of old family friend, having been hired as a tutor to my grandfather, Aubrey Herbert, both before and during his Oxford career. Befc his death, my grandfather was playing with the idea of converti. to Catholicism, and it may have been Belloc's influence whic later helped to push my grandmother over the threshold. Belloc was quite a terrifying old man with a huge white beard by the time I saw him. On our first meeting, he identified me as an evacuee child from the East End of London, of a type who were then swarming over the top floor of Pixton, and kicked me out of the Pixton drawing-room.

I was not particularly surprised. As a child, living in the nursery wing with various cousins, my status was by no means clear. Perhaps I ranked above the evacuees, but on an absolute par with children of the servants, and considerably below any gardener's boy who actually worked. I say I was not surprised to find myself kicked by this furious, bearded man, but I certainly bore resentment. It was many years before I could think of Belloc as anything but an unpleasant old fraud, through all the paeans of praise for him on every side. Before the war, he would come to Pixton every year for the wine bottling. They would buy a hogshead or barrel of wine and bottle it in the cellars, using an antique, manually operated bottling machine. Belloc insisted that this should be done in the dark by the light of a candle, which considerably slowed things up, while they all sang idiotic French songs in affected voices. As late as the early 1970s we found a cache of these Belloc bottlings in the Pixton cellars and tried drinking them. They were utterly disgusting, although my Uncle Auberon, who had no sense of taste and could not distinguish between pepper and nutmeg on his junket, swore to the contrary.

Pixton is a large Georgian house, of enormous charm but no great distinction, set in beautiful Exmoor parkland. Apart from an ugly service wing built by my grandfather, it consists of a single rectangular box of three storeys, illuminated in the centre by a huge well, perhaps 80 feet by 20 feet by 50 feet high to a sky-light at the top. The two upper storeys look on this well by a balcony corridor on four sides; at the bottom of it is one of five halls through which everyone had to pass in order to reach the dining-room, drawing-room, sitting-room, library or any other part of the house.

As a child, I once counted fifty-four rooms in Pixton. I am not prepared to attempt the feat again, and allowing for a tendency towards aggrandisement, by which a single lavatory was liable to be counted as a room, I might settle for forty. But it is a big house, thoroughly secluded and self-sufficient. A stable and garage block included three cottages. There were lodges, farmhouses and, in those days, the estate encompassed the villages of Bury, King's Brompton, Brushford and most of Upton. A great danger was that it would all be taken over by the army for the duration. Few houses survived this treatment. Even if they were not burned down, they lost their staircases, wood panelling and floors and most of their finer points. Fortunately, the chief billeting officer in the area was my beautiful young aunt, Bridget. She arranged for Pixton to receive thirty-five pre-school age children from the Westminster area of London. As soon as they reached school age, with all the greater destructive potential that implied, they were whisked away to another billet, usually a farmhouse in some distant village, where the farmers were responsible for taking them to school.

So at Pixton we had thirty-five evacuated toddlers, with five helpers under Miss Joan Haigh from Worthing. The toddlers were all put on the top floor, behind the wooden balustrade which separated them from a drop of fifty feet into the hall below. A fat Belgian woman was found to cook for them and an extra kitchen was equipped in the service wing. The helpers, for some reason best known to themselves, chose the hall underneath this great well to eat their meals. It was a foolish choice. The 'evacuees', as the toddlers were called, although not able to climb over the balustrade, could stick their heads through the balusters and watch events fifty feet below them. From their heads fell curious shapes and substances, most particularly lice, which they had either brought with them from Westminster or summoned, like so many Pied Pipers, out of the Somerset countryside. Worse than this, they became devilishly accurate at spitting. Long after the helpers had decided to eat their meals elsewhere, anyone walking through this inner hall, which connects every part of the main house with every other part, was liable to run the gauntlet of thirty-five dedicated marksmen. Visitors may or may not have noticed the 'phlitt', 'sput', 'flop' noises around them as they walked through the hall before becoming victim of a direct hit.

For reasons which I cannot explain, the texture and smell of this spittle was particularly offensive. As a grandson of the house, it was my privilege to walk through the hall whenever I felt like it, always keeping a weather-eye open for violent, white-bearded poets or jocular M.I.5 officers in the person of my Uncle Eddie Grant who might pretend to throw a dog's water bowl at me as a joke. I resented being spat upon more than I can say. When a grown-up glared at the top floor and shook his fist, the heads disappeared but I, at the age of three, lacked the authority or the ability to inspire terror. If I stood still to remonstrate, the chances were that they would score more direct hits.

But I got my revenge. At some point, the house suffered from a plague of mice or rats. Or perhaps the local rat-catcher was making a routine visit. I followed him around fascinated, holding his poison bag made of sacking and watching as he mixed poison with bait before putting it out with a collection of long-handled spoons. Pixton had an antiquated central heating system – never, I think, used in my lifetime – which included under-floor flues and passages through which a small boy could easily crawl. It was connected with the world of grown-ups by handsome, cast-iron grilles. The rat-catcher and I became tremendous friends as I followed him around, and I gave him my word of honour that I would not go back and eat any of his poison, as I very much wanted to do.

Instead, I went up to my grandmother and engaged her in conversation, as it was my privilege to do if ever I could think of anything to say.

'Aren't the evacuees *disgusting*, Granny?' I said.

'Oh, I don't know,' she replied, judicially. She often spoke as if she were addressing a committee and hoping to win its approval for some particular sentiment or course of action. 'Some of them seem all right, really. What? What?'

'No, I think they are disgusting,' I said.

'Why so?' she said.

'Well, do you know the rat-catcher, Tom? After he had been putting his bread everywhere for the rats, the evacuees went and ate it all up. Don't you think that was dirty, Granny? And *greedy*? I think the evacuees are disgusting.'

'What? What?' said my grandmother. At a hastily assembled identification parade, I picked out five or six of the evacuees, including a boy called Jackie whom I had identified as a particular enemy. They were taken away and stomach-pumped.

I do not suppose it did them much permanent harm, although it might have done, I suppose. At the age of three I was scarcely in a position to weigh up all the consequences of an instinctive act of revenge. Perhaps it had done me harm to be spat upon from a great height. I do not know. All I know for certain is that this was my first gesture of reprisal in the class war which has occupied so much of my time ever since.

Of course the whole idea of class war was deeply repugnant to the Pixton ethos, and to everything it stood for. Old England ran on a benevolent, mutually dependent relationship between the classes, most particularly between the very rich and the very poor, but as a three-year-old product of the bourgeois cultural elite, I did not really represent the threatened interests of land and property. The rich are terrified of the class war, and tend to play it down, being convinced that they will always lose it.

* * * *

I have described myself, at three, as a product of the bourgeois cultural elite, and anybody who has studied Evelyn Waugh's account of his antecedents and social background in the first and only volume of his autobiography, *A Little Learning* (London, Chapman & Hall, 1964), will be able to judge the accuracy of that. In summary my father, Evelyn Waugh, was a successful and widely revered writer; his father, Arthur Waugh, a successful publisher and respected man of letters; his father, Dr Alexander Waugh, a prosperous and surprisingly well-liked general practitioner in Somerset; his father, the Reverend James Hay Waugh, a mildly ridiculous but distinctly rich clergyman in Dorset and Somerset; his father, Revd Dr Alexander Waugh, an eminent divine in London. Before that, for four or five generations, the Waughs were prosperous yeoman farmers near Greenlaw, in Berwickshire, but not intellectually eminent.

My mother's family was altogether grander in every respect. My grandmother, Mary Herbert, was the widow of Aubrey Herbert, the legendary, heroic figure who was the model for John Buchan's eponymous hero in the novel *Greenmantle*. A full account of Aubrey's life can be found in the biography written by my sister, Margaret FitzHerbert: *The Man Who Was Greenmantle* (London, Murray, 1983). Aubrey's father, the fourth Earl of Carnarvon, was a cabinet minister in three administrations and, briefly, Viceroy of

Ireland. His mother, already a first cousin, was of the ducal and
illustrious family of Howard, which, as Burke puts it, 'stands next
to the Blood Royal at the head of the peerage of England'. My
grandmother, Mary Vesey, was daughter of the legendary beauty
and member of the Souls, Evelyn de Vesci, herself born Charteris,
daughter of the tenth Lord Wemyss and Lady Anne Anson. My
grandmother's father, the fourth Lord de Vesci, was son of the
third Viscount and Lady Emma Herbert, daughter of the tenth
Lord Pembroke, the senior branch of Aubrey Herbert's family.
Being an only child, Mary Vesey brought a certain amount of
Vesey loot into the family, including some extraordinary Russian
china in the manner of Sèvres from the eleventh Lord Pembroke,
Lady Emma's father, who married Catherine, daughter of the
Russian ambassador, Count Woronzow, in 1808...

Perhaps only professional snobs will be able to derive much en-
lightenment from my mother's pedigree, and not even they can
hope to experience quite the same degree of satisfaction as I do
when I contemplate it. But the point about the Herberts is not so
much that they were well born or well connected – many hundreds of families were just as well favoured in those ways – or
even that, through the centuries, they had emerged with plenty of
money, land, houses and furniture. Several thousand families
must have been richer than they were. The point about them –
and the Veseys, the Charterises, even, to a lesser extent, the
Howards – was that they were intelligent, witty and educated
people, moving in the inner circle of the fashionable, aristocratic
and rich. Houses and families rise and fall not only by the wealth
or possessions they enjoy, but also by the personalities in each
generation. Some great houses, like Blenheim, might be occupied
by speechless or drawling nincompoops for several generations;
others, like Badminton, perhaps, by people whose entire view of
life was restricted to the gap between the two ears of a horse. In
my grandparents' day, there were no more than half a dozen
houses which might be seen as being at the centre of things – Hat-
field, perhaps Stanway, Longleat, Haddon – and it was within that
group that my maternal grandparents, their parents and their
friends were to be found.

Somerset has many fine houses and impressive estates but
none, apart from Pixton and Mells (home of the Horners, later
Asquiths), had any claim to belong to the beau monde. At Pixton,

in Aubrey Herbert's time, you would find the Prime Minister (Asquith) staying one week-end, T.E. Lawrence the next. In my childhood the dining-room ceiling was spattered with George V postage stamps which had been fixed there by James Barrie, author of *Peter Pan*, who put them, licked, face down on a penny which he then threw at the ceiling. Maurice Baring was a frequent visitor as well as Belloc, who composed a little poem to my grandmother and her three daughters, called the 'Three Graces of Pixton':

> Three Graces – and the Mother were a Grace
> But for profounder meaning in her face.

Everybody agreed that this was very civil.

The Three Graces were still in residence, and remained so for much of the war: my mother, Laura, the youngest of them, Bridget, married to Major Grant, and Gabriel, the eldest; who had an exciting life before the war, driving ambulances and lorries for Franco's forces in Spain. She volunteered at the outbreak of the Second World War for the job of breaking the news to soldiers' families that their son, brother or loved one had been killed or wounded, but it turned out that the job did not exist, and her war work would consist for the most part of selling cakes and sandwiches to Polish airmen in Shropshire. Halfway through the war Gabriel decided to get married, and her choice fell on a small but dapper Downside man of French extraction called Alick Dru. Dru, who had lost most of his money before the war in a scheme he shared with Douglas Woodruff to make mead the national drink of England, was another of these wartime majors on the General Service list. In fact he retained this title to his dying day, although never striking me as a very military man. After the war it turned out that he was a philosopher, with a particular interest in Kirkegaard, the Danish theologian, whose study by T. Harcken he had translated in 1936, and Charles Péguy, the French socialist on whom he published a study in 1956. Apart from those two slim volumes, and a few articles in the *Downside Review*, I do not think that Alick Dru ever did a hand's turn of work in his life.

Alick Dru is not to be confused with my other uncle, Alec Waugh, who will appear in the next chapter. Alec had no hair from an early age, losing it while a prisoner in the Great War. He worked hard all his life, and wrote many books, each worse than the last. Alick, by contrast, had a fine head of hair to the very end and wrote only the two books. Alec Waugh never moved in very smart literary circles, but Dru was a close friend of Anthony Powell and discussed French literature with Duff Cooper, the Tory politician who is remembered for having persecuted P.G. Wodehouse during the war.

Dru took an interest in pig-breeding at one time. A mischievous story of my father's maintained that he would whip the pigs to death in order to tenderize the meat, but I never saw him do anything so energetic. It may have been inspired by what I believe to be a true story about Gabriel: that she travelled up to London once to record a talk for the BBC on the preparation of a calf for the table. When they played the tape and discovered how she recommended that calves should be blown up with a bicycle pump before being knocked on the head, they declined to broadcast it.

Although keenly appreciative of the good things of life, Alick was primarily a philosopher, and this may well have given him the strength necessary to face a life without work. 'I am living on my wife's money', he would explain proudly, if anyone asked. He was a generous and witty host, who seldom seemed depressed by the emptiness of his days but who lived his life as the true philosopher should, always looking forward to the next treat.

At any rate, it was to the wedding of Gabriel and Alick that I went as page, dressed up in a sailor's suit, on 6 March 1943. My sister and two Grant cousins, who were bridesmaids, were sick in the car on the way to church. After the marriage service, the couple were taken to call on the widow of the Pixton chauffeur, called Bastable, who had recently died. 'No doubt you will be wanting to see Bastable,' she said simply, and led them both – him in his smart major's uniform, her in her wedding dress and train – into the front room where Bastable's body was laid out for inspection.

Bridget, the second and most beautiful of the Three Graces of Pixton, had already had two daughters before the outbreak of war: Christine, called Polly, and Anne. They and my own elder sister, Teresa, formed a gang from which I was for the most part excluded. Polly and Teresa must already have started on some sort of religious instruction, possibly from Father O'Brien, who lived in one of the cottages of the stable block and held services in an old tin hut in the wood, or possibly from Lizzie, an old Irish washer-woman who had come from Abbeyleix and who doubled up as the priest's housekeeper and parish *catechiste*. At any rate I distinctly remember being tied to a wooden frame in the shape of a crucifix and stuck with pins by Polly and Teresa, aided by Constant, elder son of the fat Belgian cook, until I agreed to confess all my sins.

At the age of three I had very little idea of sin. Sins had to be invented to supply the demand. As a result of this forced confession, the youth Constant wrote 'Bronnie is a Liar' on a slate and nailed it, beyond my reach, to the trunk of a tree. I threw stones at it unsuccessfully, and so did Constant's younger brother, called Jean-Jean. Eventually it was destroyed, as an act of kindness, by a much older boy, called John Ledley, who had somehow joined the huge floating population of children and grown-ups at Pixton. John Ledley was my hero.

At the age of three I could see that it was true that I was a liar. Throughout all my childhood I was held up as a notoriously bad person, and I had no possible reason to dispute that judgement. However, I do remember reflecting bitterly at the age of three-and-a-half, after a tremendous row in which I was accused of pouring forty people's monthly ration of flour into a water tank in the garage: why did people not inform me that an act was evil *before* I had done it?

That year, our Amory neighbours brought their aged father-in-law up to meet my grandmother at Pixton. Old Colonel Amory was about ninety-three and stood with great difficulty on two sticks. Gaenor Amory, the mother of my friend Mark, remembers that I led her aside and told her I was going to kick the old man's sticks away. 'What do you think will happen?' I asked. 'Won't it be funny?'

Despite my reputation, I do not think I ever did anything very wicked. I might have killed some ducks with a boy called David Bottle, who was the son of a nanny called Nanny Bottle. I remember the punishment and the blame for having killed the ducks and I remember hiding under a bed in the night nursery to escape detection, but I have no memory of actually killing them, which would surely be the most memorable part of the episode. I even have a vague memory of doubting my own guilt. It is quite possible that David Bottle alone was guilty of this crime.

As for the rest, I have a memory – although it might be no more than the memory of a dream – that my self-appointed enemy among the evacuees, called Jackie, ended up being sawn in half at the Pixton sawmills. I often wondered whether I had any part in it. The sawmills at Pixton, situated about three-quarters of a mile from the house on a watercourse which in those days also supplied the house with electricity, certainly had a huge circular saw, built on a long line of rollers along which tree trunks were pushed to be turned into planks. Many comics and several horror films have featured similar machines. All I really remember is *hearing* that one of the evacuees had been sawn in half – possibly many years later – and feeling some slight anxiety about it.

*   *   *   *

On 6 March 1943 my Uncle Auberon celebrated his twenty-first birthday. This may not seem to be such an important event to those unfamiliar with the workings of an English landed estate at this time. It would be easy to forget how feudal things still were in the countryside. When my grandparents came back to Pixton after their honeymoon in 1910, they were pulled in a· carriage all the way from Dulverton station by cheering tenants – a distance of more than a mile up some very steep terrain if they used Pixton's station drive, more than twice that distance if the procession went through Dulverton, as I rather fancy it did.

Auberon's twenty-first birthday party was the second and last occasion for me to wear the sailor suit which had been produced out of some acting cupboard or other scarcely more than a month previously for the occasion of my Aunt Gabriel's marriage to her intelligent, twinkle-toed Frenchman. As Auberon never married, dying a bachelor at the age of fifty-two in 1974, there was never another occasion for the Pixton estate to parade in all its feudal glory. Auberon had an unmistakably brilliant mind and a quick if quirky wit. He was much missed when he died, in the somewhat eclectic circles he frequented. These were Polish, Ukrainian and Byelorussian exiles, for the most part, but in later life he came into some more money, through selling an almost uncultivatable valley to the Water Board, and filled Pixton once again with the young and fashionable – if not quite the *jeunesse dorée* of 1970-74, at any rate their older brothers and sisters. His mother, my grandmother, did not die until 1971, in distressing old age. Although I had loved her extravagantly, with her air of complete if benign authority over everybody in England and most people in foreign parts, one could not mourn her death under the circumstances.

Auberon, who was to die suddenly and young, probably from many years of over-eating, was a more bitter blow. Despite having no sense of taste, he was very greedy. If he had been less protected by great estates and a certain amount of money (although never enough), I suspect that life would have treated him very roughly indeed. During the war, which he served as a lorry-driver in the Polish army, he was mistaken for a German spy and severely beaten up by some Canadians. In later life he visited Canada to lecture to the tens of thousands of Ukrainians who settled there, but he never really forgave them for what they had done to him. In fairness to Canadians, however, one must admit that few people can ever have looked more like a German spy than my Uncle Auberon, with his mysterious foreign accent, his flat face, crinkled hair and rolled back of the neck.

Perhaps there was also a certain warmth lacking, a certain reluctance to commit his affections. As I wrote at the time of his death, in a life apparently dedicated to enjoyment, it was never very clear how much he had enjoyed. His twenty-first birthday party, celebrated on 25 April 1943, took place nearly twenty years after the death of his legendary, heroic father, Aubrey Herbert.

Few enough people remembered Aubrey by the time of this birthday, but in a curious way Auberon lived under his shadow. Aubrey was rumoured to have jumped across the well on the top landing at Pixton; it seems inconceivable that he did so, but everybody believed it. Auberon was neither agile enough nor brave enough to jump over the doormat inside Pixton's front door. It was decided he should follow his father into Parliament, as the obvious thing for a young man with nothing else to do. First he fought the safe Labour seat of Port Talbot in the Conservative interest, cunningly describing himself among other things as National Labour and delivering impassioned speeches about Eastern Europe in fluent Welsh to the gaping steel workers there. But it didn't work. Nor could he talk the Sunderland miners out of their allegiance to Labour. The unkindest cut was when Taunton Conservatives rejected him as their candidate in preference for Edward du Cann, a London businessman, at which point he gave up the unequal struggle.

Perhaps he was also an agent of the secret intelligence service

as he sometimes hinted. This would explain his apparently point-
less trips up and down the Iron Curtain. But I rather doubt it.

At his twenty-first birthday party I was permitted to watch
through the bannisters of the front staircase as loyal speeches
were made by Mr Chilcott, the estate's head carpenter, cheered on
by Tommy the plumber, Walter who delivered the wood, three
gardeners, Mr Crossman the new gamekeeper, Reggie the groom,
Mr Gosse the agent, and a veritable army of people who came out
from bootholes and furnace rooms, laundries and dairies in addition to tenants and farmworkers. The constraints of wartime food
rationing had somehow been circumvented by trays and trays of
faggots, made from pigs' offal by the cook, Mrs McKay, and many
helpers in the huge kitchen at the end of the service wing, with its
racks of copper moulds, its sculleries and stillrooms smelling of
ancient meat stock.

It is odd to have taken part in these occasions which belonged to
the Victorian or Edwardian eras, but I am not sure it was a very
good preparation for modern life. The entire upper class of
England – and Scotland and Northern Ireland, for all I know –
cherishes the memory of its own Pixtons. To some, they are the
Eden from which they have been exiled by social progress in
general and socialism in particular. In fact, generation after generation of the English upper class has been similarly exiled by the
savage custom of primogeniture. Some younger sons went to the
colonies, and dreamed of rose-trellised manor houses as they sat
on verandas in the appalling heat of Burma or West Africa's fever
coast. Others joined the services, where they brutalized and were
brutalized. Yet others went into Holy Orders and lived in genteel
poverty. Just a few went into business to make enough money to
start the cycle again. But nearly all lived in exile. To pretend that
life at Pixton represented some sort of norm or state of grace from
which a bad world had fallen, was always dangerous nonsense.

The Waughs, rooted in the traditions of the professional upper-
middle class, were never in much danger of falling into the trap of
supposing that the world owed them a living, a characteristic of
aristocrat and new proletarian alike. Pixton remained a good
memory, the aristocratic or Herbert side of their pedigree a
curiosity, no more – certainly not an alternative identity.

Auberon, on the other hand, never really recovered from finding
himself, an only son, the inheritor of Pixton. His enormous talents

– he spoke six languages fluently, and could make an excellent speech in any of them – were never put to any use beyond the entertainment of his friends and exasperation of his relations. He was very large, flat-footed and in his later years curiously pear-shaped. He jerked his wrists and waved them around his face when he talked, and wore an Italian scent, called Aqua di Selva, of such pungency that my father was able to detect his passage through Taunton station across two platforms after a span of twenty minutes. He was not, so far as anyone knows, a homosexual, although he certainly rejoiced in the company of young men as much as that of young women.

He was a pious Catholic, tending to Mariolatry in his private devotions: old-fashioned, superstitious but unquestionably devout. He was missed when he died, but left no monument. By dividing the Pixton estate between two nephews, and dividing the contents of the house, he effectively ensured that nobody followed him. Outside some Divine purpose, his passage through life might be seen as a minor distraction, an irrelevance, but he left little pools of fragrance behind, at any rate for a while.

*   *   *   *

Observant readers may spot that I have scarcely mentioned my parents or, indeed, my sisters (the brothers were yet to come), or made any great effort to distinguish between my cousins and the children of helpers and servants.

If asked to identify my mother from the Three Graces of Pixton I could probably have done so, but was certainly not aware that motherhood involved any particular emotional proximity. My mother had produced four children by the end of the war: Teresa, the eldest, myself, an infant daughter who died after a few days, and Margaret. Bridget had produced three: Polly, Anne and a boy called Robin. Gabriel, off to a late start, produced Angela, an infant at the time of the first group photograph taken by Compton Collier in 1944. Of this group, my only playmate was Anne Grant, the closest to me in age. Chiefly my boon companions were Willi Anderson, younger son of the French helper, David Bottle, son of Nanny Bottle, John and Ken Lowe, sons of Mrs Lowe, the housekeeper.

In some ways, I suppose, to be brought up at Pixton during the war was rather like being brought up in one of those communes which became fashionable in the sixties, believing in shared parenthood – usually with disastrous results. But Pixton was different in having an unmistakable figure of authority. Ultimately, my grandmother ruled everyone and decided everything. A clever, warm, well-educated woman, she had been accounted a great beauty when my grandfather brought her back from Ireland in 1910, although never as famous in this respect as her mother, Evelyn de Vesci. Mary Vesey was a considerable heiress, being an only child, and inherited a life interest in large parts of Dublin, as well as some lien on the considerable Abbeyleix estates. But twenty years of widowhood, of managing Pixton, Portofino, Bruton Street and her four children did not soften her aspect, and there was perhaps something a little masculine in her determined stride, her peremptory manner, by the time I was born, in her fiftieth year. It was she who instructed Auberon, on leave from the Polish army in southern Italy, to beat me and Willi Anderson for the crime of having locked my sister Margaret in the coal cellar. He beat us with a gym shoe in the spitting gallery hall at Pixton. It would not be true to say that I bore a grudge for this beating, but I think it may have precluded any great feeling of intimacy with Uncle Auberon in later life. Not to put too fine a point on it, I never quite trusted him after that experience. Where my grandmother was concerned, the reaction was quite different. From that moment, the affection in which I had always held her was tinged with a healthy awe.

* * * *

My mother, Laura, the youngest of the Three Graces, did not feature in any particular way throughout those six years of my life spent at Pixton. Much of her time was spent serving in an Air Force canteen and in other vital war work. One most uncharacteristic memory survived with her from these early years – it did not survive with me, but she reminded me often. Deciding that I was insufficiently athletic as I approached my fourth birthday, she chased me from Weir, which was the home farm on the Pixton estate, to the doors of Pixton, applying nettles to my legs. The distance involved is perhaps a mile and a quarter. Although, as I say, I have little recollection of the incident, the story has a certain ring of truth in that I have never been very keen on running or fast movement of any sort. My mother would scarcely have told the story so often if she did not think it reflected to her credit. Apart from this outrage, my mother has no separate entry at this stage in my story.

* * * *

If my mother, Laura, scarcely featured in those early years – we would happily have greeted her as 'Auntie Laudie' and settled for Bridget Grant as mother – my father, Evelyn, featured not at all. His appearances at Pixton – on leave from military training, and, later, from active service – were supposed to be awe-inspiring, but never really inspired a tithe of the awe accorded, on a daily basis, to my grandmother. My first memory of him is of his arrival at tea-time. It seems unlikely, but I remember him as being in uniform; perhaps, in wartime, army officers did indeed wear uniform to call on their mothers-in-law. As usual in Pixton, about twenty people were seated around the tea-table. On his arrival at the door of the drawing-room – the front door bell at Pixton had no authority, even if it worked, and people always walked in – everybody rose to greet him.

Well, nearly everybody. During the war, jam tarts were a great delicacy. They came with centres of two colours, red and yellow. All tasted exactly the same, but it was thought good for civilian morale to give people (or 'the people', as we were upsettingly called in those days) some illusion of choice. I had a particular passion for yellow jam tarts, but tarts of any colour were a rarity, making their appearance on the tea-table perhaps once a fort-night. The distraction caused by my father's arrival was too good an opportunity to miss. Within seconds I had cleared all the plates of yellow jam tarts and was shifting about ten of them into the pockets of my corduroy shorts, when there was a bellow from the door. My father, who attached greater importance to his paternity than I did, wished to know why his only son had not gone to greet him. The tarts, in broken and squashed condition, were extricated from my pockets and I was sent to bed in disgrace.

Shortly after this, on 13 November 1943 – just a few days before my fourth birthday – my father wrote in his diary:

There is a great deal of talk at the moment about the rocket guns which the Germans are said to have set up in France, with a range to carry vast explosive charges to London. This fear is seriously entertained in the highest quarters. I have

accordingly given orders for the books I have been keeping
at the Hyde Park Hotel to be sent to Piers Court. At the same
time, I have advocated my son coming to London. It would
seem from this that I prefer my books to my son. I can argue
that firemen rescue children and destroy books, but the truth
is that a child is easily replaced, while a book destroyed is
utterly lost; also a child is eternal; but most that I have a
sense of absolute possession over my library and not over my
nursery.

Others might have thought a child more difficult to replace than
a book, but in fairness, I must admit at this stage the indifference
between father and children was reciprocated. On 13 May 1944 my
mother gave birth to a fifth child and fourth daughter while her
husband struggled with *Brideshead Revisited* in a hotel on Dart-
moor, some thirty miles away. A week later he visited his wife and
new daughter:

I went to Pixton yesterday week and found Laura in excellent
health and her baby also. My children were much in evidence and boring.

We were much in evidence only because we were dragged out
from our normal pastimes and occupations to greet him. I would
gladly have swapped him for a bosun's whistle.

A first serious effort was made to bring us together, so that we
should get to know each other, on the day that Japan surrendered,
15 August 1945, when I was five years old. He took me to stay with
Randolph Churchill and his son, Winston, at a house they had
rented near Hitchin, Hertfordshire. It proved, I am sorry to say, the
occasion for the first major débâcle in our relationship. Let him
take up the account of it himself:

August 15 1945, *Ickleford Hitchin*:

Peace declared. Public holiday. Remained more or less drunk
all day. Collect the boy Auberon at the Eldons and drive him
to Ickleford. He behaved very politely.

August 16 1945

Another public holiday. Hangover. Winston, a boisterous boy

with head too big for his body. Randolph made a bonfire and
Auberon fell into it . . .

[Written 31 August 1945 at the Hyde Park Hotel]

The boy Auberon stayed a week at Ickleford and won golden
opinions on all sides, even mine, so that I was encouraged to
have him for a few days in London and show him the sights.

On the day we returned, Wednesday, I took him to the Zoo,
which was crowded with the lower classes and practically
devoid of animals, except rabbits and guinea-pigs.

On Friday, I devoted the day to him . . . .

But perhaps the story of that fatal Friday, 24 August 1945, had
better be told from his letter to my mother, dated 25 August 1945
and written from White's:

Darling Laura,
I have regretfully come to the conclusion that the boy Auberon is not yet a suitable companion for me.

Yesterday was a day of supreme self-sacrifice. I fetched
him from Highgate, took him up the dome of St Paul's, gave
him a packet of triangular stamps, took him to luncheon at
the Hyde Park Hotel, took him on the roof of the hotel, took
him to Harrods and let him buy vast quantities of toys (down
to your account), took him to tea with Maimie* who gave him
a pound and a box of matches, took him back to Highgate, in
a state (myself, not the boy) of extreme exhaustion. My
mother said: 'Have you had a lovely day?' He said: 'A bit dull.'
So that is the last time for some years I inconvenience myself
for my children. You might rub that in to him.

I had a very enjoyable evening getting drunk at the House
of Commons, with Hollis & Fraser and the widow Hartington
(who is in love with me I think) & Driburg and Nigel Birch &
Lord Morris and Anthony Head & my communist cousin
Claud Cockburn.

My own memory of the day is that it was only fairly interesting. I

* Lady Mary Lygon, then married to H.H. Prince Vsevolode Joannovich
Romanovsky, a caddish fellow.

had been bitterly disappointed by Maimie, who was trailed as a Russian princess, and turned out to be no more than another upper-class English lady.

Needless to say, my mother scorned to rub anything in. The first I heard that such grave offence had been taken was from my paternal grandmother several years later. I have used the episode on several occasions with my own children to point out that even five year olds cannot be too careful.

*   *   *   *

From my earliest years I was always called Bron. Only those who knew me as a child in the war have ever called me Bronnie. Practically nobody ever called me Auberon until the army, although Mr Elwood, the butler at Piers Court, always called me Master Auberon which everybody, including himself, found highly satirical.

It was curious that my father ever agreed to my being called Auberon since he had never enjoyed very cordial relations with my Uncle Auberon who, as head of my mother's immediate family, might have been flattered by the choice. From quite an early stage, my father announced that I had not been called after my mother's brother but after her first cousin once removed, the Auberon ('Bron') Herbert who, as Lord Lucas, died a hero's death over the German lines on 3 November 1916.

Bron Lucas was universally loved by those who knew him – most particularly by my grandfather, who never really recovered from his loss – but my father was not in the position of someone who had known him, being a Hampstead schoolboy of thirteen at the time of his death, while my mother was an infant of four months. In later years, whenever my father talked of 'the boy Auberon', he was referring to my Uncle Auberon, he of the enormous frame and flat feet, whose aroma filled Taunton station twenty minutes after he had left it. Nothing could really have been less boyish than that gigantic, semi-collapsed frame, except, perhaps, for a certain boyish insouciance, an enthusiasm, an excitement which still irritated the older man as both sped towards their early deaths.

It would be easy to decide that Evelyn Waugh's antipathy towards the other Boy Auberon dated back to the day of my parents' wedding. As the head of her immediate family, it had fallen to the lot of this gangling, over-sized fourteen year old to give her away. He took his duties seriously. In the short car journey from 28 Bruton Street to the Church of the Assumption of Our Lady, Warwick Street, he begged and implored her to cancel the wedding, pointing out that it was still not too late, and that she was making the greatest mistake of her life. Weeping, he argued that her bridegroom would never be acceptable at Pixton, would never fit in with anything they knew. 'Oh, Laudie, Laudie, he's such a shit', he cried – or claimed to have done, late at night and rather drunk, some thirty years later.

My mother did not bend – something for which, I suppose, I should be grateful. Perhaps she would have had a happier life if she had married someone else, but I am not really all that sure how happy anyone's life is, when one comes to examine it. She was a ravishingly beautiful young woman from a rich, clever, carefree background, who met my father when she was seventeen, was courted by him at nineteen and married before she was twenty-one. She was not available for very long, but over the years I have heard of an extraordinary number of suitors or would-be suitors who knew and cherished her in that brief two-year period between 1935 and 1937: Captain Terence O'Neill, later Prime Minister of Northern Ireland; William Douglas-Home, the playwright; her cousin, Henry Howard, who rose to be Administrator of St Kitts, Nevis and Anguilla; Lord Oxford, a Somerset neighbour, who rose to be Governor of the Seychelles.

All these people might have been suitors, and all of them, no doubt, would have enjoyed more cordial relations with my mother's brother, Auberon. But Evelyn Waugh got there first.

I would explain the antipathy which developed between the two men slightly differently. My father who, it must be admitted, rather cultivated the acquaintance of great landowners, grandees, swells, those of ancient family and possessions, could not be much impressed by the boy Auberon's efforts to act the part of the great landowner, swell, etc. When one of Auberon's sisters was reduced to penury, it was not Auberon but my father who volunteered to pay the school fees – out of his own, heavily taxed earnings. Auberon, who had never done any work and who lived entirely on family wealth which he, as the only son, had usurped from his sisters, saw no obligation to reduce his lifestyle. When one adds to this failure, a certain tendency among the young, rich and upper class to patronize their relations who are older, less upper class

and have to work for their living, then I think we can understand
how it was that no marriage of true minds ever really occurred between Evelyn Waugh and his brother-in-law, Auberon Herbert.

There might also have been a feeling from my grandmother that
writers were all very well to have in the house – Barrie, Belloc,
T.E. Lawrence – but one does not really expect them to marry
one's daughters. The result of all these pressures, for the six surviving children of Evelyn and Laura Waugh, was that the two
worlds in which they had a foothold – Herbert and Waugh, or, as I
prefer, Pixton and Piers Court – never really came together.
Throughout childhood and for some time after, there were two
possible models, two perceptions of life. Neither had the slightest
bearing on the modern world.

CHAPTER
TWO

Piers Court 1945-1956

My elder sister, Teresa, and I were driven to our new home in the last week of December 1945. Piers Court, a pretty Georgian *gentil-hommière* bought for my parents by Lady de Vesci before the war, had been used as a convent for the duration. My father, who from this moment emerged as a new character called 'Papa', had been down there for a month or two, getting the last of the nuns out and making it habitable. By the time we arrived it had a butler – Mr Elwood – a cook, Hilda, a housekeeper, Mrs Harper, a nanny, Deacon or possibly Deakin, and a cowman, Mr Sanders. Mrs Harper's mother, Gran Attwood, her brother, Norman, her sister-in-law, Gladys Attwood, and her son, Gordon, all worked at various times and in various capacities. There was a rich and varied life to be enjoyed behind the green baize doors dividing the dining-room from the pantry corridors on the ground floor, the main bedrooms from the nursery and servants' quarters on the first floor.

It was as well this was so, as not much welcome could be expected from the front of the house. On Boxing Day 1945, Papa recorded our presence in his diary:

Maria Teresa and Bron have arrived; he ingratiating, she covered with little medals and badges, neurotically voluble with the vocabulary of the lower middle class – 'serviette', 'spare room'. Only on points of theology does she become rational ... The children leave for Pixton on the 10th. Meanwhile, I have my meals in the library.

This was a practice he kept up to his death. Whenever his children or their friends were staying in the house, he was liable to take his meals in the library, advancing no more complicated reason for this than that he was bored by the company. It may make him seem a monster of bad manners, but in extenuation I must say that it was often a relief to the rest of us when he did so, and he must have been aware of this. The dejection which was liable to seize him at any moment – sparked off by little more than a bad joke, a banal sentiment, a lower-middle-class epithet – made him awkward company at any time. When he was in the grips of a major depression or melancholy, as he called it, he was unendurable. It may have been kindness as much as antipathy which drove him to eat his meals alone.

'Home for a cold New Year's Day', he wrote later. 'My children weary me. I can only see them as defective adults: feckless, destructive, frivolous, sensual, humourless ....'

After such a gap of time, it is easy to sympathize with him. By 'humourless' in this context I think he means that our jokes were not up to the standard he expected. We certainly tried making them for him. I remember in my first holidays telling him a joke I had heard at school. 'Bus conductor goes up to a lady in the seat and says, "Your fare, miss." She replies: "I know I am."'

'Oh yes,' said my father, 'that is a very funny joke indeed. My goodness, what a good joke. Ha, ha, ha, whoo, hoo, hoo. "Your fare, miss," "I know I am," Wha, ha ha.' He rocked backwards and forwards on his chair, hooting with laughter. I realized that his amusement was exaggerated, but thought it vaguely a tribute to the merriment created by my little sally. Encouraged I tried the joke on many people, but it never had quite the same success. Another bus conductor joke was told me in my second term at school. It was slightly indecent, and rather hard to understand, but, remembering the success of the first, I told it intrepidly at lunch on my first day home. A pretty young woman boards a bus carrying a parrot. Rather than pay a fare for the bird, she conceals it in her knickers. The bus conductor says to her: 'Nice day, miss.' The parrot calls: 'It's raining cats and dogs down here.'

This time the laughter was less prolonged, if equally cordial.

Papa liked to encourage his children. But my efforts to amuse him were not to be crowned with success for long. On 6 January 1946 he wrote to his friend Nancy Mitford:

> My two eldest children are here and a great bore. The elder alternates between strict theology and utter silences; the boy lives for pleasure and is thought a great wit by his contemporaries. I have tried him drunk & I have tried him sober....

In light of their inability to amuse him, it was thought better that his children should be sent away as much as possible – whether to Pixton, or to my Aunt Bridget Grant at Nutcombe, a beautiful Elizabethan manor house in Devon, or later to the other aunt, Gabriel Dru, who eventually settled at Bickham, a strange, slightly Frenchified abode near Dunster, in Somerset. My own immediate fate was to be sent to Pixton on 10 January 1946, then taken and left in a boarding school two months after my sixth birthday, on 28 January 1946 ....

> I drove to Bristol in Prothero's car ... collected Bron, a midget in new school outfit, and took him to Mells, where Katherine and Helen received him with the utmost kindness and he behaved well. Next day I took him to his school which was in a rudimentary state of preparation – ladders and paint pots everywhere ... I put him in the hands of a clean-looking matron and returned to Mells. Katherine was gayer than I have seen her for years ... I brought wine.

His undisguised glee at the prospect of getting rid of his children as each holiday drew to its close eventually succeeded in causing hurt and resentment. At this stage, though, I was too much seized by other anxieties to notice. My chief terror was of beatings which, I had been told, were frequent and ferocious at school.

However, my experiences at All Hallows, Cranmore, Shepton Mallet, Somerset belong to another chapter. Just as the conventional upbringing of the upper-middle-class male at this time encouraged him to put his experience of life and his relationships into compartments, so I propose to keep them there. School will be discussed in this chapter only to the extent which it intruded on home life, which was very little; just as home life will be discussed in the next chapter only to the extent which it intruded on school life, which was scarcely at all.

Mells, to which Papa took me in Prothero's car, was to be an island of kindness, grace and civilization throughout the ten years I spent at Cranmore and Downside, since it was close enough to both for me to be taken there for luncheon. At this time it was the home of Katherine Asquith, widow of Raymond Asquith, who died on the Somme in 1916. Mells was Katherine Asquith's own property as a Horner: a beautiful, quiet, dignified house, full of ancient Horner possessions and a gem of minor Elizabethan domestic architecture. She was my godmother and took a benevolent interest in me through many vicissitudes. Her daughter, Helen, a school inspector at that time, and a brilliantly successful Latin teacher, never married. On this occasion, the night before my first day at boarding school, she bathed me, putting on a white coat for the purpose. I would probably not have remembered the occasion if she had not been kind enough to remind me every time I went to Mells in the next ten years. What had been a perfectly normal arrangement at the age of six assumed rather more alarming proportions for an awkward schoolboy of twelve. By the time I was a self-conscious youth of sixteen I was no longer embarrassed by these reminders from Lady Helen, but found them strangely flattering as I prepared to ogle suggestively at the familiar story.

Further embarrassment at Mells was caused by a huge dog called Tarquin whose invariable greeting to any male visitor was to put his nose in the visitor's crutch and leave it there, sometimes slobbering slightly. Mrs Asquith derived a certain wry amusement from this; Lady Helen's reaction was to remonstrate noisily with the dog. Older visitors, like Lord Hailsham, a Conservative politician whose record was besmirched by, in my eyes, unpleasant attacks on P.G. Wodehouse after the war, could carry off these assaults with dignity. As a schoolboy, I found them intensely mortifying.

My last glimpse of Tarquin was at Ronald Knox's funeral, in the summer of 1957, when he howled like a woman wailing for her demon lover as we carried the coffin across the lawn in front of the house. I think the dog died soon afterwards. I took my revenge on its shade a few years later by calling a monstrous child 'Tarquin' in my first novel. Mrs Asquith wrote to object, urging me to write pleasanter novels in future.

* * * *

My first holiday from All Hallows at Easter of 1946 was marked by the third major débâcle (after the jam tarts episode and the zoo) in relations between myself and the august author of my being. This was the Great Lavery Scandal. Evelyn Waugh refers to it briefly in his diaries and briefly, I think, in his correspondence with Diana Cooper. It was represented to me at the time as something very akin to parricide. Let us first look at his diary:

Piers Court, Saturday 13 April 1946:

The children's holiday has begun. Teresa taller and more personable. It is a great surprise to see how nice they are to one another. Bron has been robbed of 10s. by a boy called Lavery.

Friday, 26 April 1946:

I fasted and gave up wine during Holy Week and attended a number of religious services. I made the disconcerting discovery that Bron's tale of Lavery's theft was pure invention.

No suggestion here of a disgust which would take years to be forgotten, although this is how it was put to me by one after another of my siblings as they reached an age when they could be told the secret. What happened, as I remember it, was that at the end of term the boys were given back all the pocket money held for them by the school which had not been spent. I had about fourteen shillings (70p) left from my pound – far more money than I had ever possessed before, at the age of six and a half. The result was that I was obsessed with money and could talk about nothing else. Our conversation went something like this:

'Papa.'

'Yes, dear boy?'

'You know ten shilling notes?'

'Yes, what about them?'

That question rather floored me, as I had not thought the matter through and had nothing further to say about them. I decided to improvise.

'You know they have a metal strip running through them.'

'Yes. What of it?'

'It is made of precious metal, and if you remove the strip, the note has no value at all.'

'I assure you that you have been misinformed.'

'Ah.'

This last was delivered by me in the tone of someone who knows better, but is not prepared to be drawn into an argument. It was a mistaken ploy. Under cross-examination, I produced as my authority a boy called Lavery at school. It was a name chosen entirely at random. I had nothing against Lavery, indeed rather liked him. Challenged on the point of why Lavery should know better, I replied that he had proved the sincerity of his belief by throwing away a ten shilling note of mine which had proved, on inspection, to be deficient in this respect. No, I had not seen him throw it away, but he had assured me he would do so.

My father went into action. He saw himself, I imagine, as defending his brood against a hostile world outside. I wrote to Lavery, with some misgivings, demanding my ten shilling note back. Papa wrote to Lavery père and, on receiving denials that either had any knowledge of my ten shilling note (although Lavery wrote to me 'Dear Bron, I remember you *showing* me your ten shilling note', which was thought highly significant), prepared to write to the Headmaster of All Hallows, Mr F.H.R. Dix.

'Before taking this step, I wish to be absolutely sure you are telling the truth. If you are not telling the truth, you must tell me now. It is not too late.'

Heartened by this, I cheerfully agreed that it was all a cock-and-bull story. But I had been deceived. It was far too late to admit any such thing. For several years, he could scarcely bring himself to speak to me, and ten years later would refer pointedly to my defective sense of honour. Lavery forgave me much sooner.

* * * *

Tuesday, 7 May 1946:

Teresa left yesterday for school. Bron goes the day after tomorrow. I found their company increasingly irksome as the holidays dragged on. On Sunday they dined with us and were obstreperous.

These end-of-holidays dinner parties became a rigid institution. Although we had lunch with our parents in the dining-room, as soon as we went to boarding school – and very gloomy occasions these lunches tended to be – we did not dine with them until the age of fourteen or fifteen, except for these end-of-holiday dinner parties, when we were waited on by Mr Elwood, drank champagne from absurdly thin, fluted glasses and made speeches at the end of dinner proposing each other's toasts. By immemorial custom, our speeches would begin 'Unaccustomed as I am to public speaking'. Papa would dress on these occasions in white tie and tails, with his military medals glittering on his chest – in a gallant war seeing action in four theatres and spending many months behind enemy lines in Yugoslavia, he had acquired a fair display of them. His own speech would be some variation on the theme of how delighted he was that the holidays were over and his children were going back to school. These sentiments would be greeted with varying degrees of obstreperousness from his children. If it had been a joke, this undisguised dislike of his children's company would soon have worn pretty thin. Since it plainly was not a joke, it became a simple fact of life. Its main result may have been in a certain indifference which his children felt for him: we held him in awe, certainly, but not in much affection at this stage. His comfort or discomfort, happiness or unhappiness were matters of indifference to us so long as they did not interfere with our own pleasures.

At these dinners none of us, in retaliation, ever made the point that we were delighted to be leaving, nor would it have carried much conviction if we had. Boarding school, throughout the late 1940s and early 1950s, was pretty hellish. We were miserable to be leaving the comforts of home and of our own company.

After the dinner and the speeches, the company would retire for what in other contexts might be called a jolly. Its constituent parts remain a slight blur: charades, dumb crambo, the game. Papa would go down to the cellar underneath the drawing-room and roar like a lion. As the children grew older, we would play poker, *vingt-et-un*, roulette. To us, these were occasions of great merriment, only slightly tempered by the threatening proximity of the school term. They, and a few outings from school, certainly provide the happiest and fondest memories of our father from these early years.

* * * *

Piers Court is, as I say, an exceptionally pretty *gentilhommière* set
in about forty acres when we lived there – the land has since been
increased, I believe – of attractive Cotswold countryside. The front
of the house is Georgian stucco, with seven bays, under a pedi-
ment adorned with the arms of Herbert and Waugh, stuck there by
my father in 1938. The Waugh arms are themselves slightly bogus.
They were assumed without proper authority by my great-great-
great-grandfather, the Revd Alexander Waugh DD (1754–1827). As
Evelyn Waugh puts it in his autobiography, 'they were displayed
illicitly and rather profusely by his descendants until my father's
time when their use, slightly modified, was regularized'.

From this it might be assumed that it was my grandfather,
Arthur Waugh, the publisher, who 'regularized' the matter by pur-
chasing himself a coat of arms somewhat similar to the one which
had been usurped. In fact it was Evelyn Waugh who, with his
brother Alec's connivance, purchased the coat of arms in Arthur
Waugh's name. The trace of *suggestio falsi* here may seem to
strengthen the case of those envious and under-endowed critics of
the Cambridge school who insist that Waugh's near-obsession
with the intricacies of social stratification derived from an insecurity on his own part, a dissatisfaction with his position and a
determination to aggrandize his antecedents. Nothing could be
further from the truth. He never claimed membership of anything
but the professional upper middle class for himself. In his determination to draw the line precisely underneath his own heels,
with no space between, he may occasionally have been in danger
of cutting off a shin or two. But the scholar in him would not have
put up with any tampering. The Waughs were as you found them:
upwardly mobile professionals, newly connected with the high
aristocracy. Mock them at your peril.

* * * *

My first impression of Piers Court, after the decaying splendours
of Pixton, was of its comparative smallness and much greater
formality. There had never been a butler at Pixton in my lifetime.
The nursery, service wing and front of the house wandered in and
wandered out of each other's orbits. At Piers Court, the front of the
house belonged strictly to my father. One detected his presence as

soon as one walked into the pretty hall, with its white and black stone floor, its glass chandelier in the well of the staircase. His presence sometimes exuded from the library on the left in a sort of miasma compounded of Havana cigar smoke and gin, or it might come bursting out of the drawing-room on the right, in a great shout of laughter accompanied by the smell of lavender; he always put Yardley's Lavender Hair Tonic on his head when he changed for dinner – a line long since discontinued, I believe. One might have thought he would have preferred some expensive preparation from Trumper's of Curzon Street, where he went to have his hair cut. It was a gentle agreeable smell which I always associated with the more festive aspects of home life.

In the pink bathroom, to which I was taken within minutes of my first arrival in this strange house, there was a printed postcard stuck above the cistern: *From Mr Evelyn Waugh, Piers Court, Stinchcombe, Nr Dursley, Gloucestershire. Dursley 2150.* Underneath it, in his own handwriting, was written: 'Should the handle fail to return to the horizontal when the flow of water ceases, please agitate it slightly until it succeeds.'

I read that message every time I urinated at home for the next eleven years, and never ceased to resent it. The downstairs lavatory in the front of the house, decorated with Abyssinian paintings, with an armchair seat upholstered in leopard skin, was out of bounds to children. So was the butler's lavatory immediately behind the business room on the other side of the baize door. Every servant had his lavatory, according to degree, down to some outside earth closets for the gardeners. Quite possibly they all had notices in my father's handwriting, with instructions about what to do at every stage of the process.

The presence, as I say, was overwhelming. He was a small man – scarcely five foot six in his socks – and only a writer, after all, but I have seen generals and chancellors of the exchequer, six foot six and exuding self-importance from every pore, quail in front of him. When he laughed, everyone laughed, when he was downcast, everyone tiptoed around trying to make as little noise as possible. It was not wealth or power which created this effect, merely the force of his personality. I do not see how he could have been pleased by the effect he produced on other people. In fact he spent his life seeking out men and women who were not frightened of him. Even then, he usually ended up getting drunk with them, as a way out of the abominable problem of human relations.

Which is a little sad when one reflects that all he really wanted to do in company was to make jokes, to turn the world upside down and laugh at it, to enrich and enliven this vale of tears with a little fantasy. The important questions of man's relationship to God and man's responsibility for the material and spiritual welfare of his fellow men could be left to private contemplation. The main purpose of human association was to share enjoyment of the world's absurdity.

One can easily forget the times when he was happy and witty and gay. He was a master of farcical invention: anything pompous or false would be turned on its head, magnified a thousand times and reduced to absurdity, usually by a process of exaggerated agreement. He would invent elaborate fantasies about the neighbours – how the local dentist, called McMeekin, had a face like a ham, and shook hands so violently that he invariably crushed the fingers of his patients. He would train us to make 'poop, poop' noises every time we passed the house of a neighbour called Lady Tubbs. But it is impossible to do justice to this fugitive art by quotation, as Boswell proves time and again, and I certainly will not try. Timing and immediacy are essential to it, but so is atmosphere. Unlike Sydney Smith, Evelyn Waugh left a corpus of beautifully polished writing as a permanent memorial to his genius, and that must suffice. But he needed an audience which could respond intelligently; whenever he met incomprehension he was liable to be reduced to the most appalling gloom. It was this, more than anything else, which he dreaded, and which made him shun strangers with a rudeness which never failed to make people gasp. 'Why do you expect me to talk to this boring pig?' he would suddenly shout at his hostess about some fellow guest. 'He is common, he is ignorant and he is stupid, and he thinks Picasso is an important artist.'

It was this fear which accounted for the coldness and exasperation towards his children when they were young, although at least one of them gave him further reasons to be exasperated. There could be no mistaking the relief of his children when he was absent, the great brooding presence was removed. Children could charge through the house, making as much noise as they liked. Outrageous breakages could be perpetrated, and the chances were that my mother would try to cover them up and conceal them before the monster's return.

The most terrifying aspect of Evelyn Waugh as a parent was that he reserved the right not just to deny affection to his children but to advertise an acute and unqualified dislike of them. This was always conditional on their own behaviour up to a point, and seldom entirely unjustified, but it was disconcerting, nevertheless, to be met by cool statements of total repudiation.

As the number of children increased – by 1950 there were six[*] of us – he spent longer periods away from home, much to the relief of us all. As I have said, even at the time, I half-suspected that he was aware of the relief we felt when he was away, that his great act of disliking his children and shunning their company was at any rate in part an acknowledgement of his tragic inability to relax with them.

In fact the most welcome aspect of him, as a parent, was his lack of interest in his children, at any rate until they were much older and became fit subjects for gossip. I have described how no noise could be made in the front of the house, but that was as far as the reign of terror extended. So long as we were out of sight and sound, we could do whatever we wanted. In that sense, he was a permissive, even indulgent parent. At the age of nine or ten I announced that I was interested in chemistry – I never studied it at school, but neither of my parents would have known that – and wished to make some chemical experiments for Christmas. Papa thought this a capital idea, and asked for a list.

In addition to the usual glass tubing and spirit lamps, I wanted a Wolff jar for distilling alcohol, large quantities of sulphur, saltpetre and charcoal, for making gunpowder some concentrated sulphuric and hydrochloric acids for various unspecified experiments I had in mind, and large quantities of nitric acid and glycerine as I was interested in the idea of going into the commercial production of nitro-glycerine as an explosive. All these things were acquired for me from a chemical supplier in London at extraordinarily low cost, and the Court Room at the back of the house was set aside for my experiments. The only substance on which he failed me was prussic (or hydro-cyanic) acid which the

[*]
1. Teresa b. 9 March 1938	4. Harriet b. 13 May 1944
2. Auberon b. 17 November 1939	5. James b. 30 June 1946
3. Margaret b. 10 June 1942	6. Septimus b. 9 July 1950

supplier refused to produce. Papa said I was not to worry, he was sure he could get some through the porter at White's, but none ever materialized.

Not many parents, I believe, would be prepared to give their sons of nine or ten bottles of concentrated sulphuric, hydrochloric and nitric acid to play with unsupervised. Some will decide that this was a deliberate, Charles Addams-like plot to get rid of me, but my parents were similarly unconcerned about firearms, which presented a greater threat to everyone else. From my earliest years I stalked our forty acres alone looking for small animals, or blasted away at targets around the house. Similarly, they were unconcerned about school rules and school reports, holding all authority in derision until the threat of expulsion brought with it the danger that children might be returned home.

*   *   *   *

We lived at Piers Court for ten years after the war, years which turned me from being a mildly delinquent six year old into something approaching a professional criminal of sixteen. These were the most intensely Waugh years, although I was liable to spend large parts of each holiday at either Pixton or Nutcombe, the home of my Grant cousins, and Papa was liable to spend large parts of them either in London, carousing, or on trips abroad. Nevertheless, Piers Court was unmistakably a Waugh stronghold. Combe Florey, when we moved there in 1956, was only twenty-five miles from Pixton, twenty from Nutcombe, fifteen from Bickham, where my Dru cousins lived with their pigs, ten from Tetton, where some other Herbert cousins had a large house of great luxury and elegance. Combe Florey was half in the Pixton ambience and Papa's presence, in that larger, lighter house, was much reduced.

For the first seven years of life at Piers Court, my time was mostly spent behind the green baize doors, apart from lunch which was often marked by the most appalling gloom. While Papa chewed his way through the unappetising meals, with his back to the window, my mother, still beautiful if slightly dishevelled in her early thirties, stared past him out of the window at her beloved cows. She never had more than six or seven of them and they cost a fortune to keep, but she loved them extravagantly, as other women love their dogs or, so I have been told, their children. She brought a cowman with her from Somerset, an elderly widower with enchanting blue eyes called Mr Sanders. I think she rather loved him, both as a reflection of her love for the cows and because he was the only reminder of Pixton in that Waugh stronghold. He lived in the top of the house, in a small attic bedroom, the floor being shared between Mr Elwood, the butler, in rather a grand attic, and another attic which must, I suppose, have been shared between nannies and nursery maids. One night Mr Sanders knocked on the door of the day nursery to wish us good-night. I said to him:

'Mr Sanders, you look very odd. I think you are drunk.'

He gave a hollow laugh and stumped up to bed. Later that night, we were told he had been taken ill and next day he died. I often wondered how they got the body down those narrow stairs, but nobody was going to tell a child. Some years later I inherited his bedroom and imagined I saw his ghost. As I lay in the dark one night the door opened suddenly. Light flooded in from the corridor outside, and a small man in trousers walked in and shut the door purposefully behind him, leaving me once again in the dark. When I turned my bedside light on, nobody was there. The experience left me puzzled rather than frightened. But Mr Sanders was a kind and merry man, at peace with the world, and it is hard to believe his repose was disturbed by my prurience.

Mrs Harper, the housekeeper – later cook – was also a kindly soul, but she suffered from bad feet and was somewhat shrill. Everybody else was in a conspiracy against her, including her brother, Norman, who worked as a farmhand and gardener and had a weakness for the drink. Always a genial figure, he became overwhelmingly so after a few pints of cider and would wave his hat in the air and bow to the ground – a stout, swaying figure – proclaiming to the children or anyone he met: 'If ever I can be of any service to you, sire.'

Every morning a bell which hung on the top of the house would be rung and all my mother's employees would assemble with the children in the kitchen for an elevenses which extended very nearly to lunch. Norman's great joke was that I was always after the women. From the age of seven, he convinced me that I was a tremendous Romeo. In fact I took no interest in the opposite sex until I was fifteen and they took no interest in me for at least four years after that.

After a succession of nannies, most of them mildly unpleasant

Vera Gilroy arrived, a terrified fourteen year old from a Catholic mining family in County Durham. Her first memory of Piers Court is of being ushered into the presence of her two charges, then respectively six and a half and eight years old. Apparently I fixed her with a ferocious scowl and said: 'Do my hair.' But she became a real friend for many years. When she married a musician-welder called Terry Grother, her cottage at the other end of the village became a centre for secret smoking until Mrs Harper learned about it. Vera also organized elaborate children's concerts to greet my paternal grandmother, always called Granny Waugh to distinguish her from the huge and powerful grandmother at Pixton, on her yearly visits.

Granny Waugh was a tiny, delicate, infinitely ladylike woman. Many years later my mother, slightly the worse for drink, turned to my father in response to some mild criticism about her household arrangements, and said: 'Anyway, *your* mother talked with a Bristol accent.' I don't think she did. It is true, as I discovered in later years, after my social antennae were better developed, that her half-brother, the Reverend George Raban, and even her beloved half-sister, Emma Raban, spoke with a distinctly odd intonation, but there was nothing regional about their idiosyncrasies. Rather, I believe it was the result of never meeting anyone else. They sat jabbering to each other dottily year in and year out for seventy years, never noticing how odd their diction was becoming. A similar explanation may apply to the various colonial accents which developed over the years, before communication between the mother country and her former colonies overseas became so much easier.

I hope Granny Waugh enjoyed these concerts. We, the performers, certainly did, but it is hard to believe they caused much pleasure to the more refined sensibilities of the grown-ups. We would act pieces from Shakespeare, give recitations, perform moronic conjuring tricks and even sing choruses, although every member of my family has always been completely tuneless. The first of these concerts marked my earliest stage appearance, in the part of Oberon, with Titania being played by Teresa. Mine was quite a small part, consisting of only two lines:

OBERON: Ill met by moonlight, Proud Titania.
TITANIA: What, jealous Oberon! – Fairies, skip hence:

I have foresworn his bed and company.
OBERON: Tarry, rash wanton: am I not thy lord?
TITANIA: Then I must be thy lady . . . .

I see now that I was being used as a foil for my sister to show off with a long and incomprehensible speech about Corin, amorous Phyllida and 'the bouncing Amazon, your buskin'd mistress'.

These concerts were only one item in an annual cycle of ceremonies and observances. Every Christmas, the Stinchcombe Silver Band came and played carols for half an hour in front of the house. Then its members would be asked in and plied with whisky. I was particularly proud to see Papa entertaining them every year, talking to these rather frightening giants with the greatest affability, and getting great roars of laughter out of them as he ribbed them about their tipsiness. The common touch was certainly not something he cultivated, but in rather a surprising way, when he needed it, he had it. Many years after his death, an enemy of his, the miserable Shimi Lovat, who had been ridiculed as 'Trimmer' in the war trilogy, wrote in his autobiography that Waugh had been detested by the men who served under him. Having no evidence to the contrary, I rather feared this might be true. Soon after Lord Lovat's autobiography appeared, when I reviewed it in *Books and Bookmen* I was surprised to receive five or six letters from people who had served with Waugh saying that the reverse was the truth. One of my correspondents, who seemed to have done some research on the matter, suggested that Lovat, although a professional war hero, had spent only about eleven days on active service, while Waugh had seen action in four theatres – Dakar, Crete, a raid on the Normandy coast and in seven months behind enemy lines with the partisans in Yugoslavia. I do not know, but I am extremely irritated when I hear the same story repeated as if it came from General Laycock or Captain Philip Dunne, rather than from the wretched Trimmer. Both these men were good and valiant friends, whom he respected as much as he despised Lord Lovat. But I comfort myself that the portrait of Trimmer will be read long after everybody has forgotten Lovat's miserable, bragging autobiography.

The greatest ceremony I remember from our time at Piers Court was the Grand Garden Fête, when house and gardens were thrown open to the public in honour of St Dominic's parish

church, of Dursley. The Stinchcombe Silver Band played all afternoon. Visitors were shown round the Works of Art – mostly
Victorian narrative paintings collected by Papa with great acuity
over the years and now, alas, dispersed. I ran a Woodlouse Derby,
whereby spectators were invited to bet on which segment of a
divided circle a woodlouse, dropped in the centre, would finally
depart from. It was an extraordinarily happy occasion. Once
again, one had the glimpse of a father who was benign towards the
human race and accepted as part of it.

Granny Waugh died in 1955, but I was not allowed to the funeral,
being in disgrace at the time. I am not sure whether this was
before or after the Great Débâcle of 25 July, but I was pretty well
always in disgrace throughout this period, with the threat of my
expulsion from Downside looming over whatever domestic
arrangements Papa might choose to make. Two earlier deaths had
left me unmoved. When Mr Sanders died, I was, as I have
described, too much overcome with prurient curiosity about the
circumstances of his death to contemplate sadness as an appropriate emotion. When my Uncle Eddie Grant died in the winter of
1947, I decided I did not know him well enough, and held him in
too much awe, to be much affected. But Granny Waugh's death
was a genuine cause of sorrow in my blighted, adolescent heart.

I had stayed with her often in her Highgate flat, which was full of
strange and ancient objects. It was my first experience of London,
with its trolley-buses and trams, and the intoxicating smell of gas
which never visited Pixton or Piers Court. Hers was a totally benevolent, unterrifying presence. On her death, the house filled with
bric-à-brac which was somehow to be divided among the children. We fought over it savagely, and swapped the spoils among
ourselves. Being better at swapping than any of my brothers or sisters, I ended up with all the loot, upon which it was confiscated
and redistributed among the children.

This was the foundation of a passion for acquiring junk antiques
– coins, stuffed birds, stone eggs – which took up a large part of my
energies until my mother's death in 1973, when I suddenly
acquired mountains of junk which I had been coveting for years.
In those circumstances of desolation, at the age of thirty-three, I
suddenly lost all desire to acquire things. Since then, I have not
minded when children broke priceless heirlooms, or even that a
burglar removed half my evidence that the Waughs were gentle-

folk – at any rate eating with silver cutlery – in 1740. Of all my youthful passions, I miss the fierce joy in acquiring things most.

* * * *

Of the other Waughs – the Alec Waughs – we saw very little at Piers Court. I stayed with them once at their pretty, redbrick Queen Anne House called Edrington, near Silchester. There I was introduced to the delights of peanut butter, Coca-Cola, and an automatic gramophone which changed records. They kept a butler in those days, who served Coca-Cola and wore a jersey. I cannot explain the strange Waugh passion for keeping butlers. Practically nobody else did by this time except the very rich. Alec stayed at Edrington only occasionally – rather, one gathered, as a tolerated guest than as a husband, home from his travels. He played me the music of *South Pacific*, which he had just seen in New York, miming the song, 'I'm going to wash that man right out of my hair'. This was made especially poignant for an impressionable lad by Alec's baldness.

Alec was chiefly famous in my family for his baldness. Before the great day that he came to stay at Piers Court, Papa warned us that he had no hair. 'What do you mean?' cried my sister Harriet, aghast. 'Has he fingers and toes?'

Alec lost his hair as a prisoner of war while my father was still a schoolboy. Perhaps it was this loss, combined with his tiny frame, which made him such a compulsive chaser after women. My father attributed it to the disappointment of his first marriage, to Barbara, daughter of W.W. Jacobs. 'I, who was called Tank at Sandhurst, could not make my wife a woman', he explained delicately, in one of his various autobiographies. That and a subsequent claim – 'Venus has been kind to me' – might serve as his epitaph. I was stricken by his death, at a great age, fifteen years after my father's, in 1981. He died in Tampa, Florida, where he had emigrated from Tangier with a third wife. We buried his ashes unceremoniously in a small aluminium flask, which his daughter Veronica drew from her handbag, next to the grave of his parents in Hampstead. There was nobody left to forbid me to attend.

* * * *

I should not leave the Waugh compartment of my life story, enshrined in the Piers Court years, without some discussion of the

Rabans. Evelyn Waugh described his pedigree at some considerable length, but was slightly reticent about the Raban half, beyond pointing out that his mother's family was descended from a long line of yeoman farmers in Penn, Buckinghamshire, before breaking out into the Indian Civil Service and the army. The Raban family lived for many years in a dignified house in the village of Hatch Beauchamp outside Taunton. Rows of handsome monuments testify to their attendance at a nearby church. The surviving head of the family, the Reverend Peter Raban, is a clergyman in the Church of England. But none of this can really disguise a suspicion that there may be something slightly odd about the name. Evelyn Waugh was prepared to mention the suggestion that it might have German origins, while pointing out that there was no evidence to support this. What nobody points out is that however you look at it, upside down or sideways, drunk or sober, the first word that springs to the mind is 'Jewish'.

This is a bit embarrassing because nobody wants to be caught denying Jewish connections too vehemently. I remember hearing the present Lord Jellicoe caught in a long explanation of how very sorry he was that there was not a single drop of Jewish blood in his mother's family, the Cayzers, how often and sincerely he wished there was.

I am in no position to give a ruling on this matter, because I simply do not know the answer. Perhaps the folder of Raban pedigree in my library, apparently composed around 1900, is a forged document put together hurriedly in face of the threat of a German invasion in the last war. Perhaps we are descended from Rabanus Maurus, the ninth-century scholar who became Archbishop of Mainz and is honoured as a saint in those parts. My friend Patrick Marnham, the writer and traveller, is in no doubt about the matter, and always makes secret Jewish signs to me when we meet. In his definitive history of the magazine *Private Eye*, *The Private Eye Story* (London, Deutsch, 1982), he ends a long and laudatory passage about me with the explanation: 'All these qualities are widely ascribed to Waugh's partly Jewish ancestry.'

Be that as it may, I have no doubt that it is to the Rabans, rather than to the Waughs, that my father, his brother Alec and their descendants owe whatever elements of fantasy or imagination they possess. Before that generation, the Waughs were uniformly stolid and unimaginative. Arthur Waugh, although recognized as a man of letters, never showed a glimmer of imagination in any part of his extensive published writings, unless occasional embarrassing bursts of sentimentality can serve in the place of fantasy. His most famous observation was to compare the poems of T.S. Eliot to the meanderings of a drunken helot, but tiresome and affected as Eliot's poetry may now seem, I cannot suppose that this piece of invective really hits any particular mark.

But the Rabans undoubtedly had a touch of fantasy. Great-Uncle George, another clergyman, would desert his pulpit to chase imaginary mice round his church with a golf club. The Reverend Peter Raban, whom I met only once, at George's funeral, when he was wearing a cloak like Count Dracula, is the father of Jonathan Raban, the strikingly imaginative novelist. I have met Jonathan only once or twice, alas, and fear I may never meet him again as, despite his marriage to the step-daughter of a cousin on the Waugh side (a descendant of the painter Holman Hunt, who married two Misses Waugh in succession), he took tremendous offence at a review of one of his books which I printed in my early days as Editor of the *Literary Review*. Hell hath no fury like a writer unfavourably reviewed. I suffer from the same problem. My first novel (or possibly my second), received a bad review in *The Sunday Times* from either Frederic Raphael or Mordecai Richler. I do not know which, but have regarded both with the deepest suspicion ever since, and *The Sunday Times* with a total loathing which becomes easier and easier to justify with every year that passes. I believe Jonathan Raban's marriage has since broken up.

* * * *

In 1954 my father experienced a financial crisis which led to all the indoors servants being dismissed except Mrs Harper, who gallantly agreed to double up as cook and housekeeper. Her cooking was so dreadful that eventually we hired an Italian cook called Tina. She brought a husband who went mad, hiding himself under her bed all day and night in the forlorn hope of trapping her in an infidelity. Much merriment was occasioned by all this.

Then, early in 1955, Papa suffered his own attack of insanity, well chronicled in *The Ordeal of Gilbert Pinfold* and various biographies. The drama passed me by, since it all happened in term-time. If he wrote me any letters in his delirium, as he did to his wife and at least one of his daughters, I did not notice anything more than usually odd about them, and threw them away after reading. But there was never any attempt to conceal what had happened. 'That was while I was off my nut,' he would explain about any odd behaviour at this time. It was easy to identify the hearing of imaginary voices as an aberration. Once they had ceased to trouble him, he could suppose himself cured, although he suffered from occasional delusions subsequently, as we all do, no doubt. Once, many years later, he convinced himself for some reason that he lived in Glamorgan and bought himself a ticket there at Paddington station, coming to his senses only just in time to catch the train to Taunton. What he never came to terms with was any suggestion that his habitual melancholia might have been a form of clinical depression. He never took any medicine for it, relying on gin, which is almost certainly not the best cure. As a young man, I was appalled by the size of the glasses he filled with gin, usually mixed with lemon barley water, a peculiarly nauseating mixture, although I suppose that at fifty my own intake is only slightly smaller.

* * * *

The final year at Piers Court was overshadowed by my last and biggest disgrace, the Great Débâcle of July 1955 for which I think my father never entirely forgave me, although our relations were much more cordial in his later years, particularly the last five when I was well married and out of the way. I will tell the story here, since it all happened from Piers Court, although its roots are to be found in Downside, rather than Piers Court. The disaster occurred when elements from three compartments in my life became mixed together. Possibly the main lesson to be learned from the episode was to keep the compartments separate.

As a fifteen-year-old schoolboy at Downside, I joined a mysterious right-wing organization called the League of Empire Loyalists, run by A.K. Chesterton, a cousin of the great journalist, and paid for by a slightly sinister figure known only by the initials 'RKJ' who lived in South America. Later I think it merged with one or another of the right-wing groups often identified by their enemies as neo-fascist, but in those days it was concerned solely with resisting the retreat from Empire, a programme it advanced by the simple expedient of heckling the Prime Minister at public meetings. I was inspired to join it by reading a copy of its magazine, called *Candour*, shown to me I think by my friend Griffin. In those early days, I even contributed an article to *Candour* explaining why I thought all its policies were correct – they included bundling the Americans out of Europe, as I remember. An editorial praised my article, saying it proved that the public schools were still turning out the right stuff. This seems a premature conclusion, in the light of what happened later. I invited the League's organizer, Austen Brooks, a young man with a flaming red beard, to address the Downside Numismatic Society, of which I was founder and chairman. The Numismatic Society belonged to another compartment of my life, but for once the compartments seemed to mix rather well, and several numismatists signed up for the League of Empire Loyalists.

Encouraged by this, the League sought other ways of proselytizing my schoolmates, and it was arranged that I would take Miss Lesley Greene, secretary of the League, to the annual Downside Ball in London, with the League paying for my ticket. The Downside Ball was not an event I would normally have considered attending, but I relished the role of secret agent, infiltrating dangerous, subversive elements and recruiting people who would be prepared to go and heckle the Prime Minister at public meetings.

Miss Greene was some years older than myself – perhaps ten years older – and we might have made an odd pair, but she was obviously game. So accordingly on the morning of 25 July 1955 I caught a bus to Gloucester and then a train to London, planning to meet Miss Greene at the League's offices in Grand Buildings, Trafalgar Square. All might have gone well, although I rather doubt it as I had no money; instead I had brought a few knick-knacks from the Granny Waugh loot and some Mecca stones I had somehow acquired from a sister, all of which I optimistically hoped to sell in London.

At any rate, it was never put to the test. Hoping to make the London visit more convivial, I removed a bottle of Booth's gin from the box under the pantry table and put it in my suitcase. Perhaps it would be more to the point to say that I stole it, although even after thirty-five years I find that natural sensitivity recoils from the word. Later, under interrogation, I swore that I had bought it at a pub called the White Hart in Gloucester and, having learned my lesson from the earlier Lavery débâcle, stuck to my story through thick and thin. My father went to his grave without knowing for sure whether the gin was stolen, but this seems the least reprehensible aspect of the whole affair. There was nothing to be gained by telling him the truth. It would not have made him any happier; it would not have brought back the bottle of gin; since he was not an ordained priest, he had no sacramental power to absolve me from my sin.

Arriving at Gloucester station, I decided it was time for the conviviality to start, and offered some of the gin, to which I added orange squash bought from the station buffet, to a railway employee who seemed similarly at a loose end. We sat drinking for perhaps half an hour until my train came in and I got on it. A slight mystery attaches to the next part of the story. I thought I had bought myself a ticket to London with the last bit of my money, but no ticket was found on me when the police later searched my clothes in the cells at Stroud police station. It was this absence of a ticket which persuaded Papa that there might be some truth in my cock-and-bull story that I had spent my money on a bottle of gin at the White Hart in Gloucester.

At any rate I was convivially offering my bottle of gin around to the other passengers in my compartment when the door opened and in walked a guard accompanied by a furtive young man who said he represented the transport police. They refused my offer of some gin and orange squash, sternly asked how old I was and took me off the train at Stroud.

I was four or five hours in the cells at Stroud police station, singing songs from Gilbert and Sullivan to keep my spirits up, before the cell door opened and I was ushered into my father's presence. We drove back to Piers Court in stony silence. It transpired that he had been summoned out of the cinema in Dursley by a police message.

Next day, in Stroud magistrates' court I stood before a chairman of magistrates who looked extraordinarily like my Pixton grandmother (she had indeed been chairman of magistrates in Dulverton for many years) and said I had nothing to say to the charge of being drunk and incapable on a train. My father was then asked if he had anything to say – it was to his enormous credit that he had not brought in any solicitor to add further weight to the enormity of my crime. Doffing a preposterous checked cap, he said:

'I beg you to regard the incident as a disastrous experiment rather than as a mark of viciousness or depravity.'

'What? What?' said the magistrate. 'Ten bob? What? What? Fined ten shillings.'

Two days later Graham Greene came to stay. I think it was the first time we had met. I do not know whether he had been briefed about my Great Débâcle, but he went out of his way to be kind to the fifteen-year-old youth who was in such disgrace that nobody would talk to him except sideways, looking another way. I told him that I had recently sold a short story about the Emperor Caligula to a naughty magazine called *Lilliput* for £15. Actually this was a lie, as I received £25 for it, but the reasons for the lie are too complicated to explain at this stage. It represented about £350 in today's money – a vast, unimaginable sum for a fifteen-year-old boy in 1955.

'Well done,' said Mr Greene. 'My advice to you is to spend it all immediately. Don't save a penny. Blow it all on a huge binge.'

My poor Papa looked sick, rolled his eyes to Heaven and no doubt said a private prayer to St Jude.

*　*　*　*

I later learned that the perfidious railway employee at Gloucester station, whom I had thought my friend, tipped off the guard on the London train that there was a drunk youth aboard. If there was a moral to be learned from that experience, regarding the untrustworthiness of the working classes, I think I can truthfully say that I learned it.

Miss Greene eventually went to the Downside Ball alone. I cannot believe she enjoyed it much. She never learned the reasons for my not showing up. I have forgotten what excuse I used in my letter. After that the League of Empire Loyalists rather disappeared from my life.

CHAPTER THREE

Cranmore Hall 1946-1952

So it was that after a thorough washing from Lady Helen Asquith at Mells, I was delivered as a boarder to All Hallows preparatory school at the age of six and a quarter on 28 January 1946. The school had just moved from humbler accommodation at Scorhill in Devon, and this was its first term at Cranmore Hall, near Shepton Mallet, Somerset, a former seat of the Paget family. It is a substantial Jacobean pile, with excellent High Victorian additions in the form of a columned arcade, an orangery and a concert room with handsome porphyry pillars.

My father and I were ushered into a first-floor drawing-room where we were given China tea in tiny cups, and ginger biscuits – a considerable delicacy in those days when everything was rationed. I ate four or five of them under the apparently approving eye of the headmaster's wife, while the headmaster, F.H.R. Dix, suffered paroxysms of embarrassment as he tried to make conversation with my father. At that stage, I noticed only his great height, his white hair and bristly white moustache, the angry gurgle in his voice and the way he carried his right arm slightly bent – from the strain of beating boys, as I decided.

Francis Dix, a classicist, married Eveleen Bird when he was an assistant master at another Catholic prep school, called Avesford, and she the school matron. Both were of mature years – she some years older – and the union was not blessed, as they say, with children, although they later adopted one of the boys in the school, called Mario Barber, who found himself parentless. There was much speculation about how poor Barber made out. It was terrifying enough to have to deal with Dix in term-time, when his fury might be directed at any one of seventy or eighty boys in the school. To have him in the holidays as well, as the one and only object of his attention, seemed a fate much worse than anything we had read about in the Japanese prisoner-of-war camps.

Dix always seemed to be in a worse temper after his moustache had been clipped. Perhaps Mrs Dix performed this service for him, and her proximity enraged him.

It was impossible to imagine any form of physical intimacy between the two of them. She was stout and efficient and kindly. As the youngest and smallest boy in the school, I was officially declared to be her pet, although I can remember no particular benefits flowing from this appointment. Many years afterwards, when I was over forty, I received a letter from her out of the blue – she must have been at least eighty-five. It enclosed a snapshot which, she said, she had found among her late husband's papers when she was going through them. It showed me playing with three other boys on the lawn at Cranmore. They were identified as David McEwen, Pips Royston and Julian Ormsby-Gore. The mystery of why she had chosen to send it to me, rather than to one of the others, was soon solved when I realized that the other three were all dead: David and Pips by sudden illness in their early thirties, Julian by his own hand, with a pistol, rather earlier. I do not know what Mrs Dix was hinting, but anyway it did not work because it was she, not I, who died almost immediately afterwards.

Dix had fought in the First World War and been wounded, a fact born out by a curious bump on his forehead which turned red when he was angry. Perhaps the wound, rather than the moustache-clipping accounted for his rages. These were completely terrifying because his power in that small community was absolute. He taught classics in the most old-fashioned way, according to which we learned the conjugations and declensions by rote, reciting them in turn around the class. If a boy erred, he would shout 'NEXT'. If three boys in a row erred, he would be thrown into a rage, and if a fourth boy erred or even wavered, he would shout:

'Go into my study, take your trousers down and wait for me

there.'

Then he would apparently forget the unfortunate child shivering in the headmaster's study with his trousers round his ankles and finish the lesson. Beatings were administered either with an evil-looking slipper, already in tatters by the time I arrived and known to generations of its victims as 'The Furry Object', or with a gym shoe called 'Jimmy'. I do not know why he always beat the boys with their trousers down, but in the mellowness of middle age I cannot grudge him whatever small satisfaction he derived from the practice. He would insist, too, on being present at the weighing which occurred at the beginning of every term. The whole school would be required to sit, naked, one by one on a red velvet weighing machine under the direction of the matron, while the headmaster smoked his pipe ruminatively above. He also insisted on personally supervising sixth form showers, which was slightly odd, as this was not the sort of task a headmaster would normally undertake. Once again, his foul pipe, with its strong smell of Three Nuns Tobacco, was in evidence. There was never the faintest suggestion that he behaved improperly towards a boy, although he was not beyond having his favourites. But he never lifted a finger or touched a boy, except to beat him and I have no reason to suppose there was anything in the slightest bit improper about his attendance on these occasions. Perhaps his interest was medical.

Under Dix's ferocious tutelage, I won a major scholarship to Downside (I think that six out of the eight boys in my Classical Sixth won scholarships or exhibitions to their public schools) and even now, without having studied a classical text for nearly thirty-five years, I have no difficulty in conjugating the whole of North and Hillard's table of Greek irregular verbs, or putting Greek and Latin nouns into the proper declensions.

Dix never attempted to instruct his pupils in what were then called the facts of life, which was probably just as well, as he would almost certainly have got them wrong. There was no homosexuality at All Hallows because we were all too young for it – only one boy in my year had passed puberty by the time we left, and his condition was the subject of derisive whispers behind his back rather than congratulation or hero-worship. But one term when Dix was away – he was suffering from some unspecified but serious illness which did not prevent him from living to an immense age – what I can only describe as an epidemic of pseudo-buggery broke out in the St Thomas More dormitory. The new craze was called 'Mating' and was no different, except unisexual, from the traditional children's game of 'Mothers and Fathers'.

Needless to say, some sneak informed the authorities. One of the problems of a Catholic school was that the traditional school-boy's code of *omertà* did not apply to anything which might be thought specifically unCatholic. I do not know who the sneak was in the St Thomas More dormitory, although I seem to remember O'Farrell came under suspicion.

A Grand Inquiry into the 'Mating' allegations was set up under the deputy headmaster, Mr Jocelyn Trappes-Lomax. Trappes-Lomax was a delightfully ridiculous person who wore shorts and smoked Pall Mall cigarettes through a cigarette holder which wiggled up and down when he talked, interspersing his words with little 'yup' noises which were gleefully imitated.

Throughout the Grand Inquiry he was deadly serious, smoking cigars rather than cigarettes to emphasize the solemnity of the moment. He typified whatever behaviour had occurred in the St Thomas More dormitory as 'vulgarity'.

'Were you vulgar with Crichton-Stuart?' he asked. 'Were you vulgar with Niven?'

Trappes-Lomax was also head of the Boy Scouts, which added a whole new range of moral pressures on top of the Catholic ones. Vulgarity was not only unCatholic, it was also unScoutlike. Scout's Law required all Scouts to be:

> "Trusty, loyal, helpful
> Brotherly, courteous, kind
> Obedient, smiling, thrifty
> Pure of Body and Mind"

On at least three occasions I let Mr Trappes down. The first was when I stole his Ribena. This shocked him dreadfully, but was not as serious as the occasion when I found a confiscated air pistol in his room and, wishing to make a stir, aimed to kick up the gravel around the feet of a boy called Gregory who was standing outside Mr Trappes's window. In the event, I shot Gregory in the leg. This was considered such a serious offence that it had to be hushed up. Thirdly, sitting at Mr Trappes's table in the dining-room, I found a lump of gristle in my stew so revolting that rather than try to eat it I threw it sideways under the table, where it could not be traced to me. Unfortunately, it landed on Mr Trappes's bare knee, as he sat in his corduroy shorts at the end of the table.

'What guttersnipe has done this?' he demanded.

I would have tried to bluff my way out of it, but for some reason I have never fathomed, everybody at the table knew I was the culprit. He walloped me with his bare hand in front of the entire dining-room.

Poor Mr Trappes-Lomax, he cannot have liked me very much but he never showed it. Later, he started a prep school of his own in Lord Portsmouth's house near Farleigh Wallop, and died in the bath there. He was an unfathomably innocent man, and there was a saintliness in his innocence. He never seemed to have any conception of how eccentric he was, in his shorts, with his curious 'yup' noises and his wiggling cigarette holder.

Sometimes, in later life, I have been accused of snobbery, but nothing could equal the snobbishness of my prep school. There was a smart set, to which I was allowed admittance by virtue of my father's membership of White's, and his acquaintance with the fathers of other boys in the group; nobody – either at Cranmore or at Downside – was much impressed by any skill he might have shown as a writer. The smart set was called 'The Clan' – by masters as well as by themselves. The nucleus was a group of cousins – Royston, McEwen, the Keswick brothers – to which the sons of members of White's were admitted to increase numbers: myself, Koch de Goreynd, Ormsby-Gore and a very thin white boy called Hercules Belville who was some relation of the famous dressmaker. Belville turned up again at Oxford, but I do not know what happened to him after that. The older Keswick brother – Henry – who led the Woodpeckers troop of the Boy Scouts, became effective King of Hong Kong by virtue of his chairmanship of Jardine Matheson, and was briefly my proprietor on the *Spectator*. The younger Keswick brother – Chippendale – who was my deputy as troop leader of the Falcons, became Chairman of Hambros and also of the Portland Club.

David McEwen was my best friend. We would pretend to be our parents, meeting in White's. I would call him 'Jock', he, after a certain amount of hesitation called me 'Evelyn'. The McEwens had a fine early twentieth-century house designed by Lorimer on the

Borders, near Greenlaw, Berwickshire, called Marchmont. It was considerably bigger than Piers Court. Once I showed him a photograph of the pretty and quite imposing front of Piers Court.

'Ah, so this is where you live,' he said.

'That is the East Wing,' I said.

David once told me, in order to demonstrate the exceptional wealth of the McEwens, that when his grandmother, old Mrs McEwen, had died they had summoned a dentist all the way from Glasgow to remove the gold from her teeth.

*　*　*　*

Up to the age of seven I suffered from an abominable squint, which did not encourage others to trust me. In my seventh year, I was sent to an eye hospital in Bristol to have it rectified. This was my second taste of chloroform. The first was a delayed circumcision performed on me by the local doctor in Dulverton when I was three. He was called Dr McKinney, a stalwart of the Catholic church in Dulverton and grandfather, as it later turned out, of the ferocious Grub Smith who served as my editorial assistant on *Literary Review* for several years. McKinney set up an operating theatre in the night nursery at Pixton for his fell purpose. Many years later, McKinney's ancient, crooked house in Dulverton was bought by an artist, James Reeve, who set aside a room in it as a sort of shrine to which he took his visitors, saying it was the room in which I had been circumcised. I believe he also showed them some shrivelled object claiming it as a relic of the occasion. Like many holier relics which might even have acquired a certain aura of sanctity through the veneration of the faithful over many years, this relic has no historical basis.

My second operation, in the eye hospital at Bristol, was even more traumatic than the first. Coming round from the anaesthetic, I found that my eyes, the source of considerable discomfort, had been blindfolded and my arms, in splints, were tied to the side of a cot to prevent me from tearing off the bandages. I think it may have been the lowest moment of my life. Although equable by nature, I have never felt such rage as I felt then.

Oddly enough, the second great rage of my life, about thirty years later, also occurred while coming round from a general anaesthetic. There was an extraordinarily beautiful lady anaesthetist at the Westminster Hospital, London, in those days, and my last memory before passing out was of her lovely face, under a strange white cap, frowning with concentration as she injected Pentathol into my veins and I counted slowly. After what seemed a second but was in fact about an hour, I awoke to find myself completely paralysed. My brain sent messages to various limbs, but the limbs refused to obey them. It was one of the most disagreeable experiences I have ever had. What had happened was that the curare used as a muscle relaxant had failed to wear off, but I thought it was some sort of punishment for my lascivious thoughts about the anaesthetist and screamed in fury for twenty minutes. In my experience, it is the feeling of helplessness which produces extremes of rage.

* * * *

My stay at the Bristol eye hospital was enlivened by my contracting a throat infection which was wrongly diagnosed as diptheria. I was promptly moved into an isolation bed, to which my father came bringing a box of white mice. He smuggled them under his overcoat. They caused total consternation in the antiseptic hospital environment, but my father's force of character was such that not even the matron dared gainsay him. He thought the mice might cheer me up, but I never liked them much. When I returned to Piers Court they escaped and bred, infesting the Court Room where I conducted my chemical experiments. For all I know they are still there.

The gift of the mice was genially intended, but the fearlessness with which Papa tackled life's problems was not always welcome. A child hopes for parents who will be inconspicuous, but this was not in Papa's nature. He turned up one Sports Day wearing a boater with a Brigade of Guards' riband, and came to give away the prizes at a school prize-giving in a grey bowler hat of which he was very proud, calling it his drab Coke. One of Dix's hobbies was to perform conjuring tricks for the entertainment of the school. Papa was fascinated by this, always referring to him as 'the Conjurer', and on Speech Day he watched his every movement with exaggerated attention as if he expected him to draw a rabbit from his pocket. I had told my friends that my father drove a Daimler. When my mother came to pick me up at the end of term, I always asked her to park her ancient, scruffy Ford station-wagon outside the school grounds so as not to shame me.

Papa's best practical joke on his son was played in my first term at All Hallows, when I was still very nervous. He told me that he proposed to change his name to Stinkbottom. When he had done so, the headmaster would summon the school together and say: 'Boys, the person you have hitherto called Waugh will in future be called Stinkbottom.' I understood perfectly well that he was joking, but one never knew how far he would be prepared to go with his jokes. School assembly was held every morning, and every morning I felt a slight tightening of the chest as Mr Dix came forward to make his morning announcements.

In fact I think I must have been quite a tough little boy after my years of struggle with the evacuee children at Pixton. Mr R.A. Jones, a history master at All Hallows when I arrived there as a new boy of six at the end of January 1946, remembered approaching me on the second day of term to ask me my name. 'I are Waugh,' I shouted at him, as if he must have been extraordinarily foolish not to know that already. In my second term, when a group of boys were chatting between lessons, a senior boy called Tony Hollander came up and asked me why I carried a large steel pen-knife. My answer: 'I use it to cut pieces off my mother's nose.'

* * * *

I think I must have been a fairly difficult child to like. My father made a valiant attempt to see the better side of me in August 1949, when I was nine years old, taking me in a small aeroplane to a dreadful seaside resort in France called La Baule, where he planned to meet Lady Pamela Berry who was staying in one hotel alone, while her nanny and three children stayed in another. I was to be put in with the children. I do not suppose for a moment there was anything remotely improper in my father's relationship with Lady Pamela, but it seems an odd arrangement, with the benefit of hindsight. In the event, there was a change of plan. As Papa wrote to Nancy Mitford from La Baule's Grand Hotel on 18 August 1949:

> I am in a town of ineffable horror. You might have warned me. There is a strip of sand, a row of hotels and sand-dunes & pines at the back. This is the worst of many hotels. I came here with my boy Auberon in an aeroplane on Monday to join your great new friend Pamela. I came to the hotel and was told she was too ill to see me & that there was no room at the

hotel . . .

I found three disconsolate, shifty urchins under the care of a nannie who knew no French at all & had no money. . . .

My boy behaves beautifully & is very happy. The more I see of other people's children the less I dislike my own.

Poor Papa. He spent every evening alone losing money in the local casino. After a week he returned to England and I joined the Berrys for a ten-day cruise on Lord Camrose's yacht. We sailed – or rather steamed, as I am happy to report it was a very large steam yacht called *Virginia* – all the way down the west coast of France and as far into Spain as Santander, then we steamed back again. It was a very agreeable way to spend the time. We were joined by Lady Pamela's husband, Michael Berry. I think he was already some sort of senior executive on the *Daily Telegraph*, which his family owned: a tall, thin, saturnine man, much more athletic and handsome than my own father. After landing at Southampton we spent the night at Hackwood, which irritated me as being obviously much grander than Pixton.

I am not sure how I disgraced myself on this trip, but I am reasonably sure I did so. There is a sad little footnote to it which appears in Mark Amory's *Letters of Evelyn Waugh* (London, 1980) where my father is describing the horrors of La Baule to his friend Nancy Mitford, in August 1949. The footnote is written by the editor, as part of his huge labour of checking facts and collating references: 'Lady Pamela Berry, now Lady Hartwell, says she has no recollection of this holiday.'

* * * *

Dix was to die on 21 May 1983, when I was forty-three years old, and it would be idle to deny that I felt a certain weight was lifted when I heard the news. His wife, who was even older than he was, died less than a year later. The last I had seen of either of them was when I was lying wounded in the Westminster Hospital after shooting myself with a machine gun in Cyprus. Dix decided, out of the kindness of his heart, to visit me there. I had shaken off the terrors of school in nine months of lotus eating in Florence. I was an officer in the army, a man who had commanded troops – if not in battle, at any rate in conditions of active service. Dix had no dominion over me. And yet I found that I froze in mortal terror as this stuttering, inarticulate man stood over my bed in the Westminster Hospital.

I do not think Dix was a sadist, as so many schoolmasters undoubtedly are, although he could be very cruel in his rages, pulling out great tufts of boys' hair. It is my observation that many pipe-smokers are cruel, although I do not know whether their cruelty is brought on by the habit, or whether cruel people are naturally drawn to pipes. Even now, I cannot smell pipe-smoke without feeling a strong urge to run away.

My poor Papa was similarly prone to strike terror without any of Dix's violent rages. He never beat his children, although he may have struck me once or twice in the heat of the moment. But Evelyn Waugh's defects were easy to see, and have been much commented on, usually by whingeing literary critics of the Cambridge and redbrick schools. It is true that he was a snob in some respects (by no means in all) although I have never been able to see that as anything wickeder than a personal preference. His chief defect was his greed.

One one occasion, just after the war, the first consignment of bananas reached Britain. Neither I, my sister Teresa nor my sister Margaret had ever eaten a banana throughout the war, when they were unprocurable, but we had heard all about them as the most delicious taste in the world. When this first consignment arrived, the socialist government decided that every child in the country should be allowed one banana. Any army of civil servants issued a library of special banana coupons, and the great day arrived when my mother came home with three bananas. All three were put on my father's plate, and before the anguished eyes of his children, he poured on cream, which was almost unprocurable, and sugar, which was heavily rationed, and ate all three. A child's sense of justice may be defective in many respects, and egocentric at the best of times, but it is no less intense for either. By any standards, he had done wrong. It would be absurd to say that I never forgave him, but he was permanently marked down in my estimation from that moment, in ways which no amount of sexual transgression would have achieved. It had, perhaps, the effect on my estimation of him that the Lavery and Great Débâcles combined had on his of me. From that moment, I never treated anything he had to say on faith or morals very seriously.

CHAPTER FOUR

Downside 1952-1956

When I arrived at Downside to put on the 'Regulation Suit' of black coat and waistcoat, hairstripe trousers, stiff white collar and black tie, I was no stranger to the place. Cranmore was only six miles away, and I had been there to be confirmed by the Roman Catholic Bishop of Clifton in the huge and rather beautiful Giles Gilbert Scott abbey church. I had also been there to box against the junior house. The fight was stopped when my opponent's nose started to bleed. I do not know why I boxed, detesting every other form of sport. I see now it was a disgusting thing to do and also rather foolish, as I was not at all athletic and never won another fight. My second brother, James, who went to be educated by the Jesuits at Stonyhurst after the appalling example I had set among the Benedictines at Downside, also boxed, even winning a Blue at Oxford for it. Again, I cannot think why. There was no physical rivalry in our family, perhaps as the result of having such a splendidly unathletic father. But the result was that I tended to look at the other boys as potential boxing opponents, and this was rather discouraging.

Partly as a result of my having gone to boarding school so young, I was only twelve when I arrived at Downside in the autumn of 1952. There were about 450 boys there at this time, more than four times as many as at All Hallows, often gangling louts in various stages of emotional and hygienic disarray. There is something quite intimidating about any large group of Anglo-Saxon youths. Violence always lurks under the surface. Even when they sang an anthem to Our Lady in the abbey at the end of term, those raucous, untrained, recently broken voices somehow managed to turn it into a war song. I decided to tread carefully, at any rate to begin with.

Partly to protect them from the savagery in store, new boys were put into a junior house under the care of Dom Simon Van Zeller, a wizened figure in his black robes with a nut-brown crew cut and bright little eyes like a squirrel. He was not popular with the boys, who credited him with running a secret police or Gestapo, encouraging them to sneak on each other in exchange for unspecified privileges attaching to the shadowy status of 'unofficial prefect'. From time to time, boys were denounced as belonging to this Gestapo and beaten up.

But Dom Simon always struck me as a witty, civilized man. He encouraged boys to play bridge and chess, complaining bitterly when one of them farted, which seemed to happen about once every five minutes. It must have been a form of martyrdom for such an intelligent man, who had no great liking for boys, to spend his time among adolescent youths, whether they were sly and crooked like me or full of enthusiasm and religiously obsessed.

There undoubtedly was another sort of secret police run by Dom Simon's deputy housemaster, a fat, bald Irishman with a deceptively jolly face called Dom Wulstan A. Philipson (Wappy). His was a spiritual secret police, trained to inform on the religious and moral health of their fellows. In a Catholic school, there was some ambivalence towards such activities. Skipping mass or any other religious service – on Sundays, we spent a good two and a half hours in church, starting at 7.30 in the morning Low Mass, Compline, High Mass, something called Sodality (a lengthy sermon), Vespers and Benediction – was definitely a school offence, and as such could not be sneaked on. Offences of a sexual nature were likely to be judged religious: with them, you were on much dicier ground. It was a Wappyite conformer called Brenninkmeyer who shopped me for trying to hold a Black Mass in the chemistry laboratory. Such people were not beaten up, merely avoided.

* * * *

On my first evening at Downside we were given rabbit pie. The food was much better than at All Hallows, but treated with great derision. The boy sitting next to me said: 'Beagle.'

'What was that?'

'Beagle. They always give you beagle on Thursdays.'

He was called Griffin, up from Worth, which was the main preparatory school for Downside, and seemed to possess immense *savoir faire*. I found myself edging away from O'Farrell who had come up with me from All Hallows, and who did not look as if he would be a very useful person to know.

Griffin became a close friend and fellow member of a gang of desperadoes calling itself 'The Clique'. We rented a room in the house of a retired poacher called Gilbert Mines where we went to smoke in the afternoons. Mines was a very stupid and disagreeable man, the first of many such landlords. There may be valid arguments against private education and the boarding school system, but one of them is not that it confines its pupils to a particular social class and prevents them from meeting ordinary people. I met many ordinary people in the sense of the semi-criminal underclass during my years at Downside, certainly enough to form an accurate impression of them. I do not think anything useful would have been achieved by meeting more.

Downside was proud of its pack of beagles, but they seldom caught a hare, and I went out with them only once. On that occasion I was with the Master of the Hunt, a boy called Poland, when we found a hare which had been caught in a gin trap. It was a particularly big hare. After much blowing of horns, the animal was disembowelled and its bowels thrown to the beagles. So rare was it for the beagles to catch anything that its head was stuffed and mounted on a wooden shield and presented to the headmaster. For the rest of my stay at Downside, it stared out from the wall of his study, witnessing all the floggings and other distressing scenes which became such a regular feature of my school life. Perhaps it is still there. If any awareness lingers in that grisly relic, it must reckon to have had its revenge by now.

*   *   *   *

Downside, initially, seemed much freer than All Hallows. There were two shops at which one could buy everything except cigarettes and alcohol. Sweets were still rationed, of course. It was the happy experience of nearly all my contemporaries, who were children through the Second World War, that with every year that passed from about 1952 onwards, the shops filled up with new and better things to buy, just as we have all grown steadily richer, with one or two set-backs, ever since. Perhaps this should have turned us into a generation of optimists, but it has not had that effect on me. I still see the privations of wartime and post-war schooling as the norm, from which subsequent freedom and prosperity are temporary aberrations. At any moment, I feel, the British economy will crash irrevocably, and there will be no bananas, let alone wine, to buy in the shops. For many years I invested any spare money I had in silver bullion and Maria Theresa thalers, having no trust in money, let alone in paper share certificates which required an act of faith that British workers would be prepared to go on working to make them profitable. Even now, my only investment, apart from some tax avoidance schemes, is in cellars and cellars of wine, so that at least I shall have something to drink when the pound disappears from sight on the world's markets.

The greater freedom was, of course, illusory, but there was pleasure in wearing long trousers instead of shorts. In those days all school uniforms were supplied by the school tailor, an obese and unattractive man called Mr Skinner, who spent an unnecessarily long time measuring the junior boys for their trousers. He lived in one of the many Nissen huts dotted around the school grounds.

Long trousers, waistcoats and stiff collars were not the only signs of our promotion. There was a classics master who said 'Good morning, gentlemen', at the beginning of his classes, and even called me 'Mr Waugh', which seemed entirely suitable. I resolved that when I was grown up I would seek him out and give him some money. He was a delightfully absurd figure called Mr Brash, with dyed golden waves in his hair, who had been at Downside for as long as anybody could remember. In extreme old age, he amazed everybody by taking a wife. Most of the other lay masters were beasts, or seemed so at the time. It may not be fair to dismiss them quite so readily, as I was an exceptionally difficult boy, who took ruthless advantage of any weakness.

*   *   *   *

My greatest friend was called Gormanston. Perhaps it was no

more than a coincidence that he was the only titled person in my year, unless you counted foreigners. He was an attractive boy, two days my junior, who, as a result of his father's disappearance early in the war, had become the premier viscount of Ireland. He also had a very attractive mother, Pamela O'Connor, whom I loved. She was not at all like the character of Lady Foxglove in my first novel, but was a cheerful, sensuous bon vivante.

The friendship was arranged by Gormanston's great-uncle, an aged monk in the monastery called Dom Urban Butler, who for some reason used to stay at Piers Court. Gormanston remained a friend through all my Downside years, but by no means all these arrangements worked out so well. When I was at All Hallows, Papa wrote to ask me to be nice to a new boy who was the son of his old flame, Baby Jungmann. I wrote back: 'It is hard to be nice to Cuthbertson. He is most disagreeable. Very weak and all the boys & masters hate him.'

My father reported his reaction to Nancy Mitford: 'I have written a tremendous homily on the nature of the English gentleman who always protects the weak & unpopular. Can't say I ever noticed it much myself.'

The vulgar idea of public schools as a conspiracy of the rich to support each other against competition from the state-educated takes no account of how public schoolboys hate each other, or how vilely they continue to treat each other whenever they get the chance. I blush even now to think of some of the things I did. Although most of my targets were figures of authority – prefects, masters and monks – there was O'Farrell from the Dix academy. He was very clever and a fellow-classicist. From his earliest years O'Farrell, whom we called Flan, was known to have an uncontrollable temper. Flan-bates, as they were called, became a regular diversion of the classical stream. First, before the class began, we would get him into a ferocious bate by the simple device of throwing books at him. When in a bate, O'Farrell would fly, screaming, at the throat of the nearest boy. Once roused, he could be activated to his full frenzy by the slightest annoyance – a rubber thrown from behind, or even a finger pointed furtively from in front. The art of the Flan-bate was to excite him to a fury a few minutes before the class started, just in time for the master to find everyone seated demurely at his desk. Then, when everyone had settled and the class had been going on for a few minutes, someone would quietly flick a rubber or point a finger. For no apparent reason so far as the master was concerned, O'Farrell would start screaming and throwing his books around before flying at the nearest boy. The classics master, a sceptical Australian called Stallybrass who quite reasonably detested me, suspected that I was to blame, but the schoolboy code of *omertà* inhibited O'Farrell from explaining his actions. I hope O'Farrell has forgiven me. Perhaps I shall send him a telegram from my deathbed.

*   *   *   *

At the end of a year in the junior house, Gormanston and I found ourselves sent to the same senior house, called Roberts after the Benedictine martyr Blessed (now Saint) John Roberts, under a wise and friendly old monk called Dom Vincent Cavanagh. In those days there was an initiation ceremony whereby new boys to Roberts had to sing a song under a shower to the whole house and then run the gauntlet while being drenched with buckets of cold water. Gormanston and I faced the ordeal together, singing a song called 'A you're Adorable, B you're so beautiful'. As he was a prettier boy than I was, he suffered more. It seems odd that this institutionalized terrorism should have taken place in front of the housemaster, but I believe ours was the last initiation ceremony. Its origins, I imagine, were sadistic and homosexual. Perhaps the monks were too innocent to understand about these things.

*   *   *   *

In April 1954 Dom Vincent was taken ill and was replaced at short notice as housemaster by a mild and genial soul, Dom Hilary Steuert. He had little experience of boys and none at all of me. More important from my point of view, he was too kind-hearted to put any force behind his beatings, which were treated as a joke behind his back, although, as I remember, we always put on an act of suffering the most tremendous pain at the time. Perhaps my acting failed to impress him, because, in a charming letter written when he heard that I was contemplating this autobiography, he stresses that although his acquaintance with me in a disciplinary way was quite brief, 'the calm and unruffled way in which you accepted my sanctions never struck me as indicating that you were desperately unhappy. Rather the reverse: you ruled your little empire of friends with ruthless efficiency and gave every impression of complacent triumph over the ineffectiveness of authority.'

The purpose of this kind and gentle priest's letter was to urge me to redress my persistent denigration of the headmaster, Dom Wilfred Passmore. I seem to remember writing quite a kind obituary of Dom Wilfred in *Private Eye* when he died in February 1976, after a rather sad period as abbot at the end of which he was ousted by a coup. But the point is well taken. I persecuted Dom Wilfred abominably in my last two years at Downside. 'In some ways it reminded me of your father's relentless persecution of the unfortunate Cruttwell of Hertford', writes Dom Hilary. 'I can only say that I think Father Wilfred was astonishingly patient and charitable towards you.'

At least the fiendish C.R.M.F. Cruttwell, Dean of Hertford College, Oxford in my father's time as an undergraduate, had given some cause for this persecution. He gratuitously wrote derogatory letters about Evelyn Waugh to Waugh's first mother-in-law, Lady Burghclere (by coincidence, my Great-Aunt Winifred, having been born Lady Winifred Herbert) at the time of his first marriage. Cruttwell died a bachelor, separated from the dogs he treated so vilely, in a Bristol insane asylum during the war, although I do not suppose my father's persecution was responsible for this sad ending to a life which had been blighted by wounds received in the trenches of the First World War.

Passmore, as I always thought of Dom Wilfred, had committed no such aggression. He had a brilliant mind and would undoubtedly have become a leading lawyer of his generation if he had not joined the monastery. He was immensely fat, the front of his black habit invariably covered with food stains. Graham Greene declared that he filed his teeth and had the cruellest face he had ever seen. I do not think he was particularly cruel, although it seems odd, in retrospect, for a highly intelligent man to have spent so much of his time beating boys. He would personally collect books left lying around in the school corridors and then summon the boys concerned for a beating. Every evening in term-time a list of boys he wished to see appeared on the headmaster's noticeboard. Sometimes it was merely to tell them that their mother had died or whatever, but mostly it was to beat them. I held the school record – possibly still do – of fourteen beatings in a single term. But I find it hard to believe he derived much pleasure from them.

Even if he did, I cannot find it in my heart to grudge him such little consolations.

At the time I calculated that if I played up the lack of sympathy between us, channelling a large part of my generally delinquent behaviour into personal attacks on him, he would be reluctant to expel me since it would look to my father as if he was acting out of personal pique. I circulated endless poems inveighing against him, of which I now remember only the opening lines of one:

Beneath that fleshy mound with laughter huge
A world of cunning and of subterfuge
A mind for all to see and fools admire
And any moneyed parent's easy hire.

It went on for pages and pages. I also raised a petition against him, to be presented to the abbot, demanding that he be replaced as headmaster. About eighty boys signed it, which was very brave of them, since the headmaster controlled not only their school careers but also any recommendations they might expect for their university or subsequent employment. For many years afterwards I divided the world's population into those who would have signed the petition – the brave, the reckless, the amiable – and those who wouldn't: the creeps, sneaks, time-servers, and men on the make. Unfortunately, I had promised the signatories that the petition would not be presented unless I had secured a hundred signatures, so the abbot never saw it, although everybody knew of its existence. It was a good thing, I thought, to have found eighty good men in the school. I do not suppose for a moment that one would find such a high proportion of good men at Winchester, or even at Eton. I remember with particular affection the two assistant masters who signed, although one of them may not have been completely aware of what he was signing.

My Great Hatred for Passmore started with an incident when we had rented a wooden garden hut in the village for our smoking club, having been turned out of the Mines's cottage. We asphyxiated a large number of the budgerigars he bred. They dropped from their perches one by one as we smoked around them. Then we rashly accused Mines of stealing our cigarettes. The garden hut did not last long either. One night we were raided by a party of prefects who broke down the door to secure entry. I became very indignant about this, seeing myself as the legal tenant, and telephoned the police to lay charges of breaking and entering against the head boy and headmaster. The police were not much impressed, but said they would speak to the headmaster.

Later, when we were lined up in front of the headmaster's desk, he expressed mild pain at our having brought the police into the matter. Then he addressed us each individually. One, Theobald Mathew, was the son of Francis Mathew, manager of *The Times*, a school contemporary of Passmore's. Passmore told him how well they had always got on together, how he had always looked upon him as a friend. I forget who the other boys were on that occasion, but each received the same treatment. Then he came to me. 'In Waugh's case, it is true,' he said, 'I have not found myself on easy terms.'

Then the beatings started – a particularly traumatic session, as I remember. I was left with a burning sense of grievance. It was bad psychology on his part, comparable to my father's eating all three of the first bananas before my anguished eyes. From that moment, Passmore was the Enemy.

*　*　*　*

It was my practice, while at home, to intercept the post and steam open any letters or reports which arrived from Downside in the course of the holidays. The school reports were enclosed in a folder, with each subject on a separate sheet of paper, so it was easy to extract those which were outrageously offensive. As a result of reading the headmaster's correspondence, it came as no surprise to me when I received a postcard from my father in May 1955 informing me that I was to change houses. He was taking me away from the mild, benign regime of Dom Hilary Steuert, and entrusting me to a small, hirsute, swarthy, Welsh medieval historian called Dom Aelred Watkin – always known as 'Bushy' – in a rival house called Caverel.

My prior knowledge of this arrangement did not diminish the shock and anger of my reply to his postcard:

> It is unprecedented in the history of the school to change house outside Junior House, let alone approaching the fourth year here. You made the decision ignorant of the constitution or opinion of the school, and could not have realized how

drastic such a course is ... nor will my circle of friends change with my house or, if it does, it will be for the worse; Caverel House, under Father Aelred's ministration as it is, is by far the most vicious of all.

My first term in Caverel, which came immediately after the Great Débâcle, brought with it the Great Fire of November 1955. I wrote home on 25 November:

Darling Mummy & Papa,
Please excuse the extreme squalor of this letter – it is being written in a prep. and must somehow look like an history essay. Thank you very much for the magnificent birthday present – I have not had an opportunity to wear it yet, and have contented myself with preening in the mirror; after my vile act in forgetting your birthday you would have been quite justified in ignoring mine entirely.

The Great Fire was immense fun; the circular you got from the headmaster kept just within the bounds of Truth, although it does not give a glimmering of what actually happened. Besides the Gym, which, as it says, is completely destroyed, three dormitories (not two) are left without a stone upon a stone, and one is badly damaged. The Linen room, containing the whole school's sheets etc. has been completely destroyed. One classroom has been pulled down because it was unsafe.

"The boys' behaviour was, in all cases, exemplary." The school divided, more or less, into three distinct sections. Those who were confined to their dormitories, not being able to escape, at an early stage, then those who gallantly tried to put the fire out, and then the reactionary group who tried to let it burn. More hoses were squirted at the boys than at the fire. The Headmaster was equally delighted with both groups – he was torn between conflicting emotion at the thought of the insurance (a claim for £40,000), the love of a bonfire, and his duty to the insurers. The other monks did not attempt to conceal their delight. Father Hubert van Zeller danced in front of the fire singing the Te Deum rather off key. Another monk rushed into Father Wulstan Phillipson's room (some thirty yards from the fire) and started throwing the wireless

out of the window, breaking pictures, jumping on gramophone records etc.

I managed to get out of the dormitory while a riot was
taking place at the other end; down in the hall I joined a
group of other boys who had escaped and were busy throwing their Corps uniforms into the blaze. I managed to grab a
hose from a semi-stupefied fireman and was the first (of
many) to squirt the headmaster. The Tusk was wildly excited
– squirting himself with synthetic foam, until he looked like a
Christmas cake Santa Claus. The flames were now raging
some 30 feet above the top of the gym. Among the junior boys
there was a general tendency to be heroic, but since there
was no one to be rescued and they had no one to practise
their Boy Scout training on, they had to content themselves
with running everywhere very usefully, and running the
gauntlet of our hoses, which knocked them down like nine-
pins.

I joined the Headmaster who was standing with the Abbot
instructing the firemen as to which parts of the building they
should let burn, and which parts they could squirt so long as
they stopped if the fire showed any signs of abating. At 3.00
a.m. the fire reached its climax. While it roared and hissed
some fifty feet above the roof, while iron girders became
white hot and crashed in twisted shapes on to the floor, while
over 2000 gallons of water were being pumped *every minute*
at enormous pressure from some forty hoses, while all this
was happening, boys were still running up and down to the
Barlow top dormitory with tooth-mugs full of water.

With that horrible bureaucratic outlook which always pre-
vails in schools, work has been resumed as usual. Boys are
sleeping on mattresses in the class-rooms, Old House, even
Old Chapel, but still things go on. Gym is being held out of
doors.

The whole of the prefabricated area of the school – about 2
acres, is now a pile of rubble with twisted bed frames here
and there. The fire was definitely a good thing.

No news – all stories in the papers about 40 boys being
rescued by monks are quite untrue – they were made up by
myself and Mark Sykes for the reporters' benefit. I was tele-
vised by the BBC and ITA hunting, distraught, for lost belong-

ings. Actually we were looting the remains of the signals room. I found one charred toothbrush.

All my love,
Bron

The Great Fire of October 1955 came so soon after my Great Débâcle that my father always suspected me of having caused it, along with the son of his friend, Christopher Sykes, who was also at Downside at the time. I never enlightened him either way. Although I knew Mark Sykes quite well at that time – in fact we shared the tenancy of Mr Mines's front room as our smoking club – he never told me that he was responsible for the fire, and I can only suppose that he wasn't.

Despite my protestations to my father to the contrary, I did change my friends when I changed house. Griffin, Innes, Farter Owen and Snowy Robson were replaced by Mathew, Pellew, Perry and others whose names I have forgotten. The new gang rented a commodious room in a farmhouse as its clubroom. As part of the new deal, I had to see the headmaster once a week and show him a book signed by all my tutors to the effect that I had attended their classes. It was rather like the electronic tagging currently proposed as a replacement for imprisonment. I also changed from classics, in which I had spent five years and secured my A levels at the early age of fifteen, to English and history. It was put to me that if I applied myself to my work and passed A levels in English and history and secured an award to Oxford, I could be out of the place at the end of the year. This is what eventually happened, but not without a fight. In the meantime I cunningly thought I might get out even earlier by appealing to my father's sense of financial prudence:

Dear Papa,
The term has run about three weeks now and it has become increasingly apparent to me, at any rate, that I am unlikely to win an award in either English or History. ... My stay at Downside is costing you a great deal of money and, should I go to university, I will cost you a good deal more. I am doing very little good at Downside for the school or myself, and I really think it is a mistake to go on paying for an education which is neither a pleasure nor a profit.

Not long ago you mentioned that you had some influence in the hotel trade. If I entered this, there would be no need for a University education. I already possess two A level passes, and if I stay on the most I can hope to gain this year is another two; if I stay on another year it is possible that I may win an award that would be either worthless or nearly worthless to you financially, and would have cost you well over £500.

It would be convenient if I could get my two years' basic training in the hotel trade before National Service. In this way I would not completely waste the next two years, which seems to be inevitable otherwise.

If you write to Father Passmore, I think he will raise no objection to my removal at the end of term; our increasingly bad relationship renders this by no means improbable in any case ...

I see that my adolescent cynicism was too overt. If money calculations were to play a part, I should have left them unmentioned. My father replied:

Piers Court, 11 February 1956

Dear Bron,
I have written to enquire at what age apprentices are taken in the hotel trade. I think you are still too young, but I don't know ... My financial interests have no bearing on my wish for your welfare. I am sorry you should suggest that they might.
Your affectionate papa,
E. Waugh

He also arranged for his friend Brian Franks, a fellow wartime Commando officer who was now director of the Hyde Park Hotel under Basil Bennett, another former Commando, to send me the brochure for a hotel training establishment in Switzerland. It included the instruction to bring three drying-up cloths. This, more than anything else, more than my father's eloquence, brought me to my senses. I wrote on 19 February 1956:

Dear Papa,

... Everything you said in your letter was absolutely true. It would be useless to pretend I had a vocation in the hotel trade or any other at the moment. I regarded it simply as a way to get out of the school. If leaving school at 16 does entail all the disadvantages you mention – a friendless life and an army career in the ranks – it would be silly to leave now. On the other hand, I can see no way in which the next two years will not be wasted here.

You mention throwing myself into school life. I have tried all the methods – I speak at Debating Societies, founded others and attend all the high-brow philosophical discussions, and even attempt to edit papers. What more could be desired? Games are quite out of the question ...

You mention obeying school rules. I am convinced that school life would be insupportable without breaking them ... My relationship with the headmaster makes any advancement in the school extremely unlikely, and even Father Aelred, with whom I am consistently on the best of terms, cannot help me in this.

My weekly meetings with the headmaster, designed to promote a sympathetic cordiality between the two of us, were not being a great success. He had kindly absolved me from organized games so that I could get on with my work for A levels and the Oxford exam. This was a major concession. My previous attempt to get out of these games had taken the form of joining the school archaeological society, then engaged in excavating a fox's earth in a cave a few miles from the school. Unfortunately, I was sacked from that for smoking on the site. Every time they dug up one of my cigarette ends we all gathered round and declared it Romano-British, probably fifth century.

But despite the headmaster's concession on the subject of games, there was no cordiality between the two of us. Perhaps our humours did not coincide. I have always had difficulty in appreciating the jokes of anyone in a position of authority over me. It is also true that even as I sat guffawing insincerely at his pleasantries, I was engaged in what I planned as my last great Downside outrage – my own edition of the *Rook*.

In the history of Downside, only two or three issues of the *Rook*

– a libellous and obscene parody of the official magazine, the *Raven* – had ever been produced. They were talked about in whispers. A boy called Mathews (not to be confused with Theobald Mathew, although I think he may have been involved too) was the prime mover. My role was merely to write most of it – a long scream of hate against poor Father Wilfred. 'I could instantly recognize the pieces you wrote,' he said to me, when a seized copy of the magazine lay between us on his desk, adding with a terrible leer, 'they were so much better written.'

Mathews was in charge of printing, production and distribution. It was by his error that the printer telephoned the school and asked to speak to the headmaster in order to check a point in the text. On balance, I suppose, I should be glad that the magazine was suppressed, but it was a bitter blow at the time. It should have been sold on the school train on the last day of term.

I never saw Mathews again after hearing that our plot had misfired. He was a brave man – a prefect to boot, which made his behaviour all the more admirable. Wherever I have gone in life, I have always found this subversive element among Englishmen in a position of authority. It does not apply to all Englishmen, of course, only to a few of them, but I think it is confined to the English, often a product of public school education. It creates a sort of fraternity. One can recognize it by a look, by a lift of the eyebrow, a chance remark – rather, I imagine, as homosexuals recognize each other. It sustained, and continues to sustain at the moment of writing, such national institutions as *Private Eye*. Of all the qualities of the British, this readiness to mock and subvert is the one which makes life in Britain preferable to life anywhere else.

I passed my English and history A levels without too much difficulty in the summer of 1956 and towards the end of the Christmas term went to Oxford to take the Christ Church scholarship. Returning from Oxford to Combe Florey for the first time, I learned I had won an exhibition in English. I think that Dom Wilfred Passmore's congratulations were entirely genuine as he agreed with my father that there was no point in my returning to Downside, although I had only just passed my seventeenth birthday. I had every reason to be grateful to Passmore, but we never met again.

CHAPTER FIVE

Florence 1957

My last terms at Downside were spent largely in the company of an artistic and theatrical set which had grouped around a monk, Dom Hubert van Zeller. Gormanston, who had remained a faithful friend throughout my vicissitudes, belonged to this set. Another luminary was 'Monster' Mlnaric, who became an interior decorator, and 'Boots' Bantock, the painter and declaimer of verse. But the chief figure in the group was Rob Stuart, a swarthy, rather rich painter.

On securing my release from Downside with the news of the exhibition at Christ Church, I was sent to Florence with Rob Stuart to spend the eight or so months before my call-up for National Service in the Royal Horse Guards (the Blues); I had decided to do my two years of National Service before Oxford, rather than after it.

The idea of Florence was that we should learn a foreign language, possibly by joining the university, if there was one – a matter on which my parents were rather vague. Later inquiries suggest there has, indeed, been a university in Florence since quite early times, but we never found it during the seven months we spent there. The time was spent quite literally doing nothing. I was given £14 a week to live on – the equivalent, perhaps, of £180 in 1991 – and Rob had the same. When money ran out, Rob, who was a gifted artist, reproduced famous Florentine madonnas in chalk on the pavement outside the Uffizi, or in an arcade on the

Lungarno, while I held the hat. We would make about 3000 lire a day – then about £1.15, or £22.50 in modern money, always from Italians who would give us a 10 or 5 lire aluminium coin as a matter of course. In the evening, we would go to a fairly smart restaurant and pay the bill with bags of these coins, often prompting the suspicion that we had raided a church box.

We stayed in lodgings in the centre of town – Signora Siringo's establishment at Via Monalda Uno between the Piazzale Strozzi and the Via Porta Rossa – which had been recommended by Andrew Sinclair, who had stayed there a few years earlier.

I had met Andrew the year before, staying in my grandmother's house at Portofino. Later, he became a famous novelist with *The Breaking of Bumbo,* describing how a young Etonian guards officer of the working class refused to serve in the Anglo-French invasion of Suez. It caused quite a stir, contributing to the glorification of the working classes which was then becoming fashionable, and adding to a general radical repudiation of the Suez adventure. When I met Andrew, however, he was quite unlike the disgusting Bumbo Bailey. Although an Etonian and a guards officer, he was by no means working class. At Portofino in the summer of 1975, he had already left the Coldstream Guards for over a year, but was to be heard harrassing his regimental headquarters every afternoon to offer his services in the imminent action. I don't know whether this little piece of literary history is of any importance.

Signora Siringo, whom we inherited from him, was a fat bustling woman with an endless capacity for being maternal. In my letters home, I describe her as having eight children, but this seems unlikely. Perhaps she had three or four. For our extremely modest rent, she supplied us with a huge lunch every day, usually piles of spaghetti followed by meat balls. Although we had the healthy appetites of young people, we could not eat all she gave us and so used to wrap up large amounts of it in newspaper and hide them in a cupboard for later distribution through the streets of Florence. Seeing our plates empty, she would give us more and more of this revolting food until the cupboard all but collapsed under the weight of the greasy bundles. Eventually, of course, she found them. After endless tearful scenes she agreed to give us smaller helpings and change the menu occasionally.

Throughout these seven months we met very few English

people. One was Tristram Hillier, the distinguished Associate Member of the Royal Academy who had been Rob's painting tutor in Somerset. We put him up at Signora Siringo's, plying him with Chianti every evening. He later claimed to retain fond memories of this episode, but I doubt whether he had any memories at all. Another Englishman turned up in the person of a school acquaintance called John Clay. We affected not to remember his name, and he was too proud to tell us it. In the course of the summer we took him to Portofino, where I led my grandmother aside and said I was sorry to be unable to introduce him as we had both forgotten his name and could remember only his school nickname which was 'Tart'. She took it completely in her stride, and called him 'Tart' throughout the visit. Needless to say, he had no such nickname at Downside.

Apart from the British consul, Ian McMaster, a former Eton master who had an unaccountable admiration for my grandfather, Arthur Waugh, our only contact with polite society was through Harold Acton, the aesthete, who lived in great splendour in his fifteenth-century palace, the Villa La Pietra, on the Via Bolognese. He was an old Oxford friend of my father, although their more recent meetings had been less happy. He did not allow this to influence his great kindness to us, although I fear we may have been a grave embarrassment to him, arriving on our Vespas in scruffy clothes to the great front door which was opened by two or three footmen wearing white gloves and gold buttons. They would pick us up when we fell off our Vespas on the gravel, and start the machines for us again. Acton shamed me into taking a serious interest in Italian painting, although his own taste for primitives always struck me as a little sissy. Unfortunately he did not open my eyes to the beauty of buildings – a passion for architecture was to come later – so I spent my six months more or less oblivious to the splendours around me.

At La Pietra I met visiting literary figures, mostly Americans. One was Irving Stone, the writer of fictionalized biographies, whose life of Van Gogh had recently been made into an absurdly over-praised film. He had come to pick his host's brains for a proposed book on Michelangelo, he explained. Harold received him with his customary exquisite politeness, wincing only slightly under a barrage of painfully explicit questions about Michelangelo's homosexuality. As a lifelong bachelor, Harold was sensitive to vulgar innuendoes and assumptions.

Apart from this, we mingled a little with the international trash which passed through Florence. One such encounter is recorded in a letter to my parents in March 1957:

> We had a very exciting week recently harbouring a confidence trickster. We met him in a bar in the cheaper part of Florence and he told us that he was a German student called Karl von Schmidt ... he wanted lodgings so we gave him the address of our own which were far cheaper than his present ones. We left the bar at about 12 and at 3.30 a.m. he burst in saying that he had lost the key of his car, and he demanded a bed. So we sat up with him playing poker dice at which he lost 3000 lire. Next day he wanted to borrow money so I gave him a couple of hundred hoping to get rid of him. Not a bit of it. He reappeared for lunch to say that he would pay the landlady a month in advance. This went on for a week, when he told us that he had paid her, which he hadn't, as we all knew. He had told her we were his friends and she now asked us to pay for him. So I picked his pocket, while Rob showed him some paintings, and extracted the necessary money. Next day we decided to expose him. The German consulate had never heard of him, nor did he have a motor car. We decided we should be armed in case he turned nasty so I solemnly filled two socks with sand from the banks of the Arno and we waited for him to reappear, but he never did ...
>
> Acton continues kind, although Rob has a theory he hates us. He is enormously amusing but very ill, I think.

It would be quite understandable if Harold had hated us, as we were an extraordinarily scruffy couple – or so it now seems to me – but if he did his exquisite politeness has never permitted him to tell me. His mother was made of sterner stuff and would not have hesitated to show displeasure. A tiny figure, usually dressed, as I remember, in some sort of Japanese kimono, she was almost completely bald by the time I knew her, and very fierce. It was her Chicago money which had enabled Harold's father to buy La Pietra and all the wonderful things inside it. After the war, she found herself so disgusted by the Italians' conduct that she refused to have any Italians in the house, which rather limited her son's social life. On one occasion, driving with her through Florence on some day of national festivity, I was alarmed to hear her instruct the chauffeur to run over some people who were walking in front of the car. Perhaps it was only the fact that she spoke no Italian, and the chauffeur no English, which averted a tragedy.

Coming immediately after the constraints of life in a Catholic boarding school, these seven months in Florence, where we were answerable to no one, represented something like an ideal of pure freedom. Certainly there was more freedom than either of us had ever known before, and probably more than we were ever to know again. My own conclusion from the experience, and indeed from my observation of life in general, is that there is nothing so demoralizing as freedom. No doubt those with strong moral constitutions can handle as much freedom as they are given, but to give almost total freedom to two youths of seventeen whose only previous conception of it had been in occasional stolen moments when they could smoke and drink freely might well have been a recipe for disaster.

Many parents would have been worried by the following letter sent to my father on 23 April 1957 after an Easter pilgrimage to Rome. My mother was excluded, being for some reason in bad odour at the time:

Dear Papa,
    ... The journey to Rome started like an early comic film. We had been told that it was 380 kilometres, but neither of us had any idea how large a kilometre was. I had always been under the impression that if one threw a stone one would be unlucky not to get it a kilometre or so – we believed the journey to be at most 60 miles. Our landlady, who has eight children, declared that we would be killed if we attempted it and it was only with the greatest difficulty that we managed to persuade her to allow us to go. Despite her eight children she is a woman with infinite resources of motherliness, and adopted us both on the first day of our arrival. We had neither of us thought to enquire the way to Rome, being under the impression that in Italy all roads lead to Rome. 3½ hours after we had been fondly embraced by our landlady, her husband and eight children, we were still in Florence when Rob's Vespa suddenly exploded. Pieces of red hot metal scattered

everywhere, and it was another hour before we left on the road to Perugia, which we believed to be in the right direction. Eight miles outside Florence my Vespa simply ceased to work, and I had to be towed by Rob all the way to Arezzo since, the day being Palm Sunday, all garages were closed.

In Arezzo there was a great Communist congress as a rival camp to the Palm Sunday festivities. There we heard Mass, received our palms, for which we had to pay, and proceeded, expecting to see Rome at the turn of every corner. At night we arrived at a charming fortress town called Castelfiorentino, where we slept. We were told that Rome was still 300 kilometres away, which was the moment of our hideous disillusionment.

Next day we motored solidly through the most beautiful countryside with monasteries on every hill and great lakes at the bottom of green, terraced mountains. We lunched at Perugia, saw the charming frescos by Perugino in the Cambio, and then went on to Assisi vowing not to stop until we arrived at Rome.

At night the only traffic on the roads is enormous, double-loaded lorries driven by the criminal population whom it is too dangerous to lock up. Over great mountain passes time and time again they tried to murder us, and at every all-night inn where we stopped they were boasting of the people they had murdered that day. It was a charming medieval pilgrimage and even if there were not gallows at every crossroads, there were the hulks of crashed motorcars as an edifying admonition. At every inn we were welcomed in the most friendly way by drunken lorry-drivers and regaled with their anecdotes.

We arrived in Rome at half past three in the morning. The streets were quite deserted, until we saw a night watchman's fire, where we drove to ask for an hotel. Sitting around it were all the prostitutes of the North quarter, drawn like moths to a light bulb, with the poor bewildered night watchman in the middle. It was a freezing cold night, and the scene was straight from Hogarth as these terrible painted hags with carefully dyed hair sat cackling over their bawdy stories around the fire. Eventually we found an hotel where we stayed for two nights before moving to pleasanter lodgings. . . .

Allowing for a few artistic embellishments and tasteful lacunae, I believe that to be an accurate description of a journey to Rome by two seventeen-year-old adolescents on motor scooters in April 1957. So far as anybody can judge his own motives accurately, I believe that its purpose was to divert or entertain rather than to cause alarm – with perhaps an element of boastfulness in the embellishment, to illustrate my own bravery, independence, etc. Many parents would have been alarmed by it, nevertheless. To their eternal credit, mine weren't in the least. Their letters contain no admonitions to drive safely, although they were later regaled with several spectacularly exaggerated descriptions of road accidents, all of which had some basis in truth.

In fact they appreciated these early attempts at wit, and responded in similar vein. Some may decide that their lack of concern sprang from indifference, and there may be an element of truth in that – they had five other perfectly good children, after all. But I would like to think that there was a streak of committed libertarianism in their make-up which harmonized with their natural inclinations towards indifference. It is a quality which I have tried to develop in myself, although I confess that I cannot know one of my children is skiing, or exploring some wretched tropical rain forest, or even driving long distances, without feeling slightly sick with worry in the knowledge of it.

CHAPTER
SIX

The Army 1957-1959

In September 1957 I joined the army for the two-year National Service which was then obligatory among all medically fit males. I had hoped to fail the medical test, since I had never been particularly athletic, had smoked like a chimney since the age of twelve, and had defective eyesight. Unfortunately the medical officer in Exeter, after glancing curiously at my tongue, seizing my testicles and asking me to cough, passed me A1. I took a train to Windsor where I had to report to Combermere Barracks, English headquarters of the Royal Horse Guards (the Blues), which had been my father's regiment while he served in the Special Air Service during the war, having transferred from the Royal Marines. I felt very small and rather frightened, but my fellow-recruits for what was to be known as the Brigade Squad – officer-candidates – were friendly and polite: mostly Etonians, with a small contingent of rather noisy Radleians and a Harrovian or two.

I was the only person who knew nobody, apart from a youth from Bloxham called Bernard Young. This might have thrown us together, but did not, in fact, have this effect. Young was rather my O'Farrell figure, I am sorry to say. He talked too much while my inclination was to be quiet and watchful at this early stage. Somebody had told him that the way to get on in the army was to tell dirty jokes, and he had arrived with a catalogue of them, freshly memorized, but they did not really work. Initially, we all supposed that this was what we had to do, and we laughed loudly, desperately trying to remember some dirty jokes from school days. But in the confined space of the Brigade Squad hut at the guards depot, Caterham, to which we moved after a few days, his high spirits began to cast a gloom, and I persecuted him mercilessly.

We were visited by two people who had gone through the process before us. The first, Valentine Thynne, had succeeded in emerging with a commission, and visited us in the mess kit of a cornet in the Life Guards, looking very fine. I bumped into him several times in the years afterwards, a gentle, friendly figure, apparently the sanest of the Thynnes. He married three times but hanged himself at Longleat in a fit of depression in 1979 while Princess Margaret was staying there. Shortly afterwards, staying the night with one of his brothers, I was surprised to hear the family break into a rousing chorus of the Eton Boating Song – 'we'll swing, swing together' – soon after his widow had retired. They all lived in close, rather strained proximity around the beautiful old palace of the Thynnes. I supposed they were putting a brave face on their loss: grief can take many strange forms.

The second figure to greet us at Windsor, known to all my Etonian companions but not to me, was Michael Cranley, greeted with cries of derisive affection by his former schoolmates. He had just failed to become an officer, and was being shipped out to Cyprus as a trooper in the Life Guards on temporary attachment to the Blues. He later secured a commission and joined the Life Guards in Aden where he distinguished himself in various ways, but at this stage he was held up as a terrible example of what would be our fate if everything went wrong. Within less than four years he was to become my brother-in-law, but neither of us could have imagined it at the time.

The move to Caterham came as a rude shock. The guards depot, Caterham, since closed, was a complete hell-hole, staffed by sadistic morons. Whenever a recruit moved, he had to march in double time. No glimmer of human kindness was allowed to show through. We were liable to be screamed at for no reason at any moment. It is said that shared suffering creates a bond – perhaps Caterham was planned to promote that *esprit de corps* which is thought essential in a fighting unit – but it did not have that effect on me.

The only officer we saw was the squad commander, Captain

Trevor Dawson of the Scots Guards. Dawson came from a rich, arms-manufacturing family which had been elevated to a baronetcy after the First World War. Two years earlier he had married an heiress of the Cowdray connection. Although we were both grinding snobs, we did not hit it off as well as might have been expected. Another recruit, Walter Kelly, reports how he was marched in for his interview with Dawson to find him sitting to attention in front of a row of directories – Debrett, Burke, Kelly . . .

Dawson looked up from his notes and said: 'I can't find you in any of them?'

Not being in any of them, Kelly suggested that 'since the Kellys were the publishers, modesty forbade them to include any reference to themselves'. When Dawson discovered that his leg had been pulled, he had Kelly doubled back to his office by the trained soldier in charge of his squad, and screamed at him: 'You're even cheekier than that ghastly little pervert Waugh!'

On the last day of the Caterham ordeal, Dawson drew the Brigade Squad together and said he was going to ask us to vote on whether it had been such a bad experience as all that. First, he said, will all those put their hands up who feel it has been a totally useless and unpleasant experience, with nothing to recommend it at all. My hand shot up, but to my amazement, I was on my own.

'Ah yes, Waugh,' said the odious Dawson, with a vulpine grin. 'No doubt that was because you had too much to say for yourself. Now I want those to put their hands up who have had a slightly bad time, but reckon to have learned something useful.'

Three hands went up, among them those of my friends Dufferin and Gormanston, who had turned up in the Irish Guards. So it went until at the end he asked for the hands of those who had had a perfectly splendid time and thanked their lucky stars for the experience. With a terrible grunt about ten hands shot up, including those of all the Wykehamists who had spent the last three months closeted together at the end of the hut.

These were the first Wykehamists I had met, and I studied them with interest. They were all in the Foot Guards – none, thank God, in the Blues – and they stuck together like maggots, singing their own horrible Wykehamist songs in the showers and talking their own private language. Then the moment arrived for the War Office Selection Board which would decide which were to be officers and which returned to their regiments as guardsmen at the end of basic training. Two of the Wykehamists failed, the rest passed. From that moment, the two who had failed were expelled from the society of the other Wykehamists. At first they sat alone, occasionally talking in miserable tones to each other. Then, like nervous jungle animals approaching a human settlement, they started smiling shyly at the rest of us . . .

All the ruthlessness of the British establishment was revealed to me in that little Wykehamist microcosm. I saw the same thing again, much later, when I tried to tackle Foreign Office mandarins on behalf of the Biafrans in the Nigerian Civil War of 1967-1970. This form of cruelty flourishes in the law and wherever public school Englishmen are given power over each other. Americans may be more obvious in their ambition but the English are the more ruthless.

A letter home which survives from this time strikes a despondent note:

> Thank you very much indeed for your letters and parcels. I cannot tell you how comforting it is to think there are benevolent agencies working somewhere outside this wilderness of malice and violence and stupidity . . .
>
> Dufferin is a charming boy. Very ugly and very funny. We have a bond in common of being the two most incompetent recruits and most hated by the trained soldier. I am appalled by my own incompetence. Were it not for two nice Etonians on either side I would not manage at all.
>
> So far two of us have been taken off to hospital.
>
> The Foot Guards next door are all animals. Poor Gormanston's life is complete hell. The cavalry are mostly the nicest. Except for one embarrassing brute who lies on his bed and tells lavatory jokes from the time we go to bed to the time we get up at 5.30. The trained soldier and he are great friends.
>
> Sweet Maria has sent me a *torta*. Do thank her. I will write soon. Do please send *Spectator*.
> Love,
> Bron

In the allocation of fatigues, Dufferin and I were appointed to the Latrine Squad, or Shit House Brigade as it was more generally called. This meant cleaning out the lavatories every morning.

About once a week the trained soldier – whether drunk, or soberly caught short, or making some obscure point about the English class system – would lay a tremendous turd overnight on the floor of the latrine hut (we lived in huts apart from the main barracks square, possibly because it was thought we would fight with the other recruits. There was no danger of our forming undesirable friendships).

Other memories of Caterham are all equally unpleasant. On two or three occasions, being identified as a member of the Brigade Square (and so a potential officer) by other recruits in the NAAFI canteen, I was challenged to a fight.

But these memories are not as unpleasant as those of simple physical torture – being made to run, with bursting lungs, round a track, carrying a bren gun over my head as a form of punishment; after being injected with TAB (anti-typhus vaccine) being drilled in double time for half an hour and then, sweating with fever, crawling on all fours in pyjamas to the latrine (or shit house); being screamed at by a drill sergeant in front of the whole battalion for having dirty flesh on parade (a shaving cut) and doubled off the parade ground. . . .

The only useful lesson I learned at Caterham concerned the resentment and hatred of large sections of the working class for such as myself. The price of privilege is eternal vigilance.

I saw Dawson only once again after leaving Caterham. The occasion was a dinner party given in the Clermont Club, Berkeley Square, by Victor 'Disgusting' Lowndes, then head of Playboy operations in Britain. It was before the Berkeley Square Ball, a charitable event which Lowndes patronized. Dawson – by now a baronet – had left the army with the rank of major and gone into business. He also had some reputation as a gambler, which might have explained his presence in the Clermont Club. Our greeting to each other was not particularly cordial. A few years later I was sad to read that his business ventures had not prospered. Faced with ruin and the loss of all he held most dear, he had only one resource left: an insurance policy of the sort which required him to die by a particular date. If he died a day later, the policy was worthless. To add to his problems, it was rumoured that he had lost much of his wife's money, and was leaving her with a handicapped child. On the day before the expiry of his policy, he attached the exhaust to the inside of his car, put a plastic bag over his head and started the engine. He died within a few hours of the deadline. The insurance company paid up. It was a soldier's death.

* * * *

The War Office Selection Board or WOSB was the next hurdle to becoming an officer. No winds of change were blowing through the regimental offices, but at WOSB we were given to understand that it was by no means automatic nowadays for ex-public school-boys to be appointed to a commission. The interviewing officer let it be understood that he much regretted this new arrangement, but I thought I detected a note of dishonesty in the sentiment and launched myself into a deeply insincere harangue about the virtues of the new people coming up from the grammar schools and provincial universities. Then he shot a trick question at me: why did I wish to be an officer?

The answer to this was too obvious to countenance: better food, better pay, the services of a soldier-servant, and the chance to be on top of all the semi-human brutes who had been persecuting me for the past three months. Instead I said that while I would be happy to serve in either capacity, I felt I would make a very bad trooper and could make a better contribution as an officer. This was because I had a burning desire to know the reason for everything, a curiosity not to be encouraged in the other ranks . . .

We were confronted with practical problems – how to get an oil drum across a ravine using three short planks – which I could not have begun to solve except that a nice Welsh infantryman told me how it was done. We had to fill in forms which asked us whether we had ever been convicted of any crime. I hesitated about this, thinking about my Great Débâcle in Stroud magistrates' court. The NCO in charge, seeing me hesitate, explained kindly: 'You write "No" in that line.' With touching docility, I obeyed.

At the end of the day, I had passed. Neither Dufferin nor Gormanston had been so lucky. They returned to their units while Troopers Birdwood, Mitchell, Baring, Pilkington, Waugh, Legge-Burke and Harmsworth went on to Officers Training School at Mons Barracks, Aldershot. I can't help believing it must have been a damned close-run thing. Goodness knows what my later life would have been if I had spent the next twenty-one months in the ranks.

*   *   *   *

The months at Officers Training School were rather trying because we were under constant observation, and expected to show keenness at every moment. On the other hand life was more comfortable. All my richer friends had their own cars – I could not even drive at this point – and there were endless expeditions to eat the appalling *canard à l'orange* in the Hog's Back Hotel, outside Guildford, or to a pub which served steak and a bottle of 1949 burgundy for £2.00. At Mons, I found my cousin Peter Waugh, son of Alec, who was hoping for a commission in the Ninth Lancers, and wearing a waistcoat to celebrate the birth of his nephew, Simon Keeling, later killed in India. Peter eventually got his commission but only after a time spent as a mess waiter in Germany, impressing us all by his agility with serving spoons and forks when staying at Combe Florey a few years later. Peter later turned up at Oxford, where we were contemporaries, before joining the wine trade for a time and then becoming a photographer, like so many of my contemporaries. Eventually he retired to a sort of hermitage in Berkshire, where he meditates on his ancestors. Alec Waugh's children all had a bit of money because every time my Aunt Joan had a baby – she had three – her Australian family sent an entire shipload of wool to England as an endowment. Or so we penniless, envious Waughs were told by our father. I have never been able to make up my mind on the point whether it is a good idea to endow children. I cannot help feeling my cousin Peter would have achieved great things if he had been a little bit poorer when he was young, and the same is true of many of my Oxford contemporaries.

My last letter home from Aldershot is dated the Third Sunday in Lent, which makes it 9 March 1958. All my letters of this period show a keen religiosity which may in part have been sugar for the bird but was also, I think, fairly genuine. In those days, Sunday church attendance was compulsory in the army, at any rate for recruits and officer cadets. The company sergeant major would shout: 'RCs, Parsees, Chinese and Japanese fall EEOUT!' and we would be marched off to our separate devotions. My letter starts with the traditional refrain:

Darling Mummy, Papa, Hattie and Meg,

Pixton Park, Dulverton, Somerset. AW's birthplace and first home.

Grandchildren gathered at Pixton for the war. *L to R:* Angela Dru, Teresa Waugh, AW (standing), Anne Grant, Margaret Waugh, Robin Grant, Polly Grant.

Above: Four
generations, 1937. *L to
R:* Laura Waugh,
Evelyn de Vesci,
Teresa Waugh, Mary
Herbert.

Left: Mary Herbert,
grandmother, and
Auberon Herbert,
uncle, outside Pixton.

Right: Auberon Herbert
1922–1974: served in the
Polish army and spoke
many languages.

Below: Piers Court,
Gloucestershire, AW's
home 1945–56.

A writer's household: Piers Court 1948. AW is bottom right.

Pixton.

Croquet-Bowls at Piers Court. The idea is to break the bottles. *(Barry Swaebe)*

Piers Court, Gloucestershire, from the back of the house.

Piers Court.

Family Group at Piers Court, c. 1949. A guinea pig, held out of sight in AW's hands, made a mess on Laura Waugh's skirt a few seconds before the photograph was taken.

EW in the library at Piers Court, c. 1949.

Above: Florence 1957. *L to R:* John Clay, AW and Rob Stuart.

Right: AW and Rob Stuart in Florence, March–September 1957.

I am sorry I have not written sooner to thank you for a most enjoyable week-end. The house was looking lovely, and I cannot tell you what heaven it is to spend a few hours there after the depravity and ugliness of Aldershot...

I go on trek on Thursday. This is the last hurdle – do you think the nuns may be enlisted? Mention too Simon Pilkington, a Life Guard, who is in equal danger of disgrace and reduction to the ranks. If all goes well I pass out on Thursday 20th – I don't suppose you would like to attend the parade, but I have been told to ask you.

This week has been occupied by things called endurance tests, which are a new form of torture designed to test our 'resistability'. In fact they are just another outlet for the sadism of the PT instructors and the masochism of our squadron leader who took them with us. Needless to say, my resistability grading was not high.

No news – tomorrow we go on an exercise to see how far away we can get and still hear each other on the wireless. I am going to Brighton with Mark Birdwood, as I am told it is most enjoyable at this time of year.

Salisbury Plain will be *very* cold without a sleeping bag.
Love
Bron

Put in command of four armoured cars with thousands of square miles of Salisbury Plain to drive on, I contrived to crash all four: they paired off to crash into each other. That night, in my tent, I heard voices, like Brutus before Philippi. I scrambled out and woke up Simon Pilkington, fast asleep on sentry duty.

'Did you hear voices?' I asked.

'I think they were angels,' he replied mysteriously.

* * * *

Somehow, miraculously, I had become an officer. I would like to think that my success demonstrated hitherto unperceived qualities of responsibility and leadership, but they have never manifested themselves since, and I am happy to accept my father's verdict that it was a miracle brought about by the convent of Poor Clares at Looe, Cornwall, whose help he always enlisted on these sticky occasions. However pompous one may become about these things in the post-Christian age, anybody who has been brought up a Catholic will retain a healthy element of superstition in his general outlook. St Anthony is demonstrably brilliant at helping people find things, and I do not know how I would have managed without him through the years. Depressed as one may be by the church's retreat from spirituality, dismayed by its inept doctrine on contraception and disgusted by the language and form of its new services, a certain philosophical theism is bound to survive if only to explain the otherwise inexplicable.

* * * *

My parents did not attend the passing-out parade at Mons, alone, I think, of all the parents involved. In a way, this was probably a good thing, as my father would probably have worn his grey bowler (the drab Coke) or Brigade boater, and my mother, although the kindest and sweetest of women, had no great sense of style. She had one fur coat, of astrakhan, but it was at least twenty years old and had lost much of its fur. She never noticed gradual deterioration in things, although if any of her cats had developed bald patches, she would have been the first to diagnose ringworm. The coat had once had rather a smart belt, but this had long been replaced by binder-twine.

So, unembarrassed by any eccentrically dressed parents, I was taken out by a brother-officer called Bruce Hargreaves whose mother came down for the occasion. His father manufactured electrical equipment in Manchester under the name of Aerialite and he constantly assured us all he was very rich. The mother took us to the Hog's Back Hotel, outside Guildford, where we ate *canard à l'orange* and returned feeling slightly sick.

* * * *

We flew to Cyprus in troop transport planes via Malta. It was a wonderful, a glorious thing to be an officer. It is true that there might be an element of sincerity lacking in the deference shown to young officers by the senior NCOs and warrant officers, but there was something profoundly comforting about being saluted wherever one went. Outside camp, the activities of the Eoka terrorists made us behave rather like an army of occupation, carrying pistols the whole time and being a little bit nervous of any sudden movement. Occasionally the strain would begin to tell.

Practically the only place in the whole of Nicosia which was air-conditioned was the long bar in the Ledra Palace Hotel, where drinks cost three or four times what they cost anywhere else, and sixty times what they cost in the officers' mess. A brother officer, visiting the toilets of this bar one evening, identified one of the lavatories as a crouching Eoka terrorist and shot it to pieces. Everybody in the bar drew his pistol and it was lucky there was not a massacre. Later everybody swore they had indeed seen some suspicious characters around the place, but I think the officer concerned was sent home.

The politics of the Cyprus emergency in 1958 were much the same as they have remained ever since, except that the island was still a Crown colony under a governor – originally Field Marshal Harding, later Hugh Foot, who became Lord Caradon in retirement. British policy was to prepare the island for independence as a self-governing member of the Commonwealth. The Greek majority wanted *enosis* or union with Greece. The Turkish minority wanted *taksim*, or secession from the rest of the island in their own enclave, which would then be united with Turkey. This last was what eventually happened after the Turkish invasion of 1974 set up the Turkish Republic of Northern Cyprus, although at the time of writing (1990) it has not yet been recognized by any country except Turkey.

The nationalist movement among Greeks, who made up 80 per cent of the population, was divided between EOKA, the right-wing more or less ethnarchist terror organization, AXEL, the communists, and EDEK, the socialists. The British army's role was to try and keep all these factions separate while somebody tried to devise a constitution with which Cypriots could face the future as an independent sovereign state. In the event, we were the pigs in the middle. Eoka shot the British, Turks massacred the Greeks and in any lull in the fighting between Eoka and the Security forces, Eoka would turn and attack the LWGCs (Left-Wing Greek Cypriots).

They were heady times for a young man whose major previous excitement had been running away from prefects raiding his smoking den. My first letter home, dated 27 April 1958, shines with enthusiasm:

Life is immensely exciting and unbelievably comfortable. Nearly every day we are out on some raid, roadblock, search or patrol. The only boring day was spent waiting outside a village in the sweltering heat for Dr Kuchuk, the Turkish leader, to arrive, which he never did. The troopers spent the time waving to [Turkish police] motorbicyclists – we are meant to fraternize with these people – and seeing how many fell off in their anxiety to wave back...

Politics here are very involved and quite interesting. One always associated politics with Auberon's boring, ineffectual discussions but here it is quite different. For instance a bomb in a petrol station will mean quite clearly that the moderate Left nationalist faction is prepared to make an amnesty for a time with the ethnarchist Right-wing extremists, whereas a bomb elsewhere will mean something quite different.

We were searching a peasant on a donkey in the mountains above Kythrea and found a tin full of snails. My squadron leader arrived, and said that he had frequently heard of secret documents, arms and ammunition being smuggled inside snail shells and so we had to search inside them all. It is so absurd, because although we destroy cigarettes and heat the paper for secret writing, we are not allowed to search women, so they can get away with anything.

We had two fires in the camp a few days ago, which were thought to have been caused by a petrol bomb, but actually it was just the Blues covering up for a trooper who left his electric iron on.

They say there are going to be street ambushes again tomorrow, but everybody rather doubts it. At the moment they are not shooting much; although one cornet claims he heard bullets whistling past him, nobody believes him. Bombs, however, are exploding at the rate of three every 24 hours, and we sometimes go rushing to the scene; quite often the Cypriots blow themselves up, as they are not very expert in handling them.

All love – is the knighthood in the bag?
Bron

I am not sure what the reference to a knighthood means. Other absurd searches on which we had to engage included digging up and opening a coffin which had been buried that day to see if it contained arms. I imagine that this must have been in deference to another intuition of my squadron leader, who was called Charles Booth-Jones. The smell was so appalling once the coffin was broken open that without a word being said, everyone standing around the grave turned and ran away. I suppose somebody else filled the grave in again next day.

The above letter earned a rebuke that I had not been sufficiently descriptive, nor reported on the fellow-officers who were sons of my father's friends. My next, and probably last, letter from Cyprus was sent in May, and is written in slightly abrupt tone:

Darling Mummy and Papa,

Thank you for your letter. I am sorry I was not sufficiently explicit in my last letter. I have met the Dunnes. I have not met Fox-Strangways. There are several species of plant in flower, but I am unable to identify them. I arise at 6.15, being called by my servant. I have breakfast at 6.35. The first parade is at 7.10. The crews then tinker with their vehicles until 12 o'clock, and then that is the end of my working day, unless we are being sent out on a patrol, roadblock or ambush. These occur about three times a week. We do not catch anyone. The last is the most boring as we sit all night in an olive grove from 7 p.m. to 4.30 a.m. and see no one and drink something disgusting called self-heating soup.

Randolph Churchill arrived here, was fêted by Colonel Julian and asked for your telephone number, which I had forgotten, but he said he would get hold of it.

Drink in the mess is enormously cheap, outside unbelievably expensive. We are allowed into only four approved bars, restaurants, night clubs, at any of which a glass of whisky costs 19/6d, in the mess it cost 4d.

The day is spent sleeping, playing bridge, roulette, pontoon, murder, backgammon, dumb crambo.

We have to carry guns everywhere. I cannot hit a human-size target at 10 yards once in twenty shots with my absurd pistol which I am constantly in fear of losing.

Love

Bron

On 21 May 1958 Evelyn Waugh wrote to his friend Ann Fleming

that 'Cornet Waugh is enjoying Cyprus top-hole.' One of the keen-
est pleasures of my new exalted status was to inspect the mess
halls as duty officer. If any trooper complained of the food, one
would taste it delicately from his plate, roll the revolting substance
round in one's mouth and say 'absolutely delicious!', just as nannies had always behaved with sour milk in my childhood.

When Evelyn Waugh wrote his letter to Ann Fleming I was
under canvas in the Troodos Hills with the rest of my squadron, a
regiment of the Ox and Bucks and a regiment of marine commandos who were horribly fit and keen, rushing everywhere at
the double. We were engaged in a mammoth search for Colonel
Grivas, the terrorist leader, who was rumoured to be holed up in
the vicinity. Armoured cars were of little use for the purpose, and
we found ourselves, on some days, acting the role of infantry,
which was thought rather undignified. I was put under the care of
Philip Chetwode, a senior subaltern. One evening I was playing
bridge with him, David Bigham and the squadron leader, Booth-
Jones. It is one of my unfortunate characteristics that if I am doing
well at bridge, I tend to gloat. Booth-Jones, who was my partner,
seemed to be having difficulty deciding which suit to lead. I
decided to help him out with a few cryptic hints. Although we
were playing for very little money – family stakes of two shillings
(10p) a hundred – Chetwode became incensed by this and said
that if I took the trick, I would regret it. I took the trick and won the
rubber. Next day, Chetwode ordered me to establish a one-man
observation post on the top of an almost sheer mountain cliff of
some three hundred feet. First, I had to climb it, carrying my
rations for the day and an unwieldy, old-fashioned radio transmit-
ter with which to report if I saw Colonel Grivas. It took me two
hours to climb the cliff. Never a natural climber, I knew that one
false step would send me hurtling to a painful and undignified
death. For the first time in my life, I discovered the horrors of ver-
tigo. I have never known such mortal terror before or since. Then
and there I vowed that one day I would revenge myself on Chetwode. I have seen him several times since – at one point, when I
was living in Wiltshire, he moved into a house in the neighbourhood with an attractive young wife. No opportunity has yet presented itself, but one day, perhaps, I shall meet him on a dark
night. . . .

Meanwhile, the search for Colonel Grivas continued. It seemed to consist of swarming over the lower parts of the mountain and pulling down terraces, many of which had probably been there for a thousand or even two thousand years. The upper reaches were similarly tackled with picks and crowbars, every large stone being rolled down the mountainside in case it concealed the entrance to a cave. After a time, the troops grew bored with this and started letting off explosive charges in the side of the mountain. The theory behind this was that if Colonel Grivas was hiding in a cave, the shock waves from these explosions, even if they failed to do him lasting harm, would annoy him very much indeed, as he richly deserved to be annoyed. One explosion was much louder than the rest, and I noticed rocks falling all around me. 'Look up, look up', they shouted, but I was brooding about my revenge on Chetwode and did not look up in time to avoid a large rock which struck me on the forehead, knocking me out. Next morning I woke up in a pool of blood which had poured out of my ear in the night. Later, it occurred to me that this injury might have accounted for the hallucinations I suffered in the British Military Hospital, Nicosia, a few days later. By then, everybody had forgotten about the head wound. The hallucinations, which involved the illusion that the hospital was under attack, and it was my responsibility to evacuate it, were attributed to a mixture of salt tablets, against the heat, and opiates, but they worried me somewhat, remembering my poor father's Pinfold experiences on a boat to Ceylon. Ever since, I have found myself oddly concerned to verify the sources of any voices I hear. To date, however, the angels on Salisbury Plain and the devil voices of the British Military Hospital have provided my only experience of insanity.

It was a relief to return to the comfort of the barracks after ten days in the field, but the day after I returned with my troop of four armoured cars there occurred the Guenyeli massacre. This was a bad moment. A party of Greek detainees who had been taken in for questioning and document-checking were dropped on the Nicosia-Kyrenia main road and left to make their own way back to their village of Skyloura. Unfortunately they were left outside the Turkish village of Guenyeli and the villagers, seeing a party of unknown Greeks, assumed they were an EOKA war party. The Turks poured out of the village and quite literally hacked them to pieces. It was a very messy business. Nine Greeks were killed and many others mutilated. Hands and fingers were all over the place and one officer wandered around, rather green in the face, holding a head and asking if anyone had seen a body which might fit it.

My troop was sent to take up a position between the Turkish village of Guenyeli and the Greek village of Autokoi on the Nicosia-Kyrenia road, to discourage reprisal raids and generally keep them apart. On patrol, we always travelled with a belt in the machine guns of the armoured cars, but without a bullet in the breech. The medium machine guns we had trained on, called Bisa, needed two cocking actions to put a bullet in the breech. The Browning .300, which we had in Cyprus, needed only one. It is most probable that I cocked the gun in a moment of absent-mindedness, but that did not explain subsequent events which were the result of excessive heat and a faulty mechanism. I had noticed an impediment in the elevation of the machine gun on my armoured car, and used the opportunity of our taking up positions to dismount, seize the barrel from in front and give it a good wiggle. A split second later I realized that it had started firing. No sooner had I noticed this, than I observed with dismay that it was firing into my chest. Moving aside pretty sharpish, I walked to the back of the armoured car and lay down, but not before I had received six bullets – four through the chest and shoulder, one through the arm, one through the left hand.

My troop corporal of horse, who had been on patrol between the two villages, arrived back at that moment and swore horribly at my driver, whom he imagined to be responsible. In fact nobody had been in the armoured car, as I explained from my prone position. I was rather worried and thought I was probably going to die, as every time I moved the blood pouring out of holes in my back, where the bullets had exited, made a horrible gurgling noise. To those who suffer from anxieties about being shot I can give the reassuring news that it is almost completely painless. Although the bullets caused considerable devastation on the way out, the only sensation at the time was of a mild tapping on the front of the chest. I also felt suddenly winded as they went through a lung. But there was virtually no pain for about three quarters of an hour, and then only a dull ache before the morphine began to take effect.

The machine gun had shot nearly the whole belt – about 250 rounds – into the Kyrenia road, digging an enormous hole in the process, before being stopped by Corporal Skinner, who showed great presence of mind by climbing into the armoured car's turret from behind. In the silence which followed, Corporal of Horse Chudleigh came back to me, saluted in a rather melodramatic way as I lay on the ground and said words to the effect that this was a sorry turn of events. He was a tough Bristolian parachutist and pentathlete. On this occasion he looked so solemn that I could not resist the temptation of saying: 'Kiss me, Chudleigh.'

Chudleigh did not spot the historical reference, and treated me with some caution thereafter. At least I *think* I said 'Kiss me, Chudleigh.' This story is denied by Chudleigh. I have told the story so often now that I honestly can't remember whether it started life as a lie.

As I was being lifted into the military ambulance with more horrible gurgles he said: 'I don't expect you will be needing your pistol any more,' and removed it from my holster. It was a 9 millimetre Browning automatic, in short supply and much prized by those, like Chudleigh, who had been issued only with a .38 Smith and Wesson revolver.

The Blues medical officer was a Catholic and an old Downside boy. He accompanied me in the ambulance to hospital and read the De Profundis to me on the way. This struck me as rather gloomy, although there was nothing else to do, but not nearly as gloomy as the surgeon, Colonel John Watts, who prepared to operate immediately for the removal of a lung, spleen and two ribs. Feeling quite happy as the morphine took effect and fortified, as they say, by the last rites of the Church in the shape of an Irish priest to whom I took an instant dislike, I said to Colonel Watts in as nonchalant a tone as I could muster:

'Tell me, Colonel, what chance do you actually think I have of pulling through?

He fixed me with his cool blue eyes and said: 'I think you've got a very good chance.'

I felt as if an icy hand had been placed over my heart, but more even than terror I felt fury.

'What do you fucking *mean* I've got a good chance? You're supposed to say I will be out of bed the day after tomorrow.'

I later learned that none of them thought I would survive, but Colonel Watts performed brilliantly, taking out the lung, spleen and ribs in a hospital whose general standard of equipment, as I later realized, was somewhere around that of a cottage hospital in the Soviet Union.

*   *   *   *

I woke up after the operation in the stifling heat of the general surgical ward, delighting Colonel Watts, when he told me that he had
removed my spleen, by asking whether that would improve my
temper. I was heavily doped and in great pain, with severe difficulty in breathing, but my chief irritation was the ward wireless
which, because there were other ranks present, had to be played
full blast all day. At night, as I have mentioned, I hallucinated. On
the second day my mother arrived, having been flown out by the
army. With enormous kindness, Sir Hugh and Lady Foot put her
up in Government House, although this was a critical moment in
the Cyprus emergency in the wake of the Guenyeli massacre. Nobody could leave Government House without the escort of an
armoured car and a personal bodyguard with sten gun. It was not
at all the sort of life my mother was used to. Perhaps she can take
up the narrative, in extracts from her letters to my father during
the three weeks she spent at Government House:

June 11th 1958

My darling,
I am staying with the Foots – I have met neither yet. There
was clearly a large dinner party going on when I arrived and
I said I would like to go to bed as soon as I had been to the
hospital. Please write and tell me how a lady behaves in
Government House when she is exceedingly shabby and fat
and has no clothes? And also what sort of tips I give?
    Everyone seems very jittery. The whole inner part of the
town is curfewed and all cars go at 60 all the time skidding to
stop at road blockades and having to produce identity cards.
All cars I have been in so far have wirelesses going all the
time giving police instructions. There is an armoured car
parked in the park of Government House. I will try and not
stand in front of it.
    All love. I will write tomorrow when I have seen the sur-
geon and Bron again.
Laura

June 13th, 1958

My darling,
I have today seen the doctors. They say they think Bron has a very good chance indeed of survival, having started with they thought none. The next two or three days are critical, after that he will be on the danger list for another 10-14 days....

His left hand is badly injured which I gather worries him almost most but they say they are certain they can give him what they call a perfectly workable hand tho' he may lose a finger but he is far too ill for them to do anything yet...

He is fully conscious & I gather has been all the time. He finds speech difficult and it is not good for him as they wish to reserve all his strength for drinking and breath. I go and visit him 2 times a day for about a ¼ hour – not longer because he is inclined to try and talk. Last night he had a very bad go and they nearly sent for me but he got round it and this morning when I saw him his breathing seemed very much better in fact I could barely hear it....

I am not allowed to leave GH without an escort with a machine gun. I have bought myself a dress because I realized I could not continue without one. It cost £7 but will do for Munich if we get there. Poor Lady Foot can never leave GH because she is not allowed out without a guard of twelve machine gunnists and she says that makes it intolerable.
All my love,
Laura

June 17th, 1958:
Randolph is in Nicosia and came to dinner last night. He was very drunk, maudlin, sympathetic and loving about you. As you may guess he succeeded in giving great offence to the Foots 1) by smoking in the middle of dinner so that Sir Hugh decided he could not propose the loyal toast 2) by his general drunkenness 3) by shouting and yelling for the prettiest girl present to sit by him during the special cinema performance 4) by barracking the cinema 5) by leaving in the middle of it and taking an affectionate leave of me but not bothering to say goodbye or thank their Excellencies.

Tues June 18th, 1958:

I really have excellent news today. I saw Bron's surgeon who says that Bron will be off the danger list by about Friday if all goes well and that he is delighted with his progress ... last night he slept well and has stopped Pinfolding.

Could you deal with a couple of farm problems. Will you tell Giovanni to give 1 spoonful of cake daily to Magdalene and Desdemona this week & two spoonfuls from next Monday. Also, if Lucy is still giving 40 lbs a day of milk she had better be artificially inseminated next time she comes bulling with the Aberdeen Angus bull. If she is not giving as much as 40 lb I do not want her served at all.

June 19th 1958:
I hope Giovanni is singling the marigolds tell him not to bother about the kale. The marigolds are on the side nearest the house and must be done. Randolph came to lunch today and was pretty sober.

June 23rd:
Bron continues to run a temperature of between 102-103 but they don't seem very perturbed about it. Today was the hottest thing I have ever known. We just sat and panted opposite each other. It was too hot to talk or think ...

June 25th 1958:
Darling,
Little news. Bron's temperature has been normal all day, which is a great improvement. On the other hand he seems to be suffering far more pain than ever before ... His surgeon whom he loves has got pneumonia and he doesn't like the new ones who have taken over. But they hope to fly him home by Comet in about 10 days time. He still has to have the lung cavity drained every other day which is a painful and beastly operation.

I hope to return either next Monday or Tuesday. So I may see you before this arrives. I long to see you all.
All my love,
Laura

My own memories of the British Military Hospital in Nicosia are mercifully few. An officious brigadier, a senior surgeon, kept trying to cut down the pain-killing drugs, for fear of addiction. After my mother returned to England and her cows, Lady Foot took to visiting me, leaving her twelve machine gunnists outside the ward. She read to me from Lawrence Durrell's book about Cyprus, *Bitter Lemons*, all about conversations with quaint Cypriot peasants as a cool, thyme-scented breeze whispered among the olive groves. Nothing could have been more kindly intended, but as I lay on my sweat-soaked bed, groaning in pain, between sessions of the crudest torture when surgeons stuck huge needles in my back to drain it, I conceived a great hatred for Lawrence Durrell. Scarcely able to speak, I eventually stammered out: 'He can't even use the word "pristine" correctly.' 'There, there,' she said. 'You must not let these things disturb you.' This hatred has never left me, and embraces the entire school of expatriates who write sensitively about sunnier climes than our own.

* * * *

Unfortunately, the abscess which had been noticed in Cyprus developed into a chronic infection of the chest cavity. It was nine months and some twelve operations later that I was finally discharged from the Westminster Hospital, where I was put under the care of Sir Clement Price-Thomas, a noted chest surgeon and senior consultant at Westminster Hospital who had chiefly distinguished himself by his unsuccessful operation on the late King George VI for lung cancer. The king died of a post-operative embolism.

In those days the young student nurses at Westminster Hospital wore black stockings and starched white apron and cuffs. I loved it. But Sir Clement kept sticking tubes into me, and after a few months he decided I was too weak and ill for the major operation he had in mind – called a thorocoplasty – so I was discharged to Sister Agnes's – King Edward VII Hospital for Officers – to fatten up.

As a serving officer, I was admitted free, which must have come as a relief to my father, who found it necessary at this point to stop the monthly allowance of £25 which he had been paying me in the army, explaining that I did not need the money in hospital and he was skint. I wept bitter tears of rage on reading his letter.

But these were good times, and I received a flow of visitors in hospital, some of whom took me out to meals. One of the most generous was my Uncle Alick Dru, always called 'Whipper' or 'Pig-Whipper', being suspected of the secret vice of whipping pigs.

King Edward Hospital

Dear Papa,

Thank you for your letter. Far from being upset by your action, I am enormously grateful that you should have been so generous as to continue my allowance up to this moment. I hope that you soon overcome your financial difficulties. Mushroom growing is said to be remunerative or you could open a lodging house.

Whipper took me to lunch at the Café Royal with a farm-hand whom he had brought to London to be tortured and eloctrocuted by a quack doctor [osteopath] of Auntie Ga's. She had a theory that it would make him work harder. We had an enormous meal of smoked salmon and roast beef, and when Pig-Whipper got too drunk to make sense I had to talk to the cowherd about harvests for the rest of the meal. It was the honest man's first trip to London and he was embarrassed by the bare-breasted ladies who decorate the walls and ceiling of the Café Royal. He stared at his plate rather red in the face. But Whipper is the best of uncles – do let him get drunk at Combe Florey sometime when you can afford it.
Love from
your affectionate son
Bron

My rich uncle, Auberon Herbert, did not measure up quite so well in the avuncular stakes:

Letters and strange gifts arrive daily from the Whippery. The great whipping man himself was here yesterday, jovial but surprisingly sober; I didn't taunt him with the second-hand wax earplugs his Wife had sent me a few mornings before. With him, and smelling like Cleopatra in her barge on her way to meet Antony for the first time, was Uncle Auberon.

Auberon brought some chicken paste and promised to bring oysters, champagne and foie gras. Whipper brought some greengages and promised nothing, but encouraged

Auberon in his fantasies . . .

My room became something of a shrine for the fashionable and good. Almost total strangers like Alan Pryce-Jones, then the editor of the *Times Literary Supplement* came calling; so did Ann Fleming, Lady Diana Cooper, Alec Waugh. . . . Of this last, my father wrote:

> The man who calls on you purporting to be my brother Alec is plainly an impostor. Your true uncle does not know your whereabouts & supposes you to be here convalescent – as witness this card which came with a volume of his describing the more obvious and picturesque features of the West Indies. Did your visitor offer any identification other than baldness – not an uncommon phenomenon? Had he a voice like your half-great Uncle George? Did he wear a little silk scarf round his neck? Was he tipsy? These are the tests.

Most of my brother-officers in Sister Agnes's seemed to be middle-aged men suffering from piles, but in the room next door to mine a charming old boy called Augustine or 'Gussie' Courtauld lay dying. In earlier times, he had been on some arctic expedition or other with my father, who had disgraced himself when rations ran short by pushing a sleigh-load of pemmican over a glacier saying he would rather die of starvation quickly than eke out life on such a revolting substance. Courtauld asked me to read to him. I was doing so one afternoon when I decided that he had died. In fact he had just fallen asleep and did not die for several weeks. But, having decided the man was dead, I tiptoed out of the room and went and told the nurse on duty, in the ghastly euphemistic language of our times, that I thought Mr Courtauld was not very well. Seeing from my face what I meant, she summoned the matron and a doctor, no doubt a mortician or two before entering the death chamber and waking the old gentleman up from his afternoon snooze.

Many years later we went to dinner with Lord and Lady Carrington in Ovington Square; I sat next to Courtauld's widow, now married to R.A. Butler, the former Conservative politician, and started telling her the story before realizing how inappropriate it was. She was a lovely person – forthright, and completely fearless

– and would not let me drop it. I ended up improvising a complete lie, involving a bed-bottle, which puzzled Lady Butler but vastly amused Rab, who said 'Ho, ho, ho' many times.

* * * *

By Christmas 1958 I was back in the Westminster Hospital for my final series of operations, involving the collapse of the chest wall and removal of a finger which had never recovered from the bullet which went through my left hand. Sir Clement Price-Thomas carved the turkey in the ward, with many jokes about ligaments and forceps, but I was spared having to eat it, as my father and younger sister Margaret had heroically volunteered to spend Christmas in London, taking me out to lunch at the Hyde Park Hotel. It was an unforgettable sight. At every other table in the restaurant there sat a single, rich, obviously unpleasant elderly person of one sex or another, eating alone, with a comic paper hat supplied by the management stuck glumly on his or her head, never exchanging a word with those similarly placed around them.

This made a profound impression on all three of us. Later in the day my father took me to White's where we saw a similar procession of disgusting old men whom nobody wanted to see on Christmas Day. My father reckoned that there must be at least a short story to be written in every case, explaining how each came to be alone on Christmas Day. He was prepared to see pathos, even tragedy in their predicament. I saw it as a parable of human selfishness, vowing then and there to marry and have children as soon as reasonably possible.

At about this time I began to be quite fond of my father, never having liked him much in childhood or early youth. As I prepared to leave home and set up my own establishments elsewhere he became more tolerant of my various failings, and in the last five years of his life we enjoyed a distinct cordiality. During these months, while I was in hospital, I even wrote him a maudlin, deeply embarrassing letter telling him how much I admired him, and sent it to my bank to be shown to him in the event of my predecease. The bank returned it to me soon after his death in April 1966. I re-read it then, but have been too embarrassed to dig it up a second time before writing this book. I have a feeling it would not fit.

CHAPTER
SEVEN

Bologna and Portofino 1959

At some time in February 1959, while I was recovering from Sir Clement's last assaults on my body, my discharge papers came through and I became a war pensioner, which I have remained ever since.

In March, I finally left hospital, weighing under nine stone. I walked into a glorious English spring such as I have seldom seen before or since. Normally, at this time of year, I would have been busy shooting young fledgling rooks on the bough, having decided I had some sacred duty to keep their numbers down and prevent them taking over the world. This year, with the bullet holes in my back still smarting, I found I had lost the appetite.

Combe Florey, the house to which my parents had moved in September 1956, is no architectural gem but it is a handsome eighteenth-century building in red sandstone of impressively large size. It is approached through a sixteenth-century gatehouse which adds to its seclusion and grandeur. The indoor staff, in those days of penury, had been reduced to Giovanni, who was also cowman and waited at table in an azure cardigan and corduroys, and Maria, his wife, who was the cook. They were not to stay very long. For the last five years of my father's life, there was only daily help which, wonderful as it was, marked a considerable retreat from the days at Piers Court when he had a butler, housekeeper, page, cook, nanny, nursery maid, gardener, cowman, housemaid and two dailies, all supported by his earnings as a novelist.

But Combe Florey was a comfortable house, furnished with an eye to grandeur rather than elegance and the Somerset country-side was never lovelier.

I stayed convalescing until June, when I moved to the south of France where I proposed to sponge off my dear, kind-hearted Great-Aunt Elizabeth Herbert, until forced to move on. She, an American heiress, had married my Great-Uncle Mervyn, a diplo-mat, and enlarged out of all recognition a minor Herbert property called Tetton near Taunton, to the designs of Hal Goodhart-Rendel, for whom she was suspected of nursing a *faiblesse*. Her French property was built on Goodhart-Rendel's estate near Valescure. We drove out there with an elderly friend of hers called Lady Shaw-Stewart, stopping on the way at the Château de Bois-bonnard, Villeperdue, the home of a distant cousin, Eliane d'Espous:

Villa S. Girant   *July 7 1959*
Valescure, S. Raphael, Var.

Darling Mummy and Papa,
A dutiful letter to thank you for my enjoyable months of con-valescence at Combe Florey, and for your indulgence which made them so pleasant. We arrived after three days on the road. After leaving the d'Espous at their country house we dined the evening after at an hotel on a dish called Langouste Amoureuse which was quite delicious and called for many coy jokes from Lady Shaw-Stewart (what words of mine can describe her beastliness? Unbelievably, she is an aunt of that agreeable fellow Jones). . . .

It took an awfully long time to find out for how long I was invited. That was a matter of Policy, you see, and Mervyn had to be consulted. 'Of course', she kept saying, 'Stay a hundred years and every minute will be a treasured memory, but won't you get a little bored of *us*?' 'No danger', I replied, and so it remained until I suppose she heard from Mervyn. Out by the 18th. O but little Mervyn is a lion in his own house, and while the cat's away the old ladies get a little tipsy in the evenings and make jokes about his waistline.

Life here is very pleasant and the food excellent. The

house is hideous, but well situated in a fir-tree area above S. Raphael. The grasshoppers are rather noisy, and I spend a lot of time killing them, which again makes Aunt Elizabeth rather tearful – she somehow associates them with Mr Good-hart-Rendel (he did not leave the place to your chum, whom he disliked, but to a cousin, whom he disliked slightly less).

'Do keep me posted re D'Amis (Darmes-D'arms?)
Best love
Bron

* * * *

This last request refers to John D'Arms, an American undergrad-uate at New College, Oxford, who had initiated what turned out to be a protracted courtship of my elder sister, Teresa. They were not married until a few weeks before my own wedding in July 1961. The earlier, somewhat snide reference to my cousin Mervyn Herbert, only son of Aunt Elizabeth and her husband Mervyn (who died in 1929), can only be explained by disappointment at having to move on from this comfortable perch. 'That agreeable fellow Jones' refers, of course, to Alan Pryce-Jones, the great hospital visitor. Even now I find it hard to believe that such a pleasant fellow could have had such a bestial aunt.

But expulsion from Valescure left me in something of a quan-dary. I had six weeks to spend before I could settle at Portofino, where my grandmother and sweet-smelling Uncle Auberon were opening the villa on 1 September, and only about £80 in cash. It was a convention with guests at the Mervyn Herbert villa in France that they should pay for the drink in the house, as well as paying for meals in restaurants. My aunt, who was the most gener-ous woman by nature, once letting me off a backgammon debt of £60 at a time when it would have ruined me to pay her, applied this rule quite fiercely. No doubt it was a quaint survival from the days of currency control, when a Labour government had re-stricted Britons travelling abroad to £20 currency allowance. But it meant that I had only £80 to keep myself in food and lodgings for six weeks.

I remembered that Bologna, when I had visited it two years earlier from Florence, had seemed remarkably cheap. There was also the vague impetus of some unfinished business with the daughter of my previous lodging house keeper whose acquain-

tance I hoped to renew. In the event I could not trace my former
lodgings, and very much doubt whether I should have finished any
business, as I was hopelessly inexperienced and painfully aware
that my chest still resembled the surface of a rather cheesy moon,
with its craters and long surgical scars representing canals.

Since I had nothing to do for six weeks in Bologna, and no
money to do it with, I resolved to write a novel which had been
buzzing round my head during the nine months in hospital. It
combined passages from life at a monastic boarding school, in the
army, and in hospital. A more experienced novelist would have
made three novels of it, but it is always the way of first novelists to
squander their material. There was nothing eccentric or preten-
tious about the decision to write a first novel; rather, in a writer's
family, it was a pious acceptance of fate, just as the eldest son of a
hosier or glover may cause *frissons* of delight in his family by
announcing that he has suddenly felt a strange vocation to devote
his life to making hose or gloves.

*   *   *   *

In Bologna, I found respectable lodgings at the Pensione Rondine,
Via Galliera, near the station. They cost 1000 lire – about 12/6d or
65 pence – a night. In the six weeks I was there, writing my novel, I
was completely alone apart from three days spent in the company
of an American girl who was travelling Europe alone. I have forgotten her name. She had long, straight, darkish hair and wore
trousers, in the fashion of the times. Everybody else in the *pensione* assumed we were lovers, but I made no progress with her
beyond intensely personal late-night conversations of such stupe-
fying boredom that I fell asleep. Seven years of single-sex Catholic
education and a year of monastic life in the army were going to
need longer than this to overcome. She was not nearly as enticing
as the student nurses of Westminster Hospital in their black stockings, starched aprons and short-sleeved shirts, and much dirtier. If
I had been more experienced and more masterful I would probably have contracted some disease. She may well have thought my
lack of initiative rather odd, having no experience of English
public schoolboys. I do not particularly regret it now, although I
regretted it bitterly at the time. It was more than a year before I
learned to make the leaps from jokes to earnest conversation to
flirtatious banter to a clear expression of sexual intent to the first

physical approach.

For the most part, I sat scribbling in my attic bedroom in the Via Galliera, working away at the novel which eventually appeared in October 1960 under the title of *The Foxglove Saga*.

My letters home from Bologna were mostly requests for money. On 11 August 1959 I wrote:

Is it still proposed that James Waugh (your son) should spend part of his holidays in Portofino? If so, it would be a great convenience if he could bring £30 or so additional to his needs, which I could repay him, or you in England. Money is also an absorbing topic in extreme youth. I propose to return to England by the twentieth of September, taking a slow boat from Genoa and going via Gibraltar. [Oxford] term starts on October 8th. I am very much relieved to see that I am entitled to wear a scholars' gown; it would have been *infra dig* for a Waugh to have appeared as a Commoner after all these years.

I think I can hold out here until the first of September, although laundry is my undoing. It costs 300 lire to launder a single shirt, a sum for which one can get hog drunk with the greatest ease. . . .

On Wednesday I finished the first half of my Book . . . I celebrated my little achievement at Al Papagallo, a restaurant which is to Bologna what the Tour d'Argent is to Paris or the George Hotel to Taunton.

Has it been confirmed that the Herberts will be at Portofino on September 1st? If not, I am undone. If I send an urgent telegram, could you send two five-pound notes in separate envelopes? My criminal acquaintances tell me that you should wrap the notes in carbon-paper to elude a device employed by the Excise men to detect the Lavery line in bank-notes . . .

Love to Mummy and Hatty

your affectionate son

Bron

My father replied, without enclosing any money, on 26 August:

. . . Your grandmother (on Harriet's authority, I think) has

told the monks of Downside that you are composing a dia-
tribe against them. I am confident you are incapable of ingratitude to those patient and magnanimous men. Pray bear
in mind that until you are 21 you cannot legally publish a
book without my consent as you are incapable as a minor of
signing a contract. I do not anticipate having to withold an
imprimatur ...
  The best restaurant in Genoa is named Pichen
  Your affec Papa
  EW

My plan to live in Bologna for six weeks on less than £2 a day required careful organization and did not really cover treats like
entertaining American women at Al Papagallo. Normally, I could
afford a *panino salami* for breakfast, a plate of spaghetti for luncheon and a two course meal with wine in the evening. There
were other, less reputable luxuries I occasionally allowed myself,
but anything else had to be taken out of the food money. Eventually, after two days of no food at all, I had the humiliating experience of being arrested by a member of a branch of the police
force called 'Vigilant' for eating nasturtium leaves from the public
gardens. He made a tremendous speech in front of a crowd which
assembled to witness my shame: 'These flowers are sown, planted
and nurtured by Italian hands in order to beautify and adorn the
city of Bologna, to give pleasure to the citizens and win respect
throughout the land for our careful husbandry. They are not provided to satisfy the gross appetites of foreigners and tourists.'
  I slunk away, crimson-faced. But within a few days my labour
was finished. I have never been able to understand how anyone
can spend more than six weeks writing a novel, if they have
nothing else to do. But perhaps my own novels would have been
better if I had spent more time on them. After finishing the book I
put it away in a drawer at Combe Florey and forgot about it, feeling embarrassed and ashamed, showing it to nobody. It was only
after suffering a 24-hour concussion in a car accident at Oxford
that I looked at it again in its more or less illegible ball-point holo-
graph and decided it was excellently funny.
  Throughout my subsequent writing career I have found there
are only two attitudes I have been able to take towards my own
work. The first is to think how shaming, how dreadful, how could I

have written such drivel? The second is to think how clever, how witty, how original – I could never write anything so good again. There is nothing in between. I think these exaggerated reactions may be quite common among writers. My father agreed that he felt the same. Only Americans and modernists convince themselves that anything they write must have the stamp of genius, that there are layers and layers of meaning to be uncovered by patient acolytes. But if I have a single serious regret about my life up to the august age of fifty, it is that I wish I had been able to spend more time revising my five novels. I do not re-read them with great pleasure now, although I very much respect the judgement of anyone else who claims to have enjoyed them. By contrast, there are certain newspaper and magazine articles – most particularly, perhaps, those in *Private Eye, Spectator* and *New Statesman* – which I read and re-read in a frenzy of self-congratulation and dread for the future.

*   *   *   *

However it was as a nineteen-year-old pensioned off ex-army officer with his first book, in manuscript, at the bottom of his suit-case, and approximately £1 in his pockets, that I eventually arrived at Santa Margherita, Liguria, the station for Portofino, to be met by my Uncle Auberon and be taken off by him in the back of an Apé – a sort of motor scooter with a cart behind it, which was the only type of vehicle which could climb the winding mountain drive to the villa.

This was to be the last time I ever stayed at the grand old Villa Carnarvon, as it was called locally, or Alta Chiara, as the family had named it in whimsical translation of Highclere, the Carnarvon seat near Newbury. I did not then know it was to be my last visit, but Auberon, whose short life was to be entirely spent in selling things he had inherited, sold it soon afterwards. It had been built by his grandfather, the fourth Earl of Carnarvon, a cabinet minister (as Colonial Secretary) in three administrations and Viceroy of Ireland, at a time when rich English noblemen had the world at their feet. Perched on the promontory with views of the harbour on one side, the Mediterranean three hundred feet below it on the other, with massive terracing to create a garden and acres of terraced vines and olive trees, it was every child's idea of heaven on earth and served in that role for all my grandmother's thirteen grandchildren as they spent their childhood summers there in rotation. It had been bashed about a bit during the war, but by the time of my first visit, at the age of ten in 1949, it had been well restored by the War Compensation Commission, with the same old servants and tenant farmers who had been there before the war, and the same old boatman to take us round the corner to Paraggi or San Fruttuoso or to wait patiently while we bathed off the *banche* at the bottom of the 250 foot cliff under the villa, approached by hazardous rock paths from above.

The house was always full of eminent people in their least eminent manifestations: the Isaiah Berlins took a cottage in the grounds with Stuart Hampshire and other brainy folk, all somehow less frightening in shorts and straw hats. The David Cecils and Muggeridges stayed at the villa and such romantic characters as Paddy Leigh-Fermor, as did an endless succession of Poles with unpronounceable names who came to talk politics with Auberon.

Auberon was at his best in Portofino, rejoicing in the part of English milord which never carried complete conviction at Pixton, and even less so in London. In Portofino he was generally known as 'Il Conte', or even as 'Conte Carnarvon', explaining that Italians found it difficult to master the complicated English laws of primogeniture by which titles went to the eldest son. But he did nothing to correct them and may well have encouraged them in their errors.

He was not in the least bit impressed by the Rex Harrisons who had a villa across the other side of the harbour, nor by any of the Greek millionaires who called at Portofino in their huge yachts. In the village, he was king. His grandmother, old Lady Carnarvon, had been mayor during the fascist years, and a handsome building for the edification of the youth of Portofino stood above the carpark as her memorial. Many of the older people in the village had reason to be grateful to the family for help during the de-fascistification processes after the war, although Auberon cannot have helped things by singing the old fascist anthem – 'Giovinezza' – loudly in the night clubs which sprang up in Portofino during these years. It ended on an inopportunely triumphalist note: 'Mussolini, Mussolini, Mussolini *IL VINCITOR.*'

The food at the villa was always delicious, starting with breakfast of fresh figs and apricots on the terrace with quite elaborate meals prepared in an ancient kitchen where the stove had to be encouraged with a feather fan, but the wine, made on the estate, was always disgusting. Auberon, who had no palate at all, praised everything indiscriminately. He served the same food and wine to the Crown Prince (later Grand Duke) of Luxemburg as he did to his poorest relations, and always assumed it was of the best.

When he came to sell the villa, Auberon did not, as others might have done, go to Knight, Frank & Rutley or some other agent and ask them to get the best price for it. That was never his way. Having perhaps nothing else to do, he involved himself in endless plots with shady Italian characters – all for the purpose of denying an estate agent his percentage. At one point, he proposed to translate the money into a shipload of pickled anchovies and bring it to England in that form. Eventually, he sold the villa to an Italian industrialist called Augusta, but kept most of the land and various small properties dotted around it. I do not know whether Fassio ever took up residence but for many years the villa was empty. On revisiting it, five years later, with my wife and first two children, we were shown round the empty villa by the gardener, Battista, in tears, before climbing further up the mountain to stay in a converted cowshed where Battista's wife, Pina, looked after us. We saw too a lift Auberon had had carved out of the living rock of the mountain to carry his growing bulk up to the cowshed.

I cannot believe it was really necessary to sell the old villa. It was just that, as I say, Auberon had nothing else to do. He spent part of the money buying an estate in Sardinia and building a huge, much less nice villa next to the sea. He brought back the rest of the money and paid it into his current account at Drummond's branch of the Royal Bank of Scotland in Trafalgar Square. For the first time in three years he asked for a statement of account, having given instructions to stop sending them as they worried him so much. He expected it to show a huge credit balance, but it showed that he was £50,000 overdrawn. It turned out that a Ukranian friend had been forging his cheques for years. He had always boasted that the friend was an expert forger and offered to help anyone who needed a forged document, as came out at the trial. Auberon cut a strange figure in the witness box at the Old Bailey. Crown counsel said: 'Mr Herbert, are you in the habit of spelling the word 'hundred' with two 'tt's"?'

'Hontret?' said Auberon in his strange, guttural accent. 'Never,

never, never.' But the miscreant was sent down for several years nevertheless. 'Mr Herbert may seem to you a somewhat unworldly man,' said the judge to the jury, in summing up.

But these anxieties were all a long way ahead in September 1959 when I found the villa in full swing, with the David Cecils staying, an elderly cousin called Lady Mary Strickland with her disturbingly pretty granddaughter called Ariel and the usual roll-call of Poles and Ukrainians. My second brother, James, was also staying there, the object of close cross-questioning by Auberon on the prevalence of homosexuality at Stonyhurst, the Jesuit college in Lancashire to which he had been sent. James pretended not to know what it was, until eventually admitting 'you get occasional cases of vileness among the younger boys'. This turn of phrase caused endless delight, and Auberon used it to his dying day, fifteen years later.

Poor Auberon, I do not suppose he ever did anything vile but he never married. A month before he died, my wife and I stayed with him in his hideous new villa in Sardinia. He suffered from a distended liver and coughed horribly. Every morning we feared he would be found dead in bed. He had discovered a whole new cast of comic gardeners, cooks and peasants to act as back-drop to his own exuberant personality, but it was no good pretending he could cut quite the same figure there. He sold part of his estate to his friend the Grand Duke of Luxemburg, and watched balefully the Aga Khan's development of the Costa Smeralda.

'Which do you think is grander,' he asked me. 'The Aga Khan, the Grand Duke, or, well, me?'

'First the Aga Khan, then the Grand Duke, then you,' I replied.

He took it manfully. 'I thought you would say that,' he said.

We saw him several times again – Pixton is only some twenty miles from Combe Florey. Then one day we left for our summer home in the Languedoc. On arrival we were met by Aymar de Laurens with a long face who said he had been telephoned by a lady from the Touraine whom he had not met for thirty years – Eliane d'Espous – with the news that Auberon had died that morning, sitting at his desk in Pixton, reading the *Sunday Telegraph*. He was only fifty-two. It was an inconsequential end to a rather inconsequential life. After serving in the Polish army during the war, he never did another hand's turn of work, but lived, as I say, from selling things – farms, woods, pieces of china or furniture or his mother's jewellery.

When Auberon turned up in my rooms at Christ Church, Oxford, a few months after I had left him in Portofino, I felt ashamed of him. He wore a duffel coat and seemed boastful as well as noisy. He was at ease only in his own surroundings, at Pixton and Portofino or, occasionally, in his London house in Knightsbridge – 11 Neville Terrace, later bought by Nigel Dempster, the social chronicler and belle-lettrist. My father once remarked that if Auberon had not been his brother-in-law, he would have welcomed and revered him as an eccentric neighbour. While Evelyn Waugh detested the modern world but did rather well out of it, Auberon Herbert loved the modern world but could find no place in it. I missed them both terribly when they were dead, and miss them both even now.

CHAPTER
EIGHT

Christ Church, Oxford 1959-1960

I went up to Oxford in October, 1959, already something of a cele-
brity by virtue of my public immolation in Cyprus. It was only now
that I started to appreciate some of the joys of having a famous
father. Others might have sprayed themselves all over with a
machine gun and thrown in a hand grenade for good measure,
and limped around Oxford unheeded. I could afford to put on a bit
of a swagger because I, almost alone among the undergraduates,
had had my photograph in the newspapers. Evelyn Waugh was not
nearly so famous in 1959 as he posthumously became with the
television film of *Brideshead Revisited*, and I do not suppose that
more than a small proportion of undergraduates had even heard
of him, but within an even smaller number he was already something of a cult figure, and it was towards this group that I tended to
drift.

In that respect being the son of Evelyn Waugh was a considerable advantage in life, for which I can only be grateful. By the
same token, I find that I have inherited a fair number of ready-
made enemies – chiefly in the journalistic and literary worlds –
and it may be that this awareness of enemies skulking in the
undergrowth has shaped the pattern of my life more than it should
have done. Others might be appalled to think of unknown
enemies, but possibly as a result of upbringing, I have always relished the knowledge and have rather enjoyed identifying them

and dealing with them over the years. At least it has given me
something to do, and kept me out of the much greater mischief of
politics.

Among the friends I appeared to have inherited were Graham
Greene, who always treated me with the greatest kindness, even
when I became a journalist on the *Daily Mirror*, and John Betjeman, who, after Oxford, became something of a close companion. He was a complicated, infinitely endearing man – tortured
and prone to melancholy under the public front of exuberant,
almost alarming geniality, put into terrible distress by the company of bores or louts or commonplace people, but burning with
affection and gaiety and generosity of spirit in happier circumstances. He was also timorous and very easily frightened. I remember having agreed to meet him once at the King Lud public
house, in Ludgate Circus at the bottom of Fleet Street, to find him
cowering with terror in the lavatories where he had fled from two
workmen – possibly printers – who were shouting at each other in
the public bar. It is lucky he had no enemies, except the usual bul-
lies at school.

My own inherited enemies divided into those who hated anyone
called Waugh, and those who hated anyone who seemed well-
connected, with an unfair advantage in life. In the first group came
inmumerable literary folk who had suffered some real or imagined
slight from Evelyn Waugh, as well as the great armies of militant
atheists, leftists and modernists who rather made up the literary
and artistic establishments in those days. The second group included almost the entire journalistic profession, as I later discovered. But I never repined as a result. Happen life's a challenge,
as the north-country working-class journalist Harold Evans is re-
puted to have said – even if his challenges were different ones.

In case anyone missed the connection between the thin, re-
tiring, rather bashed-up undergraduate and the august creator of
his being, my arrival in Oxford coincided with the launch of Evelyn Waugh's biography of Ronald Knox. Knox (1888-1957) was a
former Catholic chaplain at Oxford, and the chaplaincy, situated
in a poky Tudor building in Aldgate grandiloquently named the
Old Palace, was given over to a launch party, mysteriously referred to by my father as a *vin d'honneur*. His publisher, Jack Mac-
Dougall, of Chapman & Hall, had a daughter who came up to
Somerville at the same time, a statuesque Valkyrie called Miss

MacDougall who was said to be walking out with Lord Oxmantown.

Before the *vin d'honneur* they gave a small lunch party at the Mitre Hotel, attended by Sir Maurice Bowra, the Warden of Wadham College, and original model for Mr Samgrass in *Brideshead Revisited*, and John Sparrow, the Warden of All Souls. The idea was, I imagine, that these distinguished dons should take an interest in my progress – perhaps my father even hoped that Mr Samgrass would send termly reports as he did to Lady Marchmain on Sebastian, but although Sparrow took a kindly, avuncular interest and asked me to white wine gatherings in the summer, I never saw Bowra again after that day. Nor did I see Isaiah Berlin in my Oxford career, after so many summers sitting at his feet in Portofino, although this did not stop me boasting about how well I knew him. Eventually he gave a party for the undergraduate sons and daughters of his friends, but although he asked Martin Dunne (who had resurfaced at Christ Church, along with Sheridan Dufferin, Mark Amory, Hercules Bellville and various others) he did not ask me. Curious how these things can rankle after so many years. . . .

As I say, few enough of my contemporaries at Oxford had ever heard of Evelyn Waugh, let alone read *Brideshead*. For my own part, I knew nothing of Oxford apart from what I had read in *Brideshead*, describing one particular Oxford of thirty-five years earlier – unless you count *Sinister Street*, describing the Oxford of twenty-five years before that, or *Zuleika Dobson*, ten years earlier again. In recent years I read the autobiography of a man who had pulled himself up by his bootstraps from a slum in the Gorbals, who got himself to Oxford despite being made to eat black bread at home. I think he may have had to walk to school shoeless, with his clogs tied around his neck for fear of wearing them out. The writer was appalled, on his arrival at Oxford, by the number of public schoolboys in their change coats and grey flannel trousers, with their carefully modulated *herrenvolk* accents and air of cold disdain for lesser breeds. Well, that is his experience, his witness. My own was precisely the opposite. I was appalled by how few public schoolboys there were, appalled by the number of earnest, working-class youths whose humourless faces betokened young men on the make: they would never have time to frolic, take risks or make fools of themselves.

People will see these remarks as tasteless, or sneering. I merely record my impression. No doubt a privileged background helped towards a more carefree, irresponsible attitude, although in fact the Waughs were in much the same economic circumstances as the Gorbals hero. My father had no money when he started and he saved none; his Will, when he died, went to probate at £14,000, all of it left to his widow, who had a child still at school. What money she once had was long since spent on buying and equipping Combe Florey, which my own wife was later able to buy from her. My branch of the family has never had any money of its own, has always played the part of buccaneers – something of which the Bowras and Berlins of this world may well have been aware. Fame or literary achievement in the family may impress a few young undergraduates, but for the dons there is nothing to beat an ancient name, a stately home and a couple of thousand acres.

My income at Oxford was made up of £100 a term from my father, £300 a year from my war pension and whatever drivelling sums I received from my exhibition. My economic circumstances, as I say, were no different from those of the humblest state scholar. The great difference, as I saw it, was one of temperament. Obviously, this is not the entire truth. The state scholars saw Oxford as their means of escape from wretched circumstances such as we could only imagine. We must all agree with the puritans in our midst that it is closer to the true function of a university to train technicians and mass-produce technical qualifications than it is to harbour the idle young for a few years of frivolity before they settle down to the exigencies of earning their livelihoods. My one rider is that for an undergraduate coming up from active service in the army and nine months in hospital thereafter, nurtured on Waugh, Mackenzie and Beerbohm, the new development made Oxford a much duller, dingier place to be.

It honestly never occurred to me that there was anything to be gained by applying myself to a degree course in politics, philosophy and economics. I had chosen this subject in a foolish moment at Downside, on the grounds that it sounded vaguely clever and modern.

My exhibition had been in English, but my father advised that this was a girl's subject, unsuited to the dignity of a male. Lord David Cecil was rather upset when I told him this, staying at Portofino before my first Oxford term. I had forgotten that he was Professor of English at Oxford. But he became a good friend, asking me to stay in his house at Cranborne and never inflicting me with his opinions about Jane Austen or Philip Larkin. He was an intelligent, merry man, brilliantly good at charades. Perhaps I would have stayed the course in English, instead of finding myself lumbered with this rubbishy PPE.

In the first year we studied formal logic and the basic, neoclassical economics of Alfred Marshall. Long before I progressed to anything which could be called philosophy, or even to Marshall's theory of time-value, I met a *pons asinorum* in both subjects. People may find it tedious if I describe them, but this looks like being a long book and they can easily skip the next few paragraphs which explain why I was unable to make any progress in two of the subjects I had chosen.

Lesson one in formal logic, which seeks to reduce logical argument to algebraic symbols as a means of testing its validity, concerns a symbol called the hook, thus $\supset$. The practical function of the hook might best be translated by the English word 'therefore': A, therefore B, or if A, then B. A $\supset$ B. However, neither the consequent nor the conditional role was considered sufficiently formal, so the function of the hook was reduced still further to give A $\supset$ B the precise meaning as follows: 'It is not the case that A is true and B is false.' So long as A is true and B is true, the hook is true. If A is true and B is false, the hook is false. So far so good. Now we come to the *pons asinorum. If A is untrue, then the hook is true whatever the truth of B*. The reason for this is that the hook guarantees only that A cannot be true and B false. However, this restriction removes the hook from all application to truth or reason, and reduces it to a mathematical symbol. There are no circumstances in which 'A therefore B' or 'If A then B' automatically become true statements when A is shown to be false. If the hook does not cover either the consequent or the conditional relationship, but one of its own invention, then its only applied function must be either as a parlour game or as a liars' charter. Formal logic, like so many other things studied in the universities, must surely be a colossal waste of time. Far better play with Rubic cubes, which might impart a measure of digital dexterity which could be useful in a world threatened by a plague of RSI.

My objection to neo-classical economics was even more elementary. I stumbled and fell at the simple equation that savings equal investment. This cannot be gainsaid, since it is built into the definition of the two words as used by the disciples of Marshall, whereby they seek to create a tautology out of what is plainly an untruth. There are plenty of things to be done with savings which do not involve investment or consumption, the most obvious of which is to put them under your mattress. Although this objection is not central to the whole study of economics, as my objection to the hook was central to the current practice of formal logic, nevertheless it occurred to me that any scientific discipline which worded one of its main propositions so sloppily must be a waste of time.

My logic tutor was an intellectually tortured, socially confused, youngish don at Christ Church called Oscar Wood or possibly Woods. I think I turned in one essay in the course of my year under his tutelage – on the subject of the hook. He was never able to overcome my misgivings. My economics tutor, whose name I have forgotten, was a pretty young woman at Nuffield, although after a time I was put under the care of Sir Roy Harrod at the House – a kindly and amiable man who may have acted as unofficial economics adviser to the Prime Minister, Harold Macmillan, but who was never able to persuade me that his subject was anything but nonsense.

* * * *

Of the few Oxford contemporaries who have distinguished themselves in later life – Peter Jay, David Dimbleby, Paul Foot, Richard Ingrams, little Dominic Harrod, Ferdinand Mount – all went off to the worlds of newspapers and television. Most were the sons of famous parents. Traces of an Oxford mafia can be found in all of them. Jay married Margaret Callaghan from Oxford; when her father later became Prime Minister, he was rescued from a job on the economics staff of *The Times* to be sent as ambassador to Washington – but not before he had been profiled in *The Sunday Times* by Mark Amory, another Oxford contemporary, as possibly the cleverest man in Britain. Jay was always destined for stardom, as was Dimbleby, editor of *Isis* in my year, but several of the most promising Oxford lights never really shone out into the world. Alasdair Clayre, thought to be the most brilliant young Fellow of All Souls since A.L. Rowse, sang protest songs in cellar cafés and even involved himself with L. Ron Hubbard's Scientologists before slipping off the mortal coil under a train. Francis Hope, another Fellow of All Souls, was killed in the great Turkish Airlines disaster over Paris while still writing whimsical, left-wing pieces fortnightly in the back of the *New Statesman* – in tandem, as it happened, with me.

Paul Foot – son of my benefactors in Cyprus – joined Ingrams on *Private Eye*, where he was later joined by me, before finding fame and fortune as Robert Maxwell's in-house revolutionist on the *Daily Mirror*. His mother, as I have mentioned, used to visit me in the British Military Hospital, Nicosia, after my mother had returned to look after her cows in Somerset.

Perhaps as a result of these ministrations, Paul Foot later became a good friend. For years I would bum a bed off him in London. He would come back from addressing his revolutionary public meetings: 'Things are really moving in Doncaster. We had thirty-two people at our meeting tonight.' Perhaps he is the only genuine romantic among my contemporaries. I am not sure it is a very useful thing to be, but it keeps a few people happy.

Little Dominic Harrod was even poorer than I was at Oxford. He would kindly come and act as waiter at small parties. As a reward, a group of friends organized a whip-round to buy him a red suit but he cunningly dyed one of his existing suits red and pocketed the money. I introduced him to his first employer – Kenneth Rose on the *Sunday Telegraph* – and now he is television's greatest pundit on economics, of all subjects – having, no doubt, somehow cleared the hurdle about savings and investment.

Ferdinand Mount was not the son of anyone famous and owes nothing to his Oxford connections. I do not think he even did a spell on Kenneth Rose's diary column on the *Sunday Telegraph*, like Mark Amory and so many of us. He has risen to his present eminent position – with a charming, clever wife and a journalistic voice which is heeded in places which none of the rest of us ever reach – by talent and industry alone. But it is noticeable that like so many of us, he is seldom far away from the *Spectator*.

None of the above really belonged to the Brideshead set which centred around the Peckwater rooms shared by Mark Amory and a new friend, Bobby Corbett. Bobby was then and still is a private person, and it may seem tough to drag him out of his privacy to adorn the memoirs of one of his more exhibitionist former cronies, but he was undoubtedly the leader of the group, and he undoubtedly exerted a profound and entirely beneficial influence on us all. Looking through my father's papers after his death, I was amused to find a wadge of letters from friends and acquaintances of his youth begging him not to mention them in his proposed autobiography, which is consequently marred by pseudonyms, nicknames and omissions. Although I advertised my intention to write this book, I received no such letters. So here goes.

Robert Cameron Corbett was the fifth son of a blameless Chief Scout called Lord Rowallan whose photograph I used to salute once a week during my scouting days at All Hallows. My first vision of Bobby was when I was taken to his rooms by, I think, little Dominic Harrod on some pretext or other. Suddenly – barroom! – it was *Brideshead* all over again. Bobby was giving an impromptu lunch party – baby lobsters? quails eggs? For perhaps the first time in my life, I found afterwards that I had forgotten the food and could remember instead the company.

No doubt people have been trying to recreate Brideshead ever since it came out, from the wretched Kenneth Tynan onwards. Bobby had none of Tynan's exhibitionism – or Anthony Blanche's for that matter – but kept up a stuttering Wodehousian monologue as he invited his guests to admire his latest acquisitions. By the time I arrived on the scene, Lord Rowallan had been sent off to govern Tasmania, and Bobby more or less had the freedom of Rowallan Castle near Kilmarnock, a splendid Edwardian pile by Lorimer, to entertain his friends in the vacation. Although a handsome and dignified residence, it was no treasury of art, being decorated for the most part by the paintings of James McBey (1883-1959), a Glasgow painter for whom Lord Rowallan had conceived an admiration. Bobby's taste was nothing if not catholic. 'Your trouble, Bron, is that you look at art through blinkers,' he would say, as he hung some Bloomsbury rubbish next to Burne-Jones's original study for the angel in *The Annunciation*.

Bobby brought something else into my life in the shape of his old and close Eton friend, Lord Gowrie. 'Grey' Gowrie, as he generously invited one to call him, had the disconcerting appearance of a wind-blown street arab, with pitted face, large lips and wild hair. He seemed to have difficulty in taking in anything one said to him, and expected a thirty second silence before he answered. I saw this as a sign of stupidity, but because he was chiefly interested in modern poetry and 'art', there were many who decided that it betokened great profundity of thought. It helped, of course, that he was an earl. If he had not been, I might well have decided it would be wiser to walk on the other side of the street. No doubt he had many qualities, but I never spotted them. Although subsequent events lent a specific animosity to our relationship, I had never liked him much, deciding that he represented exactly the sort of bogusness and affectation which I had been sent on earth to avoid. He was later made minister for the arts by Mrs Thatcher, leaving the public service to make more money selling modern art to the Americans and Japanese as Chairman of Sotheby's.

A letter written in November to both my parents has the first intimations of impermanence:

Oxford is the most tremendous fun but it cannot possibly last, and either we will all get a lot nastier or we will all be sent down very soon I fear. There are more nice people than I knew existed in the country or the world. One is just beginning to settle into a rut and realize that every evening one sees the same faces, but they are such delightful faces that I cannot believe one misses anything. ...

Later that month I was driven with a party of other undergraduates to a party in Hampshire by Simon Lennox-Boyd. Simon was a good man and a fine driver, but on this occasion he and the driver of an agricultural lorry were unable to avoid each other. I woke up two days later in the casualty ward of a hospital in Aldershot with a policeman by the side of my bed asking how much we had all had to drink. In fact we had had nothing except possibly a glass of Guinness – Simon's mother's family made it, and Simon was later to be deputy chairman for a time. But so far removed were we from the Police Terror of the 1980s and 1990s that I could not for the life of me think why the policeman wanted to know what we had had to drink. I racked my brains. Crème de menthe? No, I could not remember drinking any crème de menthe. Luckily, I resisted the temptation to launch into any mendacious undergraduate boasts, but it was only later that I realized what a narrow squeak Simon had had.

After a few more days in hospital I emerged with a cracked skull and lingering symptoms of concussion, but no permanent injury. In fact I was more light-headed than usual and, on returning to

Combe Florey, picked up the novel which I had written in Bologna in the summer, and hidden away in a drawer out of shame and mortification. Far from finding it embarrassing, I thought it was exquisitely funny, and sent it off to Jack MacDougall at Chapman & Hall. Perhaps it would have been more seemly if I had sent it to some other publisher under an assumed name, but I was very short of money, having spent Christmas and New Year at Rowallan, and seemliness had to give way to the main chance. MacDougall telegraphed me in the first week of the new term: 'Accept *Foxglove* with delight, horror and deepest admiration. Suggest advance of £150.'

The rest of that term passed in an alcoholic haze. At the end of it I took prelims – the first year qualifying examinations – and failed them in both logic and economics, to nobody's surprise. One paper I passed with flying colours was the French set book – Tocqueville's *Ancien Regime* – which I had not actually read, but on which I had enjoyed two discussions, one with Mark Amory, the other with Dominic Harrod. My chief regret, in the light of my amazingly high marks, was that I could probably have managed without little Dominic's dissertation.

* * * *

At the beginning of this second term I realized that I had fallen seriously in love – in a hopeless, incompetent, mooncalf sort of way – with an undergraduate in St Hugh's. It would be intolerable to parade this unfortunate lady before the public gaze for no better reason than that I fell in love with her thirty years ago, so I shall confound everyone by calling her Beatrice and implore any reviewer or gossip columnist who knows her identity to hold his peace under pain of an orphan's curse.

Beatrice was eighteen years old on 27 February 1960. In the time-honoured fashion of gawky youths, I had seen to it that she knew I fancied her. I gave her an onyx bead necklace for her birthday, to match her lustrous brown eyes, and she wore it faithfully for the next four months or so. So I cannot claim that I received no encouragement. I was just incapable of taking advantage of it. We smiled at each other. I treated her with elaborate chivalry. She waited and waited, but I never made a move. It seemed, then, an inexcusable infringement of her personality to push myself on her and demand what I craved for. Oh dear. If I had been to a coeducational school I would have realized that the opposite sex craves for these things, too – sometimes, anyway – but I had little or no conception of this. 'My advice to you is to treat her like a woman; stop treating her like a doll' said my good friend Bobby in an uncharacteristically gruff, avuncular moment. Better advice was never given, but I was psychologically incapable of following it. My trouble was the ghastly old Dante-Beatrice syndrome, a product of Catholic guilt and inexperience.

And then the subtle, swarthy Lord Gowrie started stealing her from under my nose. Although he had not been to a coeducational school either, he had spent the time when I was in uniform as art master at an expensive girls' school. Black, and an earl, and said to be a poet – the combination was clearly irresistible. One of his former pupils, called Bingo, would visit him at his lodgings outside Balliol. She later became his first countess. For the moment, however, I had to watch him practise his Afro-Asian wiles on my Beatrice. Quite possibly Gowrie would have carried the day even if I had put in two years' National Service in a girls' school – with his earldom, his exciting touch of the tar-brush, his interest in modern art and his so-called poetry. But I was in the throes of this Caliban-like passion and have never been so miserable in my life.

My letters home from that disastrous summer term of 1960, when I might have been preparing for my second bash at prelims, say nothing of a soul in the extremes of a ridiculous, self-inflicted torment:

Darling Mummy,
Oxford is much the same – all the faces are exactly the same and although they are all very nice I feel that it has no more surprises. I now share a tutorial with a very funny Arab called Surrowoggy who keeps winking at me; whenever the tutor's back is turned he points and rolls his eyes and sticks out his tongue and rocks with derisive laughter. I never know whether to be priggish and pretend not to notice, or whether to try and enter the spirit of the thing and point, too. Instead I give half-hearted little giggles which make my poor tutor very anxious.

Miss McDougall failed prelims, so did B. Corbett, so did S. Dufferin, so did N. Fleming and many others. So did Surrowoggy.

Surrowoggy, who I think probably came from Ceylon, had an uncanny resemblance to my tormentor, Lord Gowrie, needless to say. My parents would have been quite unable to spot the unbearable pathos of the first sentence of the next letter, nor the pluck behind the brittle gaiety of the gossip which follows:

Christ Church, Oxford
Dear Mummy and Papa,
Oxford is quite exceptionally pleasant at this time of year. There is not much news to relate – a friend called Henry Berens killed not one but two cows last night returning from the Betjemans, which I thought quixotic and creditable. D. Harrod was his only passenger; he is still in the Radcliffe Infirmary.

Sir M. Bowra offered Henry Harrod free tickets for the Wadham Commem Ball if he could get Emma Cavendish to come. Don't you think that rather sordid?

I have decided that when I grow up I want to be a printer. I have just corrected the galley proofs of *Foxglove* for Chapman & Hall.
Love from
Bron

As the summer went on, social chitchat becomes ever more frenetic.

Dear Papa,
Thank you for your letter. I made no plans for the long vacation for the reasons you so delicately suggest; but shall start making them now . . .

I spent last week fishing in Norfolk with the Harrods. We caught hundreds of tiny crabs, but as they were unfortunately not eatable we just had to put them to sleep as humanely and effiiciently as possible, which was great fun. The week-end before we went to the Boyds' house in Bedfordshire which is a tiny two up two down cottage . . . B. Corbett danced with four duchesses at the Lambtons' ball and has been insupportably stuck-up ever since.

· Yesterday we went to see Cliveden and the Iveaghs' house nearby which is fairly small but costly with lots of Guardis and tapestries. Next weekend I am going to stay with some people called St Just for my first debutante dance of the year, but I doubt its being much fun.

Mr Sparrow has taken to giving soirees for the sons of his friends at which he serves very nasty white wine cup and cigarettes.

"I do not know what my vacation plans will eventually be. I think I shall apply for the post of tutor to some wop . . .
Love
Bron."

He could not have guessed what agony of heart was disguised in the bitter suggestion that I might take a tutorial post in Italy for the long vacation.

My last letter from Oxford before the end of term does not read, now as if it was the work of an entirely sane person:

Dear Mummy and Papa,
I shall be returning home in time for dinner on the 22nd, if that is convenient. I shall have to go away for the night of the 24th and also the night of July 1st unless that is inconvenient for you. I have spent a very busy fortnight making plans and doing things . . . The dustcover has come for *Foxglove*. I think it is rather pretty. Last week-end I spent at an awfully pretty house near Andover called Welbury. . . . The night before I went to a very rum dance given by Douglas Fairbanks Junior in his London house. The lavatory seats all had written on their underneath: 'Good, Goody Daddy's home'. The night after to a sort of barn dance given by Mrs Betjeman. The week-end before I spent at Wantage with them, and Mr Sparrow came down to play progressive ping-pong, at which he is quite nimble . . .

Last night I was at a very pleasant dance given in Sussex at which there was a room entirely given over to middle-aged love, and all the little débutantes stared wide-eyed through the windows at the gross figures sprawled over the sofas.

My examinations start tomorrow and so I am spending a quiet evening with my books. I should be disagreeably surprised if I do not distinguish myself.
With love from
Bron

* * * *

The suggestion that I would be disagreeably surprised not to distinguish myself in the examinations might be read as pure bravado or even, in the light of what had gone before, as what is nowadays called a cry for help. I had done no work and realized that I had no chance whatever of passing. But there was a more disreputable reason for the bravado. My father had generously said he would pay for the long vacation holiday on condition that I passed prelims. Since the results would not appear until the end of the vacation, he had to accept my assurance that I would pass.

By the end of term, Oxford had lost its charms for me. The sight of Beatrice walking her radiant way over the lawns and gardens of Oxford was a constant source of torment, even when she was alone and without her swarthy admirer. Oxford consisted in seeing the same faces day after day, and hers was always among them. I had only my own incompetence and cowardice to blame. It was time to move on.

I also had a first novel coming out in the autumn, and foresaw that the role of a published novelist among the other undergraduates would be an odious one, requiring endless displays of modesty and self-effacement. They were mostly slightly younger than I was, since I had chosen to do National Service before university, and I could see no future joys. So it was in the almost certain knowledge that I would not be returning to Oxford that I left my strange little room in the Old Library building, with its bedroom let into the sitting-room like a horsebox.

The holiday which I had swindled out of my poor father took me to Dubrovnik and Corfu with George Clive, his sister Alice and Martin Dunne. On my return I spent a month in Siena alone and wrote most of a second novel, but it was no good and I never finished it. I seem to remember it was about two young men living in Florence – the only part of my life's experience I had not already used up in *The Foxglove Saga*. The inevitable Oxford novel was to come later.

Then back to Combe Florey to face my father's disappointment. I drove to Oxford to collect my belongings in an extraordinary sort of furniture van my mother used for driving her vegetables to the market. I stopped at Cliveden on the way for a ball given for a pretty girl called Amanda Morris. Lord Astor, still untouched by scandal, was a most agreeable host at dinner. I remember explaining to him that I rather hoped one day I might myself live in a house like Cliveden, which had been designed by the same architect as Highclere, where my grandfather spent his childhood. Lord Astor quite understood. At the ball afterwards I decided I had seen Lord Gowrie, although it might easily have been some innocent saxophonist in the band. I climbed into my ridiculous furniture van, parked outside Charles Barry's stately front elevation, and drove away.

There was a brief moment of acute misery, stripping my room and attendant horsebox of its pictures and *objets de vertu*, its endless bottles of strange and disgusting liqueurs, its twelve brandy glasses of different sizes which had somehow accumulated over the year.

From that moment on, at the age of twenty, I always managed to support myself, with the help of my war disability pension which grew imperceptibly over the years whenever my wife had another child, or whenever a government of the day grew worried about its votes. I have always managed to support myself in tolerable comfort. I think it may have helped to know that there was no money in the background to bail me out if I ever stopped working. Many of my friends have had their lives completely ruined by possession of a private income. The sum of money which I tricked out of my father for the summer vacation – I think it was £100 – proved to be the last he ever had to give me.

CHAPTER
NINE

Clarges Street 1960-1961

'There are only two possible careers for a man who has been sent down from Oxford. You must become either a schoolmaster or a spy', said my father, on my return.

In fact I had not been sent down from Oxford, like Paul Penny-feather, for outrageous behaviour. I had merely been rusticated. It was open to me to apply for re-admission by re-taking the pre-liminary examinations in a few months time, if I wished, but I had decided to forgo that option. Following my father's advice, I wrote off to Sir Roger Hollis, an old drinking friend of his from Oxford days, who was head of M.I.5 at the time, and also to Church and Gargoyle, the well-known firm of scholastic agents, really called Gabbitas and Thring.

Sir Roger, who was also the brother of Christopher Hollis, my godfather, replied that I was too young for his service, but that he had sent my letter and other details to the Foreign Office Depart-ment sometimes called the Secret Intelligence Service or M.I.6, but known on its writing paper by the less exciting name of Co-ordination Staff. I was duly interviewed in Carlton Gardens by an admiral and a man from the department who knew my Uncle Auberon and had, indeed, stayed at Portofino (where Donald Maclean also stayed, although I tactfully did not mention this). After that I was sent to the Civil Service Selection Board in Savile Row, whose chairman, John Goldsmith, I immediately identified

as a communist agent on the strength of some mildly liberal re-
mark or other. After my unexpected success in the War Office
Selection Board I was cocky, and thought I would swim through.
When I learned I had failed I brooded long and hard about Mr
Goldsmith, and even put him, heavily disguised, into a novel five
years later. I think he may still be alive, but surely too old to sue.

Three years later, in different circumstances, I applied again
with the same result. By then several of my friends from Oxford
and elsewhere, including Martin Dunne and David Winn, had
joined, although neither lasted long. I attributed my second failure
to the reference Martin gave me, on which no sane person would
have hired the once-off services of a shoe-cleaner. While paying
tribute to my powers of imagination, it dwelled at length on my
irresponsibility and carelessness with facts. I was rather bitter
about it at the time and drew some harsh conclusions about
Etonians generally, but in the mellowness of middle age I can see
they were all quite right. I would not have made a very convincing
spy, despite my nondescript appearance and almost obsessive re-
ticence.

My application may not have been helped by an interview with
two spies, a civil servant and a psychologist, where they grilled me
on my attitude to race. I was anxious to prove myself as liberal as
possible, and averred how much I admired the new independent
states which were beginning to emerge all over Africa.

'You don't think they may have some problems?' asked one of
the questioners.

'I feel sure they will overcome them,' I said. 'You see, they may
not be as good as us at our particular skills, but they are much
better than us at other things.'

'What sort of things?'

My mind went blank.

'Well, climbing trees,' I suggested weakly.

Efforts to find employment in the teaching profession were
more successful and I was offered two jobs almost immediately,
both in private preparatory schools. One headmaster made the
mistake of inviting me to join him at his table in the school dining-
room. Suddenly, it all came back: the revolting food, the smells,
the noises and the terrors of school. Scarcely pausing even to
make my excuses, I stood up and fled.

I eventually landed a job on *Queen* magazine, then owned and

edited by Jocelyn Stevens. My job was researching a centenary
volume under the editorship of Quentin Crewe. My co-research-
ers were Katie Sachs, daughter of a High Court judge, and Judy Innes, sister of a Downside friend and a famous beauty whose Cambridge friendship with the novelist Andrew Sinclair had already
been recorded in his novel and musical *My Friend Judas*. In my
time I had stayed at the Innes family home in Brentford, but Judy
was by now a figure of crippling elegance and smartness. We were
supposed to find illustrations for the book, and sat giggling nervously all day in the outer office at pictures of Victorian invalid
chairs while in the inner office Quentin dictated letters from the
wheelchair to which he has tragically been confined for most of
his life. We were in something of a conspiracy against him, as I
suppose nearly all low-paid employees are against their boss – we
received £9 a week for a six-day week. His secretary, Angie, pretended to join our childish conspiracies, but I suspect she was spy-
ing on us and reporting back. This is because Angela Huth, later to
become the famous novelist, was to emerge even sooner – in fact a
few months later – as the second Mrs Quentin Crewe.

My arrival at the *Queen*'s offices in Fetter Lane coincided with
the publication of *The Foxglove Saga*. It was greeted by a peculiarly savage review in the *Sunday Express* which appeared on the
day after my first week of work:

> I can say without doubt that it is one of the most heartless,
> disagreeable books I have ever read. Contempt reeks from
> every page. Monks, doctors, nurses, soldiers, nannies, ser-
> vants, all are despised and mocked.
> *For what*? For nothing but the hope of a joke. A joke which
> never comes. No sadistic, perverted, vulgar trick is missed.
> No object is achieved.

Heady stuff, this, for a young man of twenty, made all the head-
ier because the author of this extraordinarily violent review was
none other than Quentin Crewe, my boss at *Queen*. Later in his
long review, he explained the reason for his violence:

> Yet it may be said, if I feel so harshly about young Waugh's
> first book, why write about him at all? Why pillory the poor
> young man?. . . .

The answer is that Auberon Waugh is no ordinary author. Because he is the son of his father, the literary establishment has gone to work. Only a son of the literary establishment would have got this book published with so much publicity. Pages of advertisements, great billows from the publisher (Evelyn Waugh's father was a director) far more than any first novel could reasonably expect.

It is a poor system that produces this: that ensures attention for any books by the Sitwells but leaves other authors unnoticed.

This slightly mysterious reference to the Sitwells can be understood only if you know that Sacheverell Sitwell had recently written a book about Japan, which had been received with reasonable politeness by most reviewers except Crewe, who himself had a book about Japan coming out a few weeks later.

Crewe undoubtedly had a point. The novel came out with glowing testimonies from John Betjeman and Graham Greene. Mr Greene, never one to mince his words, had written: 'Only once this 50 years, I think, has there been a first night like this. It is superb, your book, in its fun and deceptive ease. A thousand congratulations.'

It was certainly true that through having met Mr Greene and Mr Betjeman – and through my father's friendship with them – I had better access than was available to most first novelists, although I liked to comfort myself that they would not have written so enthusiastically if they had not genuinely enjoyed the book. But Crewe took a very dim view of it:

In my opinion Betjeman and Greene should have known better. Unless we want to see our leading authors nominating their successors – like the tally clerks of the London docks.

My own attitude to the innumerable injustices of life has always been a philosophical one, especially when they have tended to operate in my favour. A player in life's poker game can use only the cards he is dealt. It is not the sign of a clever or compassionate player who is dealt three kings if he trades one of them in for a jack. Most hands have good and bad cards in them. Others may

have been born richer or more athletic than I was, better at singing or dancing or drawing in charcoal. I was born with a famous
name and a certain fluency in writing – and also with sufficient
acumen to see that neither of these gifts would endear me to
everyone in my chosen line of business. Writing is a jealous profession, and journalism even more so. If I had not already been
aware of it, I was soon to learn of the unbudgeable resentment
which these two advantages would cause in many quarters. In
those early days there were unknown 'enemies' behind every
other bush, few of them prepared to reveal themselves as soon or
as openly as Quentin Crewe, some of them prepared to go to extraordinary lengths behind my back to do me harm. If this sounds
like persecution mania, I must also testify that I have thoroughly
enjoyed hunting these people down so as to catch them from
behind.

My only revenge on Crewe was to send in pictures of ever more
absurd Victorian invalid chairs as proposed illustrations for his
centenary volume of *Queen* magazine. When the book eventually
came out it was a tremendous flop. Practically nobody bought it.
No doubt this added to his bitterness.

* * * *

I celebrated my twenty-first birthday on 17 November 1960 while
still working for *Queen* with a small lunch party at Wilton's. My
father sent me a copy of his children's pedigree which he had had
printed and bound.

> Combe Florey House,
> Combe Florey,
> Nr Taunton
> 16 November 1960

My dear Bron,
I congratulate you on reaching your majority and hope you
will spend an enjoyable day. I hope that in later years you will
look back on this birthday as the opening, not as apogee, of
your career.

I should not wish you to enter man's estate encumbered by
debt. My present to you is therefore to remit your debts of
honour to me. I note from this account which was left on the
morning room table that I advanced you £50 beyond your

[Oxford] allowance. There is also the £50 which was to have bribed the examiners. You may well have calculated that the gold watch or other trinket I might have given you would have cost less than £100. You were probably right.

I send you your pedigree – not illustrious on my side, but none discreditable.

Yours ever affec.

E.W.

If I had had the slightest intention of repaying him the £100 I could easily have done so when he presented the account which I left on the morning room table. I had sold the serialization rights in *The Foxglove Saga* to the *Daily Express* (which had printed a rave review by Peter Forster, who became a very good friend) and the American rights for $2000 to Simon & Schuster. Even by the standards of the times, I was quite a rich bachelor, as well as being an elegant one. Rather than pay my father I bought a new mini-car for £559.6.8d. But it was good to know that there were no hard feelings.

13 Clarges Street, Piccadilly, was to be my home for the rest of my bachelor days and, indeed, for the first few months of my marriage. The house, a small Georgian one where Charles Keane the actor once lived, converted into service flats in the Edwardian era, has long since been demolished to make way for a hideous modern block put up by Reed International. When it was being demolished I happened to walk along Clarges Street and saw the wallpapers I had put up hanging out of the window. It was run by Mrs Norrie Iago, an eccentric Irishwoman, who spent most of her time inveighing against the Jews. I would return from idyllic week-ends at the Goldsmids' palace in Kent and listen to her tirades. I think she had formed a poor opinion of the landlord, a man called Mr Benjamin.

These months were indeed the apogee of my social standing; even in my own family I was a figure to whom people deferred. In November I wrote home:

The Frasers gave a party last night. Whipper was drunk, Mervyn courting someone French and chic, Mr Woodruff amiable, Alice ill, [John] Chancellor trying to hire me to write about tooth decay and whales for a children's magazine

which he is editing, and I was rather the Lion, which was
very nice. When it is all over they will be ashamed of having
lionized me, I am afraid.

Neither parent would come to a party given by my publishers as
a combined twenty-first birthday party and book celebration – *The
Foxglove Saga* sold 14,000 copies in hardback, which was a considerable achievement. As I wrote rather tartly after the event, it
was probably better that they had not come, as they would almost
certainly have embarrassed me in one way or another. They were
not great attenders of events, failing to turn up for any of their
grandchildren's christenings and attending their children's wed-
dings only after long and bitter complaints. After the experience of
the grey bowler hat at my prep school sports day, I did not mind
too much.

The rent in Clarges Street was twelve guineas a week, appre-
ciably more than the £9 I was receiving from *Queen*, so I applied
for a post on the diary column of the *Daily Telegraph*. I was recommended by Kenneth Rose, who was just leaving it to start the
Albany feature on the *Sunday Telegraph* which he has been writing ever since.

The Editor of the Peterborough column was a shrewd, wry professional called F.J. Salfeld. At the interview, Fred Salfeld seemed
uninterested in my efforts to convince him that I could write,
chiefly concerned to stress that I was a person with connections
which would be useful to a newspaper diarist. 'I can see that with
your contacts you have an advantage over some applicants who
might be better in other ways.'

I started sizing him up, but Fred was no enemy. He was just
making the point. I worked happily under him for the best part of
three years, writing little pieces which were often about the birth-
days of octogenarian generals. This is one of my masterpieces
printed on Monday December 11, 1961:

General Sir Reginald Hildyard, who is 85 today, will celebrate
his birthday quietly at his home, South Hartfield House, Cole-
man's Hatch, with possibly a drive in the evening.

It was a fondness for motoring which led to his resignation
as Governor of Bermuda in 1939. A motion to allow him him a
car was greeted with laughter in the Bermudan Assembly

after it found no seconder . . .

'Ironically, a few months after Sir Reginald's resignation, war broke out and the ban was lifted. Since then, Bermuda has never looked back – if that is the phrase.

Another occasional type of entry took this form:

My note last week about 'the late' Lieut. Gen. Sir Adolphus Appleyard may inadvertently have given some readers the impression that General Appleyard was dead. In fact, as his daughter tells me, he is very much alive at 94, and will be taken out today as usual to be shown round the garden in his Surrey retirement home.

Although he has had to give up the rugger he loved, 'Dolly' Appleyard takes a lively interest in what is going on. Recently, he was heard to remark of the Orpington by-election that it was 'a b - - - dy poor show'.

* * * *

The other members of the Peterborough team were Richard Berens, eldest brother of the cow-slayer, Sean Day-Lewis, a son of the future Laureate, and Bill Deedes, who, as a cub reporter on the *Morning Post*, had been with my father in Addis Ababa when my father was the *Daily Mail*'s special correspondent to cover the coronation of Ras Tafari, otherwise Haile Selassie, and the subsequent Italian invasion. These expeditions produced both *Black Mischief* and *Scoop*. My mother liked *Scoop* least of Evelyn Waugh's novels, for reasons which I have explained, and he deferred to her in the matter, but it has been my experience that every journalist worth his salt adores the book. During the 1970s there was a pathetic attempt – emanating chiefly from *The Sunday Times* – to project journalism as a serious profession, even statesmanlike in its responsibilities. Whenever I heard of a journalist who disapproved of *Scoop*, I marked him down as a prig and a fool, someone not to be trusted.

Bill Deedes had no such problems. My father's novel about journalists was his Bible. Although by the time I met him in December 1960 he was forty-seven years old, had fought gallantly in the Second World War, been a Member of Parliament for many years and even a junior minister under Churchill and Eden, his promotion in the world of journalism, as of December 1960, was to be deputy editor of the *Telegraph's* diary column: Peterborough, London Day by Day. My father always referred to him affectionately as 'Young Deedes' and rather to my surprise, that was how he was known in the office. I have never known a man with less side to him – always cheerful, always friendly, always polite, always one of the boys threatened by authority from above, whether it was Michael Berry, the Editor-in-Chief of the *Telegraph*, or Harold Macmillan, the Prime Minister. It was the schoolboy quality in him which was irresistible. The relationship between him and Michael Berry could scarcely have existed in any other country. Although there were only two years between them, they appeared to remain on a prefect-junior boy basis throughout their entire association. During my time on the *Telegraph*, Bill was summoned to Downing Street and asked if he would like to join the Cabinet and Privy Council as Minister Without Portfolio in charge of information and press relations in the run-up to the disastrous 1964 election. He came back to ask Mr Berry (as he then was) for leave of absence and was told there could be no guarantee that the job would still be waiting for him when he came back.

Bill eventually became Editor of the *Daily Telegraph*, where in my few dealings with him I found him living in exactly the same schoolboy terror of the fifth floor. On retirement he was made a lord. Virtue is sometimes rewarded.

* * * *

One incident occurred during my first employment on the *Telegraph* which threatened a major débâcle on the Lavery scale in the still-fragile relationship with my father. It was entirely my fault, and I tell the story here as much as an act of penance as in the form of a cautionary tale. In 1959, my father had published his *Life* of Ronald Knox, in the course of which he had disguised the identity of an undergraduate on whom Knox had had a platonic crush while at Oxford before the First World War. The undergraduate concerned, cryptically called 'C', was Harold Macmillan, the then Prime Minister. 'C's' identity was revealed by Malcolm Muggeridge in a diary column in the *New Statesman* after Muggeridge had heard it from my Uncle Auberon who heard it from me. This provoked a violently contemptuous letter from Evelyn Waugh on the evils of gossip and journalistic tittle-tattle which, in the light of his own predilections, may have seemed to be riding a dangerously high horse.

After the book came out, Macmillan wrote to Evelyn Waugh offering him the CBE, which Papa turned down, saying he would wait until he had earned his spurs. He reckoned he was too old for a CBE. Anthony Powell, an inferior artist and a younger man, had been given one by Eden four years earlier.

Then, in June 1962, Macmillan (still the Prime Minister) wrote to Evelyn Waugh again, asking him to an official luncheon at Downing Street in honour of U Thant, then Secretary of the United Nations. This invitation was refused with even more alacrity. If Macmillan thought he could discharge his obligations by a free meal, to be shared with an impenetrable Burmese gentleman, he would have to think again.

A few days later I mentioned this circumstance to my friend and colleague, Kenneth Rose, who turned it into a characteristically witty and good-natured piece in his *Sunday Telegraph* column, as he was perfectly entitled to do – mentioning also the Knox connection.

Papa decided that the culprit was Lady Pamela Berry, wife of the *Telegraph*'s editor-in-chief, at whose house he happened to have had lunch and discussed the invitation. He wrote another furious letter, this time to the Editor of the *Sunday Telegraph* who showed it, ashen-faced, to Kenneth Rose, who showed it to me. I decided the time had come to take evasive action and wrote, shamefully, to my father on 5 July 1962: 'I have just read your letter to the *Sunday Telegraph*. They are delighted with it. It was not I who sold you to them, although I have a theory as to who did.' Readers may observe how, with typical Catholic casuistry, there is no actual untruth in this letter, as I had not sold the information to Rose, merely told it to him by way of passing the time of day. Papa wrote back from Combe Florey on 6 July:

My Dear Bron,
Of course I never suspected you of betraying me to the *Sunday Telegraph*. The culprit was Pam who is now known alternatively as 'little Miss Judas Sneakhostess' and 'Lady Randolph Grubstreet.' Alas pressure from Prime Minister has obliged me to withdraw the letter – or rather compassion for his secretary P de Zulueta, a decent young man, who got into

very hot water with PM for instigating me to write.

There used in my youth to be much indignation & contempt for 'sneak guests' – impecunious young men who sold gossip to the papers. 'Sneak hostesses' of ample means and no motive but malice are a new development.

I have contented myself with warning Michael against his butler who as the only person in the room besides Pam when I spoke of U Thant, must be in illicit communication with one of his editors.

The breach between Pam and myself is final. I do not think this will affect your position in any way. You got there without my assistance.

Although the Berrys must have had a very shrewd idea about the provenance of Kenneth Rose's diary story, they never penalized me in any way.

* * * *

This unsavoury episode was still in the future when I took two friends to stay at Combe Florey for the week-end of 13 February 1961 – Bobby Corbett, whose failure to pass prelims a second time made him my inseparable companion in London, and Teresa Onslow, sister of Michael Cranley the dejected trooper in the Life Guards I had met on my first day in the army. Teresa and I had been seeing much of each other after meeting at the house of Berens the cow-slayer in Hampshire. When I walked into the Berens drawing-room to meet her for the first time – she had heard of me from Boyd and Amory in Greece, I had heard of her from Boyd – all the lights in the house fused simultaneously. Obviously this was some sort of portent, whether for good or bad.

During the course of the week-end my mother announced that as I now had my own establishment in London, she was taking away the bedroom I had commandeered for myself, segregated with its own bathroom in the older part of the house, and giving it to my two younger brothers, James and Septimus, who were being brought in from a dilapidated, unheated and isolated wing. For the first time, I felt that I had been expelled from the nest, that Combe Florey was no longer my base. In fact I more or less vowed never to set foot there again, announcing my decision in typically oblique and odious fashion in a letter written late at night in the

Daily Telegraph's sub-editors' room on 6 February 1961:

Dear Mummy,
Thank you very much for entertaining me and my friends so
lavishly over the last week-end ... I hope that the invasion
did not disorganize life too much, although it must be rather
galling to be treated as a week-end hostel for London office
workers. I shall not be returning this week, nor indeed for
some time as everything seems to happen at the end of the
week these days, and the comfort of Clarges Street is overwhelming, if comfort can be said to overwhelm. But I shall
give you good warning several weeks ahead if ever I need a
bed in Somerset.
    I am at a loss to understand why you chose my bedroom to
give to the boys – they expressed no desire for it, and you
could not have chosen a room which gave more pain to at
least one member of the family. . . . However, I must not
whine on – I could not have expressed myself more strongly
when the scheme was suggested, and there is no reason why
you should share my feelings – but if it had been a scheme for
keeping me out of the house it might have been successful.

My mother wrote a pained but unyielding letter back. My father
reported to various of my sisters that I had gone mad and was
bombarding his poor wife with insulting letters. I could see that I
had lost the battle. It was time to move on. I wrote a conciliatory
letter back, explaining that I had been suffering from a fever at the
time, was full of penicillin, etc:

Can I really have said all that? I am terribly sorry about the
letter if it was as bad as you make out – it was written in a
moment of pique not at yourself but at the late night chief
sub-editor, a fiendish and greasy mechanic with a vile temper.* I must remember not to write letters when sub-editing
late at night. Also, I had a particularly virulent type of tonsil-
itis. The logic in your letter is unassailable, and I can't think
what entered my head to question the wisdom of put-

---

* Winston 'Peter' Eastwood (1914-1991) became Night Editor then managing director of the *Daily Telegraph* 1965-1986.

ting the boys in my bedroom.

I followed this letter two days later with another which announced my intention to marry. The letter is once again written on expensive, embossed *Daily Telegraph* writing paper (stolen from the fifth floor), which suggests another late night subbing ordeal, but declares itself to be from 13 Clarges Street, Piccadilly, W.1:

Dear Mummy and Papa,
I wondered if I might return this week-end to Combe Florey although I am afraid it will be a fleeting visit, to arrive on the Saturday and leave on the Sunday.
   I would like to discuss with you a plan about which I am afraid you may have misgivings, to say the least. I propose, despite my extreme youth, my only moderately secure financial position and my uncertain and at times *irresponsible* temperament on which it has been your painful duty from time to time to remark, to take a wife and marry her.
   I am terribly sorry to be doing something which might incur your displeasure. I only ask that you accept the matter and, if you can, give us your blessing.

After a little more in this vein, I named my prospective bride, and proceeded:

Although extremely young, I do not think that celibate existence has many more surprises, lessons or pleasures for me. I am *extremely lucky* to have such a charming and lovely girl fond of me, and feel confident it will not happen again. My hair and teeth are falling fast, and if I do not marry soon I shall have to be content with Miss Catcheside.
   Lady Onslow suggests a wedding in July . . .
With love from
Bron

The reaction was quite cordial. My mother wrote that I could knock her down with a feather, my grandmother (Herbert) approved, having been a best friend of my bride's great-aunt, Dorothy Onslow, and indeed a bridesmaid at her wedding to Lord

Halifax, later Viceroy of India and Foreign Secretary. My Aunt Bridget approved, having been a friend of my father-in-law, Lord Onslow, and having stayed at Clandon in its grand days before the war (so had my mother, but she had forgotten) and my father arranged to have lunch with my prospective mother-in-law. I wrote to him from Clarges Street:

> Dear Papa,
> I hope you enjoy your luncheon with Lady Onslow. It is very kind of you to put yourself to all this trouble. You will find her a nervous woman, but not unintelligent. I should say that it is a great sorrow for her that her daughter is marrying a Catholic, although she is determined not to influence her in any way in the matter. . . .
> I hope I shall see you at Combe Florey this week-end. If not, or in any case, I should very much like you to see Clarges St before I move to more humble lodgings. Would Thursday 6.30 be any good?
> Your affectionate son,
> Bron
> P.S. Please don't overdo such depreciation of your son as you may feel politeness demands.

*   *   *   *

The outcome of it all was that I was married to Teresa Onslow on 1 July 1961, a day of insufferable heat, at the Church of the Assumption, Warwick Street. The reception was held on the terrace of the House of Lords. On the same day, the Princess of Wales was born, which is a sobering thought. An alternative diversion was the wedding of Lady Eldon's son, Johnny Encombe, in Brussels. As the two families had been fairly close in the west country – Lady Eldon was inaccurately called Cousin Magdalen – there was a certain amount of rivalry over who would choose to go to which. My Uncle Auberon caused great relief to my father, great annoyance to me by choosing Brussels. So, I think, did Thomas Pakenham.

Our honeymoon was spent in La Rochelle, where my bride introduced me to the delights of French cooking, which soon became an obsession, and to the French culture in general. She was already trilingual in French, Italian and English. Afterwards we returned to Clarges Street for a few months, while our new home in 44 Chester Row was prepared for us.

I was now more than twenty-one and a half years old, my bride some three months younger. It was plainly time to settle down and live happily ever after.

CHAPTER
TEN

Chester Row 1961-1964

I stayed working on the Peterborough column of the *Daily Tele-graph* for another two years before beginning to feel restless. In fact I did not really feel restless myself, and if left to my own devices would probably still be there today if my wife had not sug-gested it was time for a change. Fred never sacked anyone, although one of his young men was once removed after being found in the women's lavatories with a mirror.

Work on the *Telegraph* was well suited an idle man. So long as each member of the staff turned in one or two paragraphs a day – seldom requiring more than a telephone call or a lunch engage-ment – Fred Salfeld could be relied upon to supply the rest of the copy from the post. The great disadvantage of the job was that junior members of the Peterborough staff – Day-Lewis and I but not, I think, Berens – were required to stand in for the night sub-editor in charge of film, theatre, music and television reviews, which could be delivered in those days as late as eleven o'clock at night. The night sub-editor concerned was the great Harold Atkins, known as the Culture Sub. When I was sitting at his desk in the sub-editor's room and the telephone rang, I had to answer it 'Hello, Culture'.

The first part of the evening would be spent putting the Peterbo-rough column to bed, which was not much problem. Like a boy at school presenting his report to the headmaster, the sub had to take the copy to the editor's office and stand in front of the desk while Sir Colin Coote read it. 'What's all this about? I don't understand this one. I remember Reggie Hildyard well when he was in Southern Command. They wouldn't let him drive a car then. We certainly don't want to encourage them to let him drive around now he is eighty-five. Got turned out of Bermuda for trying to drive all over the place, and that was twenty years ago. I don't think we can use this piece.'

The second half of the evening was spent putting headlines on the late reviews and then accompanying them down to the stone where the pages were made up. Looking at the headlines I composed, I see they are almost uniformly gloomy:

TITO GOBBI NOT ON FORM
OUR IMAGE OF THE GERMANS
SCRAPPY BILL SUNG OFF PITCH
DOCUMENTARY FILM SHEDS NO LIGHT
PREDICTABLE VARIATIONS
NO THRILLS BY VISITING SWEDE
TRITE EXCHANGES ON CONTINENT
UNADVENTUROUS LIST
UGLY STAGE SET
AFRICAN PLAY MISSES ITS AIM
SPACE JARGON MEANINGLESS
TELEPATHY NO USE
BALLET TEACHES NOTHING NEW

But the worst moment came at the end of the day. By ancient tradition, nobody was allowed to leave the compositors' or make-up rooms until the last page had gone to the foundry – in those days, newspapers were set line by line in hot metal; the foundry was where the impression of the made-up page was sent to be cast into the plates which would eventually print it. The culture page was always the last to go. A distinguished reviewer like W.A. Darlington would wander into the subs' room at eleven o'clock at night, dressed in a dinner jacket, his review exquisitely written in blue ink. This gave the sub about ten minutes to get it printed, correct the galley, cut it down to the right size, compose a heading and see it safely into the printing frame, being careful never to touch the metal type for fear of provoking a strike.

Nothing would have mattered if the wretched sub-editor had not been required to go down to the stone, where the type frame was assembled. Perhaps there were only fifty or sixty people waiting to go off work, although it seemed like several hundred. They would begin with catcalls and whistles, then they would start hitting the metal lamps over their benches with steel rules. Finally, they would break into a horrible chorus of 'Why are we waiting?' while the sub struggled to make sense of a review of some tone-poem by Schoenberg which needed twelve lines taken out and a new heading to replace one which had bust.

The atmosphere on the *Daily Telegraph* in those days was still tremendously public school – I think I wore a stiff white collar to work most days, although this might already have been thought eccentric – and the greatest odium in the whole public school demonology is reserved for the cad who is rude to servants. It was odd, but none of my experience with the evacuees at Pixton, or in the army, or during nine months spent for the most part in the public ward of a national health service hospital, had equipped me for a situation where the servants were not only outstandingly rude to public schoolboys and plainly held them in the greatest dislike – that, perhaps, I had seen in the army – but were also much better paid. Proud as I was of my £25 a week pay packet, these angry men were already being paid five or six times as much for a job which I felt I could have done after half an hour's instruction. One night I decided I would try and see how long I could keep them up, but after twenty minutes the head printer called down my enemy the chief sub, and it all ended ignominiously.

* * * *

Yet I could so easily have stayed on the Peterborough staff of the *Daily Telegraph* for the rest of my working life. I was less adventurous when I was young than I am now, and the general, all-pervading air of caution would have got into me before very long. I would probably have been promoted to second-in-command of the Diary by now. It seems unlikely they would ever have trusted me with the top job. Every year continues to produce its crop of octogenarian generals to celebrate, or to mourn.

It would have been a pleasant enough life, no doubt. I was saved from it, as I have said, only by the determination of my wife, who decided she was too young to dedicate herself to such a husband. A life of placid London existence on a shoe-string, with week-ends in the houses of people much richer than ourselves, was not for her. It was time for us to go and live abroad, most particularly in France. And so we did. When I married, being drawn by face, limbs, laugh, a sympathetic manner and a shared sense of humour, I had no conception of the strong and virtuous character which would emerge over the years, keeping me within nearly acceptable range of the straight and narrow path. I had no conception that I had married a wife who, in the process of raising four children, running a large house and attending on a husband who spent long stretches in hospital, would embark on university life as a mature student, emerging with first class honours. I did not dream that in addition to translating numerous books from French and Italian, she would write a series of novels, setting out an original philosophy of response to the modern world which would be recognized and acclaimed by a growing number of discerning readers. A cynic might say that these are risks which all men take who marry too young. At any rate, a first inkling of this strength of character emerged on her insistence, early in 1963, that we should leave England and live for seven or eight months in France while I wrote a novel and she looked after the baby, Sophia, and practised her linguistic skills on the French.

By good fortune, the *Catholic Herald* was looking for a columnist to comment on political and current affairs on the leader page. For this the princely sum of eight guineas a week was offered. I had very few views on current affairs, and even less knowledge – since my flirtation with the League of Empire Loyalists at Downside, I had more or less dropped the whole subject, which was probably just as well, as the *Catholic Herald* was a distinctly pinkish paper. Otherwise, I had written an unpublished letter to the *Tablet*, complaining about a book review, of which they might have heard. Their choice may seem odd, but perhaps they were influenced by the famous name – here precisely valued at eight guineas a week. This, with my war pension of nearly £7 a week was to be our sustenance for eight months. Staying at Pixton one week-end we met my venerable cousin Pat Smith, who had been in love with a French girl before the war and said he was sure she would have an empty cottage on her estate near Castelnaudary, in the Aude, which she would let us cheap.

Pat Smith thus became our great benefactor. He was a member

of White's who lived in Brussels with his Belgian wife Monique. All my life he had been visiting Pixton for no apparent purpose. He was famous for having had a very good war in the RAF. When the RAF scientists wanted to find out how far a man could fall without a parachute and survive, they took Cousin Pat up in an aeroplane and threw him out. Then they counted the broken bones, and took him up again. Or so my father always claimed.

Further tips were given us by the head of my mother's family, Lord Carnarvon, who was making a rare visit to Pixton about this time. He taught me a card trick on the proceeds of which – or so he claimed – he had supported himself for over a year in the United States as a young man. You shuffle two packs of cards, put them side by side, and then ask the assembled company for odds against the chance of your turning over two identical cards simultaneously as you go through both packs. He taught me the patter to go with it:

'Nah then, I didn't hear ten to one, did I? That's ridiculous. Wown't anyone give me sixty to one? Twenty to one? Come along, we're not at Woolworth's *neow*,' he called out in his rich Cockney-Jewish accent.

At sixty-five, Cousin Porchy was a man of immense wealth, and at the height of all his various powers. This was his gesture towards equipping his impoverished young cousin to set out in the world. The real odds, he explained, are thirteen to four on, and you clean up every time.

Those who have the misfortune to be born without aristocratic connections often rail at an unkind Providence which has allowed others to be born with so many unfair advantages. I think I can honestly say this is the only benefit I have received from mine. At the moment of writing, I have never had occasion to put my august cousin's tip to use, but I have had it in reserve for more than twenty-five years.

Thus equipped for a new life, we set off for France, pausing only at Asolo, near Treviso, as guests of Freya Stark, the veteran Arabist.

Freya is one of those writers who are universally respected, even if few have ever read her. 'I confess I am not a close student', said my father, evasively, when challenged. Her house was full of strange, middle-eastern jewels and other objects. She lost an ear, when young, on her mother's silk loom, and was briefly, unhappily married to a homosexual. Old, upright, brave, hospitable and warm and gloriously unaware of her own absurdity, she represents a tradition in English letters which has continued well enough into the declining stages of the modern movement. She adored the Arabs – 'the Arabs have many human qualities', I once heard her explain, unblushingly – and liked a glass of wine – 'this is most exquisite wine, redolent of the very essence of water', she said to me once, in praise of a bottle I had bought her in the Café Royal.

While we were in Asolo, Freya generously suggested that Teresa might care to go and live with her and look after her in what she saw as her approaching old age. I think I was included in the invitation. It seemed a possible solution to the problems of having no money and wanting to write. We nearly accepted. Twenty-seven years later, Dame Freya (as she became in 1972) is still alive. It would have been a long stint.

* * * *

I left the *Daily Telegraph* at Easter 1963, being told that while of course they were sorry to see me go, they could not guarantee that my place would be available when I came back. I vowed that I would never return to writing the London Day by Day column, never reapply for a place on that agreeable, neglected shelf. This is one of the few professional vows I have kept. At other times I have vowed never to work on a gossip column, never to review books, never to be a political correspondent, never to involve myself in the precious, self-regarding world of literary magazines and literary prizes. But at least I never went back to the Peterborough column.

As soon as my first columns starting appearing in the *Catholic Herald* at the beginning of February 1963, the newspaper was deluged with Hang Waugh letters calling for my instant dismissal. It seemed unlikely that I would survive for long. This would mean that we had only my war pension of £7 a week to live on – what little income Teresa had was more or less dissipated by the purchase of the lease on 44 Chester Row.

However, I held the *Catholic Herald* job for eighteen months. My articles were modelled on Douglas Woodruff's roving, panoramic leaders in the *Tablet*, written without any of his enormous knowledge of the world, but oddly enough they do not re-read too badly. As it turned out, I was to be writing at least one weekly column every week ever after, sometimes four or five a week, but I did not know it at the time. These first attempts were possibly the most reasonable and politely argued of all my essays in this genre over the subsequent twenty-seven years. It may have been because for the first time in my life – and I hope the last – I was genuinely frightened of the sack. The letters which poured in brought my first awareness of an altogether larger circle of hostility outside the circle of those who disliked me because they knew me. To the hatred of progressive Christians for conservatives, I had to add the hatred of large numbers of people for Evelyn Waugh, the hatred of older people for the young, the hatred of the underprivileged for the privileged and the hatred of humourless people for anyone who tries, however unsuccessfully, to make jokes.

And so to France, which will be described in the next Chapter.

*   *   *   *

We returned to Chester Row at the end of October 1963 for the publication of the novel I had written in the first ten weeks of our stay in France, and also for the birth of our second child, due at the end of December. The book was *Path of Dalliance*, a novel of Oxford life which I have not read for twenty-five years and do not propose to re-read now. The child, which turned into my elder son, Alexander, by contrast, has been a source of growing pride and pleasure ever since.

Apart from a determination not to reapply to the *Daily Telegraph*, I had no very clear idea of what I wanted to do. I reapplied to the Foreign Office for employment as a spy, but once again was able to get no further than the Civil Service Selection Board. Goldsmith had just retired as its Chairman, and as a Civil Service Commissioner, but I suspected that his baneful influence lingered. I also applied to the BBC, where Harman Grisewood was wrongly thought to be pulling strings. The truth, as I discovered, is that in such huge bureaucracies as the BBC, the real grandees have no power at all. You have to know people much lower down. I knew nobody lower down.

The weeks of unemployment turned into months. I had the advance on my second novel to spend, and we also had some accumulated rent from the tenants who eventually took Chester

Row in our absence, but I now had even greater commitments. In our last weeks in France, we had taken on a young French girl of Spanish extraction called Lolita Gordo as maid of all work, or 'mother's help' as it was then fashionable to call such underpaid slaves. She was very small, but she worked incessantly. *'Madame a peur de me commander,'* she once exclaimed incredulously, on first glimpsing the traditional English diffidence towards their servants. My father uncharitably compared her to a large, hairy spider. I humoured him to the extent of elaborating the conceit that we had caught her in the Pyrenees with nets, and imported her in a cardboard box with holes punched into the sides. We grew very fond of Lolita in the three years she stayed with us, but it would be idle to deny that her beauty was chiefly in her soul.

When my son was born at the end of December, a nurse also joined the payroll and things began to look desperate. A month earlier, on my twenty-fourth birthday, my father had written from Combe Florey:

Dear Bron,
My best wishes for your birthday. I hope the coming year will find you the father of a son as worthy of your devotion as you have been of mine. Also that you will be in honourable and remunerative employment. Pray choose yourself a present to the value of £10 at any of the shops where I have an account – Turnbull & Asser, Heywood Hill, Fortnum & Mason, Carlin, Berry – and charge it to me.
    If you visit your niece, pray salute her in my name.
My love to Teresa
Every yours affec.
E.W.

I do not think, as others may decide, that the second sentence was intended ironically. Or at any rate, not very ironically. It certainly was not intended as an embittered father's curse.

The mention of a niece refers to his second grandchild, Emily FitzHerbert, born to my sister Margaret on a night when all of us (except, obviously, Margaret) took a Pullman coach to Brighton and back in a revival of the Oxford University Railway Club organized by John Sutro.

I suppose this is the sort of event one should mention in one's memoirs. It is hard to think of any reason for organizing such an occasion unless someone is going to mention it in his memoirs. The older generation was represented by E. Waugh, C.Connolly, looking hideously uncomfortable and being mercilessly teased throughout by C. Sykes, H. Acton, who made a witty speech, Lords Bath and Antrim, to add tone, Sir R. Harrod, to add *gravitas*, J. Sparrow to add glamour, Lord Boothby, for no particular reason that I could gather, and Mr Terence Lucy Greenidge, a sort of Poor Bitos figure who had disappeared into obscurity since his Oxford days and recently suffered a leucotomy. The younger generation was represented by myself, Desmond Guinness, Henry Harrod and little Dominic, my brother-in-law Giles FitzHerbert ... but perhaps, on second thoughts, I will leave Dominic to write about the episode in his autobiography.

Soon after the birth of my son, I find myself writing to Papa to thank him for a sustaining dinner at the Café Royal, suggesting that the extra nourishment may have saved our bacon:

It may make the difference between honourable impover-ishment and public disgrace. I now feed six mouths com-pletely, as well as clothing and keeping them warm. Lolita eats three loaves of bread a day, and even our daily woman has taken to eating my food, which makes a seventh mouth. I shall see that the servants starve first –
Your affec son
Bron
P.S. Did I tell you that Mr Grisewood was sponsoring me for the BBC? Very friendly of him. Some irons in the fire are beginning to get warm.

My father's reply, written four days later, on 24 January 1964 from Combe Florey, shows traces of the melancholy which des-cended on him with renewed force in his last two years, and which he generally managed to keep out of his letters:

Dear Bron,
I was very sorry to have to ask you & Teresa to postpone your visit. The truth is that the house has been too much fre-quented of late; we have no servants; I have work to do and there is much to be done in securing the home against bur-

glary, during our absence. We hope very much you will both come in the spring.

I think of having some heraldic engraving on a piece of silver for my grandson's christening. Can you tell me the arms of his maternal great-grandfather – are they Beckett of Grimthorpe?

I hope you insinuate yourself into the BBC – a safe and reasonably honourable concern. The *Sketch* would be shameful. Provincial papers have a way of suddenly ceasing publication.

I hope you can make Lolita keep to a diet of bread. Much cheaper than the fresh meat demanded by English servants. Love to Teresa.

EW

* * * *

I had indeed been offered a job as political reporter on the *Daily Sketch* by its then editor, Howard French. I had not liked him much at the interview and once again he made it plain that he was hiring me for my 'contacts' rather than for any wit or skill at writing I might possess. As I had no contacts whatever in the political world, beyond acquaintance with a handful of unimportant back-benchers and one Cabinet minister, long retired, I decided not to take up the offer.

In the event, I took advantage of my mother-in-law's acquaintance with one of Mr Cecil King's daughters to write a letter to the Chairman of the Mirror Group. King summoned me for an interview and then handed me over to Hugh Cudlipp. In those days Cudlipp had a very fierce reputation, and was certainly not one to kowtow to his chairman's wishes to employ spare public schoolboys. Oddly enough he took pity on me and always treated me with the greatest kindness. I was hired as a 'special writer' at £1,600 a year and given a desk in the main newsroom, opposite that of Mr Pat O'Hanrahan, who was in charge of circulating newspapers and magazines throughout the building. Sitting at that desk, while messengers and copy boys ran around and reporters telephoned hectically to the three corners of the earth, I eventually wrote the best part of two novels. The secret of success on the *Mirror* was never to try to get anything into the paper. That stirred up endless resentments among your fellow scribes. So long as I sat scribbling away at my novel, everybody assumed I was engaged in some special writing for Hugh Cudlipp. Although they did not approve of my presence in the newsroom, I presented no threat. In fact, I later learned from Derek Jameson that a gang of younger reporters on the *Mirror* had decided to put me in Coventry, but I never noticed this during the three and a half years I sat there. I attributed their taciturnity to the ordinary awkwardness of their class, or possibly to the natural shyness of those who had nothing to say.

My first problem, however, was to break the news that I had joined the *Mirror* to the august creator of my being, who was no admirer of anything it stood for. If he thought the *Daily Sketch* would be shameful, what on earth would he think of the *Mirror*? In fact I had always rather admired the *Mirror* – and still do – even if the main reason for my accepting employment there was that I was in desperate straits. My second novel, *Path of Dalliance*, had come out to a loud chorus of unpleasant reviews. Perhaps it was foolish to write a novel about Oxford, but I had nothing else to write about, with the predictable result that every single reviewer compared it with *Brideshead*, and all compared it unfavourably. My letter in reply to Papa's of 24 January 1963 shows sign of strain, I feel. I have cut long passages of mendacious and boastful descriptions of my new job, which I find too embarrassing to re-produce ('I shall be one of the four people responsible for all foreign and home political events which demand comment. . . .'):

44 Chester Row,
S.W.1.   *29th Jan. 1964*

Dear Papa,
Thank you for your letter. I am sorry to hear the house has been too much frequented of late, and would not wish to do anything that might aggravate such a state of affairs.

Your grandson has two maternal great-grandfathers – Onslow and Dillon. The Onslow married a Bamfylde, of un-impeachable ancestry, the Dillon married a Beckett whose claim to be related to the Lords Grimthorpe, always stoutly advanced by herself, was never recognized by the Lord Grimthorpe of the time. However, she made free use of the Grimthorpe crest, and it seems likely that she was a distant cousin. . . .

I am at a loss to understand why you should find the *Sketch* so shameful. More poisonous, illiterate rubbish appears each week in the 'quality' newspapers than in the two tabloids.* It would be a worthy aim in life, I think, to try and bring the lower classes to their senses. The educated and upper classes are too deeply committed to wrongheadedness to make the attempt worthwhile.

I was offered a most remunerative job on the political staff of the *Sketch* but, on reflection, turned it down because I thought the *Sketch* a poor paper. It has a dwindling circulation and moribund staff. Instead, I wrote to Mr King and, rather to my surprise, have been offered a job of much greater importance, although of smaller salary, on the *Mirror* ...

Lord Thompson, inebriated by his recent ennoblement, did not even answer the letter I sent to him. My *Mirror* salary – £1,600 – is probably less than a third of that received by my three colleagues, but I have no doubt that it will provide more interesting employment than anything the BBC might eventually have offered. Any literary employment is bound to be undignified, but I see no reason why I should suffer boredom as well as indignity. Since the job will be more enjoyable and more worthwhile than anything I am likely to be offered, I have no regrets for having accepted it.

Yr affec son,
Bron

In three and a half years on the *Mirror* I undertook perhaps four major projects, always the brainchildren of Hugh Cudlipp. The first was a three-part report on the state of Britain's sexual morals – 'Our British Morals by Auberon Waugh: A Brilliant Young Writer Reports.' Research for this important inquiry took me to all the strip-clubs of Soho, to interviews with Paul Raymond and on a mad outing to Manchester with Lucinda Lambton, then an up-and-coming photographer.

Our purpose was to photograph scenes of abandon in the Mecca ballroom, where photography was strictly forbidden. On the way up there in the car, Lucy asked me what I thought of Henry Har-

* In 1964, these were the *Mirror* and the *Sketch*.

rod, an Oxford acquaintance. On the spur of the moment I gave him rather a poor reference. Lucy went into peals of mad laughter and said she was so glad I had told her that as he was the man she loved most in the world whose proposal of marriage she had accepted the day before.

This might have cast a blight, but did not seem to do so. We checked into a desperate lodging house on Moss Side where the sheets were made of nylon and curious notices were stuck all over the walls: 'GENTLEMEN are Requested to Put Out their Cigarettes Before Getting into Bed' and 'LADIES!! Please do not put unmentionables in the Toilet but in the Receptacle Provided'. By night we crawled round the Mecca ballroom in the half-light, photographing couples on the dance floor who thought they were unobserved, but at the end of the day Lucy discovered she had forgotten to put a film in her camera so we came back empty-handed. Instead, she persuaded some young friends to pose for her in compromising situations, as being vaguely indicative of modern British morals. However, it turned out that some of them were under age: furious mothers turned up demanding to see the editor and took the pictures away again.

I wish I could think that the final Report on Our British Morals, which ran throughout April 1964, was worthy of the effort we had put into it, but the truth is that I never really mastered the art of writing for the tabloids. Perhaps I lacked a sense of rapport with the readers.

*   *   *   *

In the middle of my stint on the *Daily Mirror* I decided I had been living in London long enough. Our house in Chester Row, although quite commodious by London standards, was not big enough to share with two children and Lolita. I also thought I was yearning for the sound of rooks calling to each other in the tree-tops, the sweet, fresh air of the West Country and the sight of green fields. This is a common feeling among town-dwellers, of course. At any rate we found a pretty, old village house in Wiltshire about halfway between London and Combe Florey. We sold the lease on Chester Row and moved into the Old Rectory, Chilton Foliat, in the winter of 1964. But before arriving at Chilton Foliat, we must look at the French connection which started at Easter 1963 and ran, as a separate compartment in our lives, until the moment in 1990 when we gave the property to our eldest daughter.

CHAPTER ELEVEN

Lauragais (1963-1990)

In metropolitan France, the small southern town of Castel-naudary, in the Languedoc between Toulouse and Carcassonne, is sometimes used to mean 'the back of beyond', 'the sticks'. Or so I later learned. I did not know it when I said farewell to my wife at the end of November 1962 and sent her off to find a house for us to rent in the neighbourhood.

Twenty-four hours later she arrived at the railway station at Castelnaudary, Aude, intending to stay with Pat Smith's pre-war inamorata who lived five or six miles outside the town, while she looked around for a house for us to rent in the neighbourhood. Arriving at eleven o'clock at night, she found that she had lost the address of her hostess and forgotten her name. There was no one at the station to meet her. She had very little money, she had left her young baby behind in London, she had nothing but some vague memories of a crazy conversation with my aged cousin, who lived in Brussels, and who had assured her that she would be well looked after by his old friend, Jacqueline. Teresa later described this moment of desolation as the worst in her short life.

Within a quarter of an hour, however, her hostess had arrived, and whisked her off to La Ramejane, where she was introduced to another world of family and social relationships which were to prove an alternative, summer background to our lives for more than a quarter of a century. Jacqueline de la Motte St Pierre, as the beautiful Jacqueline de Laurens whom Pat Smith wooed and lost thirty-five years earlier had become, lived in a large house dominating the village of La Pomarede, of which she was mayor. Her husband, retired from the Foreign Legion with the rank of colonel, had been the chief cook and catering officer in that fearsome body of men. He now lived a rather fierce, withdrawn life in a flat on the top of La Ramejane, emerging only occasionally at mealtimes. At other times he would make himself felt by shooting with a pistol out of the windows of his flat at any of the neighbours' dogs he saw walking in the garden or park around the house. Many of the dogs in the neighbourhood walked with a limp as a result.

Jacqueline de la Motte ignored such distractions, busying herself with running a house for five children – four of them already grown up – and nine grandchildren, overseeing the farm and village and looking after her own dogs, to whom she was devoted. Two of her sons-in-law were in the French navy – one, Henri de Mauvesain, from a noble family in the region of Toulouse, the other, Jacques Bonnemaison, who was later to rise to the rank of admiral and command France's fleet of nuclear submarines.

In Teresa's honour, on the evening after her arrival, they served *demoiselles d'oie* – the carcases and backs of geese which are a local delicacy, available only in the season of making *foie gras*. There was one per person. Teresa mistakenly took two and ate them. Monsieur de la Motte arrived late for dinner in a fury and demanded to know of the assembled wife, children, sons-in-law and grandchildren which of them had eaten his *demoiselle*. Monsieur de la Motte in a rage was quite a terrifying sight. Silence fell on the company. After a short pause, Jacques Bonnemaison rose to his feet. 'Je regrette, mon père, c'était moi.'

The Bonnemaisons – Jacques and Jeanne, their five children, each more beautiful or handsome than the last – became firm friends ever after. When, later, he was posted to London, we saw them constantly. When Jacques was commander of the French nuclear submarine base at Lorient, in Brittany, we attended a New Year's *reveillon* at the base, dancing between suspended nuclear weapons in a huge cave.

There was never any possibility of doubting his nobility of character from that moment. I had to face a similar test a little before: when staying with the Glasgows in Scotland, I ate Lord Glasgow's kipper at breakfast. In response to his furious questions, I contented myself with keeping my eyes on my plate and quietly eating the skeleton, while everyone else watched me impassively.

* * * *

Madame de la Motte found us a little house outside the neighbouring village of Labécède-Lauragais. It was not a beautiful house, having been built since the war by a simple-minded recluse of good local family, called Villefranche, who had married his cook, and become, as the locals put it, *tout à fait déclassé*. Both died in the fullness of time. The neighbour was an elderly, widowed farmer called Pelissier, who lived in almost unbelievable simplicity with a simple-minded *bonne à tout faire* who could speak no French, and who spent her time bawling at Pelissier's six cattle in the Languedoc patois; the language of the troubadours, in its time, but now restricted to a dwindling band of elderly, illiterate peasants. Pelissier slept above his cows, the *bonne* slept with them in the straw. They ate nothing but bean soup and the occasional potato.

The story was told of a neighbouring farmer who had contracted cancer: scorning doctors, he consulted the local vet-cum-witch doctor, who recommended that he drink petrol. Either this or the cancer killed him, but the body was not found for several days, in the course of which it had been half-eaten by rats.

It is hard to imagine now how backward the French countryside was in 1963. Practically none of the houses in the village had water. Clothes were washed communally by the wives and old women in a stone and lead *bassin* through which cold water trickled. Our own water came from a spring in the field above us, which dried up intermittently throughout the summer. We shared it with Pelissier who was furious that we used water for washing ourselves and the baby. His own needs, he explained, were limited to two litres a day, which he used for his soup. His idea of a day's work was to go and shout at his *bonne* who sat in the field watching his six cows. She would then shout at the cows for a few minutes and he would retire happily to watch over his bean soup which hung in a cauldron all day over a smoky wood fire.

There was nothing very picturesque about the life of these peasant farmers, and no philosophical conclusions to be drawn about the superiority of simple country ways. The only lesson was that such a life was extremely uncomfortable. Land holdings were tiny, the result of the French laws of inheritance, but every square metre of land was jealously defended.

The local shops and restaurants, too, were extraordinarily primitive in those days. There was nothing except the barest essentials to buy, and the food was terrible, never having progressed beyond the local speciality of cassoulet, or bean stew with lumps of sausage, pork and pig-skin. In fact, the *cassoulet de Castelnaudary* is famed throughout France, if not (as they fondly believe) throughout the entire world, and makes a perfectly acceptable course if taken perhaps once every three months. To eat it every day, for breakfast in the morning and dinner in the evening, as the more prosperous farmers did, was no recipe for the good life.

More seductive aspects of La Vieille France were open to us through Madame de la Motte, whose kindness to us was unfailing. Most weeks we would drive to dinner with her and a game of bridge with her family and neighbours, driving back afterwards in a state of blissful intoxication from the foul red wine she made at the Ramejane, which stained the mouth purple for several days afterwards, and the ancient, very strong rum which she received from her husband's estate in Madagascar. She had two surviving brothers – a third, who had stayed at Pixton and was well known in my mother's family, was killed in the war. The younger brother, Comte Aymar de Laurens, lived in the main family property, Le Castelet, a few hundred yards from La Ramejane. Aymar, a man of intelligence and endless amiability, was the king of the neighbourhood. The Castelet, formerly a huge and forbidding chateau of great antiquity, had been burned down by the Germans in retreat at end of the war, and rebuilt as a comfortable and commodious residence by the War Reparations Board, with only a turret here and an old gateway there to mark the former building. Aymar and his wife Aliette had six children, mostly younger than us, and built a huge swimming pool at Le Castelet to keep them happy in the summer months. It became the social centre for the whole neighbourhood. By great good fortune, we were invited to join the circle, which comprised first the Laurens children and their children, as and when they married, then the la Motte children and their children, then the relations of anyone who had married a Laurens or a la Motte, then the friends of any relations, then certain approved neighbours, their friends, relations and guests. . . .

Arriving for a swim, with wife and child (later children) in tow, one might expect to shake twenty or thirty hands, in the formal French manner. Perhaps there were sixty or seventy adults with access to that swimming pool, and innumerable children. All knew each other and gossiped about each other behind their backs, but a high level of politeness and geniality was always maintained.

Over the years, I have watched the children, whom we 'tu-toied' so patronizingly, grow up into dignified young men and sometimes embarrassingly attractive young women. Several have married and had children, some have been less fortunate and ended up with thirty-year prison sentences in the Far East. The Lauragais, revisited practically every year ever since, has offered an alternative panorama of life, a twenty-seven-year soap opera which is still running and will continue to run long after I am dead. It has its joys and tragedies, a constantly recurring cycle of birth, marriage, very occasional divorce and death.

First of the deaths was Pelissier, our neighbour in Labécède. He was travelling in the back of a lorry which overturned. I never heard why he was travelling in the back of the lorry. It was normal among the peasant farmers in those days for the men to travel in the front, the women behind – a tradition inherited from the Arabs who once occupied this part of France, many hundreds of years earlier.

Next Monsieur de la Motte crashed into a tree on the road from Castelnaudary to Revel. I do not think he was much mourned by his family, but a book could be written about how this handsome, dashing young aristocrat from Anjou came to end his days shooting at dogs with a pistol out of a window in the Lauragais.

The father of one of the *jeunes filles de la région* who came to be our *au pair* in Wiltshire blew himself up in his car when he lit a cigarette and threw the match towards a petrol can on the back seat.

Even more tragically, one summer we were expecting some neighbours to dinner – Paul-Médéric de Fleurieu and his wife Ghislaine – when there was a knock on the door. Two Bonnemaisons were there with the agonized, embarrassed grin of people with seriously bad news. The evening before, Paul-Médéric – a man considerably younger than I was, and infinitely fitter, the father of a young family – had been to dinner with his parents-in-law, the Fontanges, in their house which is about half a mile from the Castelet. In the middle of dinner, for no apparent reason, Paul-Médéric fell to the ground, dead.

Finally, saddest of all, Aymar de Laurens died, apparently the victim of some unsuccessful surgery.

After a few years of revisiting the neighbourhood, either at Labécède or as guests of Madame de la Motte or the Bonnemaisons (who had converted an outlying farmhouse on the Ramejane estate), we found a farmhouse there – La Pesegado, on the ridge of a hill looking down on the plain where all our friends lived. A year or two later, we built a swimming pool there, and so rather retired from the Castelet ceremonial, which was just as well as it was becoming uncomfortably crowded. But we continued to see them all, at dinner parties in our own and other people's houses, at market in Castelnaudary and Revel, at the annual Fête de Puginier, and even in England, where a few of them occasionally ventured. Aymar never came to see us in England, but his benevolent presence continued to fill the Lauragais with the warmth of his intelligence, his good manners and his natural generosity.

* * * *

La Pesegado was still a ruin when we eventually moved into it in the summer of 1971 – two derelict cottages and a barn situated half a mile from the nearest house approached by cart tracks in four directions. It stands between the villages of Montmaur and St Paulet, in the shadow of the Château de St Paulet, once a very minor property of the Princes de la Tour d'Auvergne, but now their major property in the Midi.

* * * *

But I obviously can't keep up this level of excitement. The narrative, where I left it to digress about the whole French experience, had Teresa and me, both aged twenty-three, with our daughter Sophia, aged one, living in the bungalow at Labécède-Lauragais (built by the potty Comte de Villefranche for his unsatisfactory wife) in the summer of 1963.

It took, as I say, a couple of years for us to find La Pesegado, and it was a couple of years after that before we obtained possession. It had seemed quite a good idea to beat the politicians and join the

Common Market at the receiving end as French farmers, but we encountered some opposition along the way. The first came from a colony of French spiders, some of them only the size of kittens, others growing to frolic around like spaniel puppies. Next came the mice. Our first night, spent in camp beds on an earth floor, was made unendurable by mice running all over us. On the second night we set traps on every beam and rafter, with the result that we were kept awake by hideous snapping noises, after which dead mice and traps would rain from the ceiling.

In those early days, the children threw themselves into their new French identity, collecting snails after every rainstorm until Teresa eventually refused to cook them. We gave them instead to a workman called Fat François, or more simply 'Le Fat', as a reward for plastering and rewiring the entire house. We had borrowed this François from Jacqueline de la Motte, for whom he worked as agricultural labourer, gardener and major-domo, but he was also an expert carpenter, electrician, plumber, plasterer, glass-cutter and everything else. He was quite easily the fattest man I had ever seen outside a circus, and also the most dignified.

François personally drank four litres of wine a day and was never noticeably either worse or better for it. He worked very hard indeed, with a mere two hours off for lunch, and was the only man I ever saw standing literally in a pool of his own sweat, as he helped plaster a ceiling on a hot day.

After work, he picked bunches of wild lavender which grew around the house, explaining that he liked to have wild lavender in his underwear drawer. At one point, his wife suffered some form of nervous breakdown – quite a rare complaint in those parts. When I asked him how she was getting on, he replied: 'She is completely deranged. At breakfast today, I had to ask her three times before she passed the cheese.'

A normal breakfast for the working man in those parts was, as I have already intimated, cassoulet, with its traditional ingredients of white beans, lean pork, sausage, skin of pork and garlic. The cowman of a neighbour, describing to his employer how ill he had been the day before, explained that he had found it necessary to push this mixture down his throat at breakfast with his finger, because he was unable to swallow.

Our next-door neighbour but one at La Pesegado – perhaps a mile away – was a farmer who spent his entire day watching his cows as they grazed. He had thirteen of them, several up on old Pelissier, at Labécède, and sometimes he spoke to them in a high-pitched, angry voice, always in patois. On one occasion he introduced them to me, very formally, one by one: Frissone, Blanchette, Rosalie, Trompette, Mayot, Grissetto, Fanje. . . . When it rained, he sat watching them from a Citroën Deux Chevaux, parked in a corner of the field. That was what the Common Market had done for French agriculture at that stage. But I never cracked the patois language, despite many hours spent conversing with Blanchette, the most communicative of the thirteen cows. It appeared to mean whatever one chose it to mean, as in Wonderland.

* * * *

At an early stage I was told by Madame de la Motte, who fancied herself a little as a local historian, that the name of our property, La Pesegado, was patois for a place where mud was weighed. *Gadou* survived as a slang word for 'mud', and *peser* is the normal French word for 'to weigh'. Apparently the inhabitants of the farm spent all their time in this diverting and harmless occupation, before the French Revolution came, destroying all ideas of harmony, degree, social order and traditional values. Nowadays, there was not even any mud around, so one could not have weighed it even if one had the time, inclination and necessary machinery.

Then I met the Mayor of Montmaur who told me that the name derived from its alternative meaning of a footprint. There used to be a huge stone on the track outside the farm – he had seen it often – which showed the impression of a foot, with toes clearly marked. Legend had it that this was the footprint of an angel who had landed on the hilltop many centuries earlier. Then in 1940 the farmer who owned the place grew fed up with having an angel's footprint on the doorstep and blew up the stone with dynamite.

This story illustrates not only the robust attitude of the countryside to ancient monuments, but also the amazing ambiguity of the Languedoc language. If patois speakers could never be sure whether they were talking about an angel's footprint or a place for weighing mud, it scarcely seemed worth the effort to pursue my studies.

On a subsequent meeting with the mayor, he changed his story a bit. Far from its being an angel, it was Our Lady herself who had landed on the hillside, and the event was commemorated for many years by a chapel on the site, called Notre Dame de Peze-gade. But he still agreed that the chapel and stone had been destroyed soon after the war.

A few years later we invited an elderly neighbouring farmer to lunch. He was a friendly sort who very much enjoyed conversation but unfortunately, as he talked in a mixture of patois and the heavily accented French of the Midi, it was seldom possible to understand much of what he said. This was discouraging for the listener, who had to guess whether the old man was telling an amusing anecdote about rabbits or describing the death of someone very dear to him. He was a kind man, without malice or guile, and one would not have liked to make a mistake.

Towards the end of a very long lunch, I came to realize that he had been telling us once again the story of La Pesegado. My guest favoured the version that it was Our Lady who had landed on the hillside so many years ago. In this he was supported by his wife, who had seen the footprint often, and testified that it was much more like the Blessed Virgin's footmark than that of a mere angel. However, when the old man came to the end of his story, we began to note a significant difference. He had been present when the outrage was committed twenty-five years earlier and spoke of it as quite a jolly occasion. But there was no mention of dynamite. Under a sudden barrage of questions, he admitted that there had been several of them present, and they had merely tipped the rock over a cliff down the side of the mountain. Was it still there? He supposed he could find it.

So, after a heavy lunch, our expedition set off: myself, my younger brother Septimus, the old farmer and his son. We had to pause from time to time to allow the old gentleman to relieve himself, but we found the Pesegado without difficulty. It lay half-buried in the earth on the scorched mountainside where it had lain all those years since being tipped there by a group of over-excited and probably tipsy farmers.

My brother Septimus made the first disquieting discovery, that the footprint had four big toes and three little ones. As if this was not horrible enough, he also noticed that the footprint was thirty-six inches long. According to Professor Philip Tobias, of Witwatersrand University, the length of a human foot is about 15 per cent of total stature. This would make the Virgin Mary twenty feet high. Those who are interested in such things can visit the relic, where we eventually manoeuvred it, outside the front door of the house named after it. With the revival of fundamentalist religion, it may come to be an important piece of evidence.

* * * *

In June of 1963 I wrote to Papa announcing that Teresa was expecting her second child in December, which meant that she would probably have to spend Christmas in hospital. I added, rather poignantly as things turned out: 'I hope that at least some of these grandchildren will be a source of delight to you in your old age. Will you let them pull your beard?'

Papa had always promised to grow a long white beard, like Belloc's, as soon as his hair grew white. By the end he was prepared to admit that the gold had turned to silver, but he never got round to growing the beard. What neither of us could possibly have realized, of course, was that he had scarcely more than two years left to live. He wrote back in bullish mood:

Thank you for your letter and the good news that Teresa is to have another child. Please give her my love and congratulations. The date of birth is very opportune. It give me a perfect excuse to spend Christmas in London to keep you company.

The fact that he was still looking for excuses to avoid the family Christmas in the penultimate Christmas of his life suggests there was still a spark of resistance left. In the same letter, he commented on my *Catholic Herald* column and the correspondence it was exciting: 'Some lunatic this week suggests you were brought up in affluence. Little does she know.'

The 'lunatic' concerned was called Mrs T. Cobb of Caernarvonshire, who wrote in the *Catholic Herald* of 26 July 1963:

One fears that the young man is the victim of a too-affluent upbringing, which seems to have deprived him of any dis-

cernible sense of understanding of the problems of those less
fortunate than himself.

No doubt Mrs T. Cobb had a point. Over the years, it has been a
constant refrain from the enemy camp that nobody but those of
working-class background can possibly have any understanding
of anything. But the circumstances of Mrs T. Cobb's letter were
rather strange. Letters of complaint had been appearing regularly
ever since I started the column at the beginning of February. On 8
June I wrote to my father that I expected the sack by every post. It
was a gloomy prospect because without the eight guineas a week
my wife, child and I would actually have starved. Instead of giving
me the sack, the editor planted a letter in the correspondence
column, written by the business manager, Otto Herschan, under
the pseudonym of 'Oliver Martin'. It raised the question about
whether or not the *Catholic Herald* was right to employ me. The
editor added a note to the bottom of Mr Martin's letter, which
appeared in the issue of 12 July 1963:

> Columnists are usually allowed freedom of expression for
> opinions but not if their policies are consistently at variance
> with that of the paper. Do other readers agree with Mr Mar-
> tin? – *Editor*

I do not know how many letters the editor received, but he
printed about twenty-eight of them, some taking one view, others
the other. Both sides almost invariably threatened to cancel its
subscription unless its advice was followed. I read the correspondence, which continued for many weeks, in trepidation. If I had
been in Britain, I could have organized friends to write in my support, but I was helpless. What astounded me was the strength of
opinion on both sides. What I had thought were moderately conservative, good-natured pieces, written perhaps with a bit of nose-
twigging here and there, turned out to have been inflammatory
calls to a counter-revolution. It is one of the problems of a journalist's life that, choosing to live in whatever company he finds con-
genial, he loses touch with those whose company he would not re-
lish; making little jokes as he goes about his business, he loses
sight of those to whom any sort of frivolity is deeply repugnant. My
own conclusion, after thirty years on the job, is that it is quite right

to ignore these people's objections, just as one shuns their company. There are plenty of other publications catering for their preferences. In a sense, the more one annoys them the better. But a writer, like anyone else, has got to know his enemies, both in the sense of identifying them correctly and understanding their likely responses.

I hoped that my three-and-a-half-year stint on the *Daily Mirror* might teach me a little bit more about how the other half lives and thinks, but practically nobody on the *Mirror* showed any of the symptoms of the hostile correspondents on the *Catholic Herald*, or of the hostile reviewers who greeted each of my novels with a chorus of self-righteous horror, or of the thin, sour trickle of disapproval which has accompanied most of my appearances everywhere. Few of the *Mirror*'s employees were embittered, few were unintelligent or humourless and none was poor. My grand philosophical conclusion at the end of the day is that humanity does not divide into the rich and the poor, the privileged and the unprivileged, the clever and the stupid, the lucky and the unlucky or even into the happy and the unhappy. It divides into the nasty and the nice. Nasty people are humourless, bitter, self-pitying, resentful and mean. They are also, of course, invariably miserable. Saints may worry about them and even try to turn their sour natures, but those who do not aspire to saintliness are best advised to avoid them whenever possible, and give their aggression a good run for its money whenever it becomes unavoidable.

In the Lauragais there seemed to be no bitterness, no aggression, no resentment, very little vice of any sort. It was a garden of Eden which we left after seven months to return to the hatreds and jealousies of London, where I would have to find a job, Teresa would have another baby, I would be presenting a second novel to a literary world which did not seem, at that stage, to be quite ready for it.

I suppose there was, indeed, such a literary world as the one I imagined, but in fifty years I have never quite discovered it. My father never belonged to a literary world, although he had a few friends who were writers. Perhaps his father, the publisher and critic Arthur Waugh, belonged to such a world. If he did, it rather confirms what I have come to suspect, that literary circles are rather dim areas of society, populated by critics, publishers and literary agents more than by writers. A few minor writers, jostling for fashionable status, may frequent them, but nobody who is any good has much time for forming societies, groups or 'movements', excluding outsiders and issuing manifestos. At best, they afford the benefits traditionally associated with matrimony, of mutual society, help and comfort. At worst, they exalt mediocrity and encourage affectation.

On our return from France, we did not know that we would be making a second home in the area, or that we would develop alternative identities in its alternative society. One year, to celebrate the fact, I grew a hideous revolutionary moustache, and paraded myself in a beret. The moustache was allowed to stay only a few weeks, but the character somehow stuck. It was a character which later emerged, behind a fake beard, in the *persona* of the *Private Eye* diaries. I sometimes think, in whimsical moments, how nice it would have been if we had spent all our adult lives in La Pesegado, but the truth, of course, is that we would have died of boredom.

CHAPTER TWELVE

Chilton Foliat 1964-1971

Our retreat from London took us eventually to the Old Rectory, Chilton Foliat – a pleasant village in Wiltshire on the River Kennet just across the county border from Hungerford. The Rectory was and is a charming early eighteenth-century redbrick house set back from the Hungerford-Swindon road in a large garden. With six or seven bedrooms, and four recep. it was large without being oppressively grand. I had always hoped for something a bit grander myself, but Teresa was delighted with it. Hugh Cudlipp, my patron and supporter on the *Mirror*, now had a bright idea. I was to be the new Godfrey Wynn or Beverley Nichols, star of the women's magazines which the *Mirror* had acquired. Both Wynn and Nichols were still alive, but Cudlipp detested them both. I was to be the new Wynn for the New Woman. As a preliminary, he sent me on a gigantic tour of the country to write a report on Woman at Work for *Women's Own*. There had been a marked growth in the number of mothers of young children returning to work. I was to go round factories and offices interviewing them. Cudlipp took me to meet the then Editor of *Women's Own*, whose name I have forgotten. We did not take to each other. He resented Cudlipp's interference – I think Cudlipp was then Deputy Chairman of the International Publishing Corporation, which had taken over George Newnes, which owned *Woman's Own*. The Chairman of Newnes was called in, Alex MacKay, a good man who later joined Murdoch's News International, only to have his wife kidnapped and murdered in atrocious circumstances by the brothers Hosein who mistook her for Mrs Murdoch.

Even Mackay's bluff cordiality could not soften the heart of the man directing *Woman's Own*. For my own part, I identified him immediately as an Enemy. He sucked violet tablets, and it occurred to me that they might be responsible for what seemed a distinctly blue tinge to his hair. He told me that when he was a child, his family had been tremendously poor. Cudlipp and MacKay beamed their congratulations. His mother had had to take in washing, he said. I commiserated. My mother had washed for forty evacuee children throughout the war, I said, lying recklessly. Ah yes, charity work, he sneered, puffing Parma violets at me.

I spent a month away, touring factories in Belfast, Glasgow, London, Manchester and Burnley, Lancashire. It was the first of a number of such solo tours for which, in later life and in other climates, I developed something of a taste. All the time I was interviewing women at their work-benches. They were incredibly friendly and trusting, with none of the terror of publicity normal among the middle classes. There was no aspect of their lives they were not prepared to lay bare for the benefit of *Woman's Own* readers. Teresa and the two children went to stay at Combe Florey while I was on my tour. My father was taken with the idea of me among the women of Burnley, and walked around the house singing:

> What will the women of Burnley say
> When Auberon Waugh has gone away
> Leaving them all in the family way
> With the Deuce of a doctor's bill to pay?

But when I got home I had to prepare my 8000-word report and deliver it to my smirking, blue-haired, violet-scented persecutor. He handed it over to one of the woman writers on his payroll who rewrote it from beginning to end in special woman's magazine English, and it was thus that it appeared under my by-line. Mercifully, I don't think anyone I knew ever saw it.

The rest of the year I spent travelling into the *Mirror* building in Holborn Circus where, sitting at my desk in the newsroom, I wrote my third novel, called, rather mysteriously, *Who Are the Violets*

Now? It is about a poor young hack journalist working for a woman's magazine whose editor sucks violet tablets until his hair goes blue.

The *Woman's Own* commission marked the end of my attempt to inherit the crowns of Godfrey Wynn and Beverley Nichols. At about this time, Hugh Cudlipp relaunched the crumbling old *Daily Herald* as the *Sun* and introduced me to its editor, Sidney Jacobsen. Sidney was a wise and kind old bird – later ennobled, like almost everyone on IPC in those days: Jacobsen, Cudlipp, Beavan, Pickering. He saved me from many errors. I remember once, when I had written a peculiarly bitter attack on the young Nigel Lawson, then a city journalist who had somehow acquired a large interest-free mortgage from the London County Council, he said to me: 'Journalists are unpopular enough as it is. We don't want to help our enemies destroy us. Let's leave it to them to attack the press.' It was the first time I had heard the dogs-don't-eat-dogs doctrine enunciated.

At the time, I wrote truculently home:

> I have found a new *métier* in journalism. A newspaper called *Sun* prints a weekly sermon, rather on the lines of my old *Catholic Herald* pieces, but pays 25 guineas a time. So far they have had the moral beauty of suffering inflicted by fireworks, the wickedness of allowing state-supported undergraduates to demonstrate, the idiocy of allowing Old Age Pensioners free medicine and the injustice of free public school education for children of the working class. Money for jam.

A neighbour, who became a close friend at this time, was Woodrow Wyatt, the Labour MP for Bosworth, who for an intoxicating period between the elections of 1964 and 1966, held the government of the country in the palm of his hand, along with his colleague Desmond Donnelly. Harold Wilson had been elected in October 1964 with a majority of four. It needed only two Labour members to switch their votes to the Opposition for the majority to disappear. Wyatt and Donnelly, two Gaitskell supporters, were both set on the path which would take them away from the Labour Party – in Desmond's case, to the National Front and a sad, lonely death ten years later; in Woodrow's, to a Thatcher peerage and an influential right-wing column on Murdoch's *News of the World* – actually the same I found myself writing for a time in 1969/70.

Woodrow's marriage to his second wife, the dashing Lady Moorea Hastings, was breaking up at this time, and he felt lonely. He filled his house with all the beautiful people he could find. I had met him through my Uncle Alec Waugh, who, I suspect, may have had a passing fancy in his time for Lady Moorea. We had visited their palace off Regent's Park several times before moving to the country, and he had been to Chester Row. In Wiltshire, we fell into each other's arms. Teresa supplied the beauty and I was more than usually good at croquet, if I say it myself, even playing by his absurd rules. It was a marriage made in Heaven.

On Easter Day 1966 we went to lunch at Connock Old Manor, near Devizes, where Woodrow held court. Among the guests was the young journalist called Nigel Lawson who had just been appointed Editor of the *Spectator* in succession to Iain Macleod, the Conservative politician who was later, like Nigel, to become Chancellor of the Exchequer. In retrospect, it was a meeting which changed my entire life. At the time, it seemed fairly unimportant. Lawson made little impression on me on this occasion. He seemed a smart, clever young journalist, a trifle pompous in his deliberations but obviously well informed about everything. I did not yet glimpse the gigantic intellect before which I would eventually prostrate myself. I had an uneasy memory of a bitter attack on him which I had written in the Odham's *Sun,* but could not remember which parts, if any, had eventually appeared even as I wondered vaguely if he had read it. Under the circumstances, we made our excuses and left early, after a more or less cursory thrashing of all opponents at croquet.

* * * *

Returning to Chilton Foliat, I found a policeman waiting outside the door with a long face. Was I Auberon Alexander Waugh of this address? For a terrible moment, I thought that something had happened to the children, left behind with Lolita who still spoke no English. It came as a conscious relief when he said that my father had died suddenly in Somerset.

* * * *

It transpired that after a Latin mass, said by his old friend the Jesuit priest Philip Caraman in the parish church at Wiveliscombe, he had failed to turn up at lunch and been found dead in the downstairs lavatory. To die on Easter Sunday, after communion, among friends, with no lingering deterioration of the faculties, must be reckoned a merciful death. When I arrived at Combe Florey towards midnight – only my brother-in-law Giles FitzHerbert had stayed up, everyone else having gone to bed – the house still smelled strongly of paraldehyde, the foul substance he took as a sleeping draught after poisoning himself with chloral and bromide in the Pinfold episode. In the heightened awareness of the moment, that familiar, revolting smell seemed to have the property attributed to Padre Pio, of an odour of sanctity. The body had been taken for investigation by pathologists, but it came back two days later, boxed up in a coffin, to await burial, lying in the library attended in shifts by members of the family.

The night of his death there was a fire in the house. Somebody had left a door of the Aga in the old kitchen open, and it became red hot, setting various other things alight. Firemen tramped through the house, squirting things, before being given glasses of Guinness and sent away. On arrival, I had noticed a small pile of excrement on the carpet outside the downstairs lavatory. Others must have noticed it too, but, being Waughs, they all pretended not to have done so until the daily help arrived, when it vanished without anything being said. My mother, the Widow Waugh as she became from that moment, remained in her bedroom and did not emerge through all the night's alarms and excursions.

*   *   *   *

My feeling of relief on hearing of Papa's death remained one ingredient in the mixture of emotions. In his later years he had lost all terror, becoming bland and benevolent, and genuinely pleased to see his eldest son, daughter-in-law and grandchildren. He visited Chilton Foliat only once, but approved very much of all he saw. In his last year he had many of his teeth drawn, choosing to have it done without anaesthetic, for some impenetrable reason of his own (the vulgar new school of literary biographer would undoubtedly attribute it to some strain of sexual masochism, but I am not persuaded by this). In the event, his teeth seemed to have been drawn not only physically but also metaphorically. Where before he had been gloomy, bad tempered and on occasions aggressive, he became benign and affectionate.

But he still projected an immensely powerful presence. Just as school holidays had been happier and more carefree when he was away, so his death lifted a great brooding awareness not only from the house but from the whole of existence. Papa possessed to an unusual degree the power of making other people want to please him – not just in the relatively undemanding sense of winning his approval, but of keeping him happy in a hundred ways, for instance sending him presents of pictures and artefacts, rare wines and delicacies; more particularly, he sent family and friends into the world to supply him with information and gossip to keep his imagination fed. Nothing ever happened to me while he was alive but I mentally sub-edited it into a report which would be sent to him in my next letter. The last letter which survives from me is dated 15 March 1966, less than a month before his death, and describes Teresa's great-aunt, Lady Iveagh's funeral at Elveden in Suffolk. Reading the letter again after twenty-three years, I see that one of my major functions as an informant, was to present Papa with a version of the world as he would have had it be:

Lady Iveagh's funeral was sheer delight. Poor Lord Iveagh (he is 93) recognized no one and slept soundly throughout, being wheeled around by a strapping nurse. Occasionally he woke up and smiled beatifically around: 'Now Gwennie's dead I can go to lunch at the Brewery' – and went to sleep again. He also plans to go to Italy and do everything else which Lady I. had been preventing him from doing for 60 years. The assembled Guinnesses were a very queer crew. We lunched in freezing cold at Elveden, a vast mansion with a fine Indian marble hall. Prince F. von Preussen brought his own bottle of port and caused great offence by offering it to nobody else. 'Very Teutonic', they all muttered. Otherwise they gossiped about each other in different corners. Lord Moyne was getting off with his cousin Mrs Stux-Rybar, Benjamin Elveden, heir of all the millions, offered us cheap *rosé* wine with great aplomb. We sat at a corner table for poor relations with legless Richard Wood, and each one made a point of coming over to patronize us when the coast was clear of other Guinnesses. Teresa cried at the funeral. I was rebuked for laughing, she for crying. The evening ended with a drunken rout at the house of Teresa's cousin, Eliza Nugent, another Guinness.

* * * *

It was many years before I could break the habit of viewing every event with half an eye to the bulletin I would send to my father. Even now, I find that when I hear a funny story about someone in whom he would have been interested – the child of a friend, perhaps, or some grandee – I mentally store it away to repeat to him. There always follows a pang of bereavement when I remember that he is no longer around to hear it. But the strain of living two lives, one on my own, and the other through his eyes, was greatly relieved by his sudden death. Perhaps nobody is completely grown-up until both his parents are dead. For many years afterwards I continued to go to church faithfully every week. It was only when I came to accept that the services would be completely unrecognizable to him, that the new religion had nothing whatever to do with the church to which he had pledged his loyalty, that I felt I could distance myself.

It is hard to believe that these kindergarten assemblies bear much relation to the ancient institution of the Church as it survived through the Renaissance. The new Mickey Mouse church of Cardinal Hume and Archbishop Worlock is surely not a reduction of the old religion. It has nothing to do with it, being no more than an idle diversion for the communally minded. Whatever central truth survives is outside it, buried in the historical awareness of individual members. Or so it seems to me. But whenever I have doubts, it is my father's fury rather than Divine retribution which I dread.

* * * *

The obituary notices which greeted Evelyn Waugh's death were, with few exceptions, extraordinarily grudging. He died unhonoured by the country to whose literature he had made such a salutary contribution, and very largely unsung by his contemporaries. He had never been part of any literary group, and was deeply resented by the new wave of left-wing mediocrities who had come to prominence in the forties and fifties behind the Spenders and Isherwoods. Even among his acquaintances, there was a loud noise of worms turning. People who would never have dared insult him in his lifetime reckoned the coast was clear. About a week after his death, Nigel Lawson telephoned to ask me to write a piece for the *Spectator*, which had already marked the event with a decent tribute from Anthony Burgess and a tiresome but not, I think, malicious, memoir by Alan Brien of an occasion he had met Waugh with Randolph Churchill in White's.

To my slight shame, I took advantage of the moral high ground occupied by orphans and widows to write what I would probably now see as a petulant and intemperate reply to the encircling enemies. I remember it as a shrill, Bookerish and self-righteous piece of journalism. I am glad I was not able to trace a copy. It was written under pressure from the family. My mother, understandably distressed by the turn things had taken, was baying for blood. It is often a relief, in moments of shared bereavement, to find a common enemy. I myself have played the part on various occasions, and am always heartened to think of the comfort afforded. I do not, in fact, believe that much harm is done by insulting the dead. Beside the real pain of bereavement, the anger it excites comes as welcome relief. But it is obviously rather a dangerous occupation.

* * * *

My days on the *Mirror* were not quite over. Europe was all the rage at this time. Partly to acquaint his readers with their European future, but chiefly, I believe, out of the kindness of his heart, Mr Cudlipp sent me on a grand tour of European capitals, taking Teresa with me to write about the woman's angle. This added up to six weeks of staying at first class hotels in Lisbon, Paris, Bonn, Rome and Vienna, writing perhaps a thousand words on each. Michael Frayn mocked our efforts in the *Guardian*, which made me very proud at the time.

As 1967 got under way, it became apparent that even Hugh Cudlipp's ingenuity was beginning to be strained by the need to keep me employed. I was writing occasional pieces still for Odham's *Sun*, which had been launched on the promise of being an independent newspaper, in reaction to its former dogged acceptance of the Labour Party line. But I think there may have been a certain amount of dismay among the writers in what was, after all, still a newspaper of the left, if the price of calling themselves independent was to print my own reactionary Catholic burbles. I did not see much of the people on the *Sun* apart from Sydney Jacobsen, although I rather liked Dee Wells who was another columnist. For the most part, I was happy to keep my head down over my desk in the Mirror newsroom, and push on with my fourth novel, *Consider the Lilies* (1968) about the tribulations of a modern clergyman living in a huge rectory in Berkshire.

February 1967 also saw the birth of my third child and second daughter, Daisy. The *Mirror*, which had allowed me to write two novels in its time, also supplied me with two children.

Hugh Cudlipp managed to produce one more idea for my employment on the *Mirror:* Auberon Waugh's ABC of Beauty. This was a series of captions to photographs of bathing beauties. Unless one has a particular aptitude for this form of writing, it is not easy. One day when I was struggling with a caption, Hugh sauntered through the newsroom, smoking a huge cigar, with the air of a man who had enjoyed a good lunch. He stood back, pretending to admire my work: 'M stands for Matiness. Most men would be very happy to get matey with 21-year old Sharon Tudale . . .'

'It must be a wonderful thing, Auberon, to have had such an education,' he said. 'I never had one at all, you know.'

* * * *

In May 1967 I was asked by an American magazine called *Cosmopolitan* to write a piece about the two Profumo girls – Christine Keeler and Mandy Rice Davies – four years after the scandal. Keeler refused to see me unless I would pay her £10,000, which put an end to that side of things, and Mandy was living in Tel Aviv as the wife of an El Al steward. Then the Six Day War started and New York heard that Mandy had turned over a new leaf, had embraced the Jewish religion and was working as a nurse in a front-line hospital tending the wounded. I was asked to get out there immediately.

This was all very well, but in wartime greater priority is sometimes given to other cargoes than women's magazine journalists: bandages, blood plasma, and that sort of thing. However, by making a lot of noise and pulling every string in sight I managed to get enough bandages, blood plasma, etc. taken off a plane for me to squeeze into a flight to Tel Aviv. The trouble was that the story did not quite stand up, as we journalists say. Mandy, although

cheering enthusiastically for the Israeli side in the Middle Eastern
war, was in fact busy managing her discotheque in Tel Aviv, pro-
viding rest and relaxation for the troops. When we heard on the
radio that Russia was supplying tanks to Egypt, she exclaimed in
anger: 'And to think what I have done for those Russians!'
Although she was taking instruction in the Jewish faith – Israeli
laws on property and citizenship added impetus to her spiritual
awakening – she was some way from acceptance, and had to face
several tests, including a court of High Priests and Elders whom
she needed to convince of her sincerity. When I asked whether the
prospect intimidated her, she replied: 'I've been in court before,
you know, my dear.'

Mandy became a good friend. Much later, she employed my
elder daughter, Sophia, to help put her various books together. On
this occasion, we travelled to newly liberated Jerusalem and
posed together in front of the Wailing Wall. Not wishing to disappoint my sponsors, I bought her a nurse's uniform and she
posed with wounded soldiers at the Tel Hashomer military hospital. She was a great success there. All the wounded heroes waved
their stumps in the air and cheered. When it came to the point, I
lacked the gall to persuade readers of *Cosmopolitan* that she had
been working full-time as a nurse, but we got some nice pictures
of Mandy in nurse's uniform, posing with some most attractive
young Israeli children, into the centre-page spread of the *Daily
Mirror*. Worse crimes have been committed in the name of wartime propaganda.

* * * *

One result of all the pain and sorrow in being orphaned was that
my writing started to appear in the *Spectator*. Until that moment, it
had noticed me only with exceptionally snubbing reviews for my
novels. Nigel Lawson commissioned me to write a review of my
father's obituaries. It was a start. Later, he seemed keen to rescue
me from the tabloid grave I was digging for myself. He said he
would welcome some pieces on general subjects, which I duly
supplied. A year later he found himself in need of a political correspondent, when Alan Watkins went to join his brother-in-law
Tony Howard on the *New Statesman,* and offered me the job. But it
was Evelyn Waugh's death which gave me first entry into the
higher journalism. He was always a *Spectator* man, using the

magazine as a vehicle for many of his squibs. I think it would have pleased him to know that his death provided the means of my joining the magazine to which I have remained attached, with one or two interludes, ever since.

*   *   *   *

When I joined the *Spectator* in September 1967 as its political correspondent at £2,500 a year I knew practically nothing about politics, but Lawson made good that deficiency, telling me everything I needed to know on the issues of the day. He was and remains by far the cleverest person I have ever worked with. My only qualification for the job was a certain scepticism about anything I was told and an unbudgeable suspicion of political motives. Lawson, in at any rate part of his magnificent mind, shared both these prejudices. My predecessor, Alan Watkins, who had already helped me with one or two articles for the Odham's *Sun*, took me under his wing, showed me the ropes and introduced me to his friends and acquaintances in the Labour Party. My godfather, Lord Longford, was still holding on to a Cabinet post by the skin of his teeth, and Ann Fleming gave some lunch parties to introduce me to her friends in government. Lawson gave a lunch for me to meet Dick Crossman, whom he hoped I would find a kindred spirit.

So I might have done – we parted with mutual exclamations of regard, and his firm promise to keep me acquainted with every leap in his agile imagination – except that a few weeks later, when I telephoned to check a point on the November 1967 devaluation crisis, he made himself unavailable, while acquainting other, more favoured correspondents with the way his mind was working. I wrote quite a nasty little piece describing how Crossman had been seen wafting through the corridors of power leaking like the *Torrey Canyon* (an oil tanker which had just been sunk by the RAF, causing devastation on the Cornish coasts). The Prime Minister apparently seized on my piece as evidence that Crossman had been briefing journalists (as indeed he had) and gave him a severe dressing down in the Downing Street kitchen. Crossman's reaction was to summon me to the Lord President's office in Whitehall – a very grandiose room, with green silk wall coverings – and bawl at me for twenty minutes. I can understand this reaction – Crossman always had more than a streak of the bully in him – but it achieved nothing other than to relieve his feelings. He became my sworn enemy for the rest of my time on the *Spectator,* and indeed I carried the enmity with me to *Private Eye,* denouncing him as a former Nazi sympathizer of German extraction who had almost certainly been parachuted into this country disguised as a nun. . . . We made it up, later, when he became editor of the *New Statesman.*

But it was a foolish way for a politician to behave. They really cannot afford unnecessary enemies. The *Spectator,* despite its small circulation, was widely read in the Conservative Party, where it was thought to be influential. It was also thought to be read by the more intelligent Labour leaders. Perhaps it is still read by all these people, although the new Conservative members give little evidence of reading anything much beyond the *Sun* newspaper, and the new wave of Labour MPs give little evidence of reading anything at all.

* * * *

The year 1968 saw the beginning of my involvement in the Nigerian civil war which was to occupy much of my time for the next two years. I had no knowledge of West African affairs and no interest in Nigeria when, in the summer of 1968, Nigel Lawson proposed that I should go out as the *Spectator's* special correspondent to report on the Biafran war. The former eastern region of Nigeria, mostly populated by the Ibo tribe, had seceded from the federation and declared its independence as the Republic of Biafra in May 1967. The reason for this was that the Ibos, who although Catholic were sometimes described as the Jews of West Africa by virtue of their greater commercial acumen, had over-reached themselves in January 1966 by staging a coup to take over the federal government, killing a few northern statesmen in the process. By the end of July, a second coup had more or less restored the status quo. Then the massacres started. Ibos poured back to their eastern heartland from the north of Nigeria, where they had always been resented by the stupider, less well-educated Muslim Hausa-Fulani. The military governor of the eastern region, Colonel Odumegwu Ojukwu, an Ibo, sought guarantees for his people from the new head of the federal government, Colonel Yakubu Gowon, and when these were not honoured, he started making preparations to secede.

One of these preparations was to send emissaries to London and

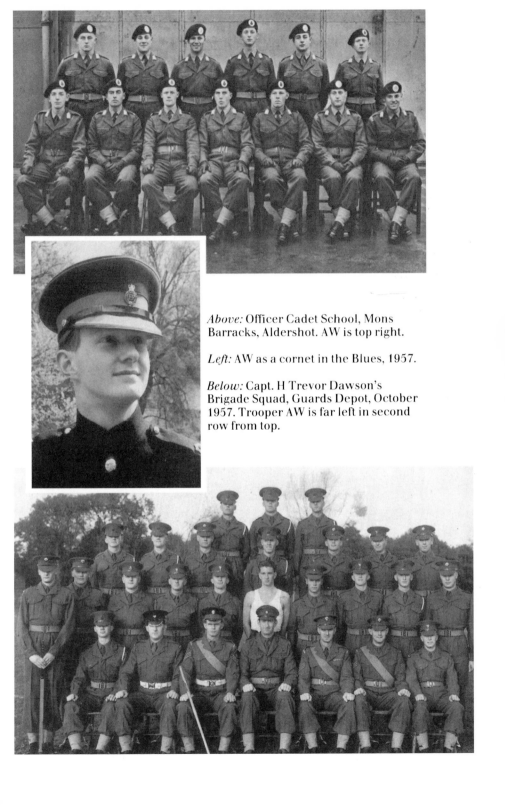

Above: Officer Cadet School, Mons Barracks, Aldershot. AW is top right.

Left: AW as a cornet in the Blues, 1957.

Below: Capt. H Trevor Dawson's Brigade Squad, Guards Depot, October 1957. Trooper AW is far left in second row from top.

At Combe Florey, where the family moved in 1956.

AW in Bologna, writing *The Foxglove Saga*, June 1959.

La Ramade, Labécède-Lauragais, Aude. First French house, March–September 1963.

A gruesome moment at Combe Florey, summer 1965.
Top, L to R: AAW, Teresa Waugh (his wife), Alexander Waugh (his son), Teresa D'Arms (sister), Justin D'Arms (nephew), Margaret FitzHerbert (sister), Claudia FitzHerbert (niece), Giles FitzHerbert (brother-in-law), Emily FitzHerbert (niece), Harriet Waugh (sister).
Middle: Septimus Waugh (brother), Laura Waugh (mother), Mary Herbert (grandmother), Evelyn Waugh (father), James Waugh (brother).
Bottom: Sophia Waugh (daughter).

AW at La Pesegado, his French home in the Aude, 1968.

The Old Rectory, Chilton Foliat, Wiltshire, where Auberon and Teresa
Waugh lived 1964–71.

At *Private Eye*'s reserved table at the Coach & Horses. *L to R:* Martin Tomkinson, Richard Ingrams, Auberon Waugh and Nigel Dempster.

AW, Terence Wogan, Kingsley Amis: a moment to record for posterity.

At home at Combe Florey: *L to R:* Nathaniel Waugh, Daisy Waugh,
Countess of Onslow, Lady Teresa Waugh, AW, Alexander Waugh.

other world capitals to plead the eastern region's case. Among them the Chief Justice of Biafra, Sir Louis Mbanefo, caught the ear of Arnold Goodman, the solicitor whom many Labour potentates consulted on their personal problems, as much for his wisdom and ability to arrange things as for his legal knowledge. Goodman convinced Lawson of the justice of the Biafran cause, and Lawson had little difficulty in convincing me that it would be a pleasant diversion from the House of Commons Press Gallery to go out and see for myself.

By the time I arrived in Biafra, in July 1968, the civil war had been running for a year. Biafra had lost the major town of Port Harcourt in the south, and with it the oil port of Bonny, as well as its capital, Enugu, and the university town of Nsukka in the north. In fact, Biafra was reduced to the towns of Aba, Umuahia and Owerri, with an airstrip at Uli bringing in vital supplies of ammunition and medical equipment and possibly less vital supplies of journalists to report on the war.

The only way into Biafra was as part of the arms airlift from Lisbon. This involved taking an ancient plane which refused to take off until the pilot was paid in cash – a wait of three or four days – which then put down at Bissau, in Portuguese Guinea, and on the Portuguese island of Sao Tome just on the equator to the south of the Nigerian coast. The flight into Uli – in fact a stretch of main road converted into the second biggest airstrip in Africa – had to be done by night, lying on top of crates of ammunition. Although the federal air force had Mig fighters supplied by the Soviet Union, in some cases with British pilots on secondment from the RAF, it managed to shoot down only two or three planes in the entire course of the war, scoring a few more on the ground at Uli. Even so, I was glad when I arrived, to be hustled out of the plane at enormous speed as it was unloaded and turned around for the flight back to Sao Tome.

This was my first visit to Africa and it was easy to be seduced by the charm and cheerfulness of the Biafrans. Other journalists had been taken to the federal side and been similarly convinced of the justice of the federal cause. The difference, as I saw it, was that the federal cause was being advanced by a system of blockade with the avowed intention of starving the Biafrans into surrender. The International Red Cross reckoned that 3,000 of them were dying of starvation every day during the period I was there, and anyone who chose to doubt this figure could actually see them starving all around. The British government under Harold Wilson, with the particular, almost fanatical enthusiasm of Michael Stewart, the Foreign Secretary, was supplying arms and diplomatic support to the federal government. If it had been the case that the Biafrans had been bullied or deliberately misled into supporting Ojukwu's secession, there might have been some case for supporting the integrity of Nigeria's frontiers as laid down for the administrative convenience of the imperial power in the previous century. But the Biafrans were plainly disenchanted with the federation, and one could have no sympathy with a federal government which was prepared to starve millions of its former citizens to death for the purpose of forcing them back into an association they had rejected. Biafra had everything needed to make it a viable state, including a large part of Nigeria's oil resources, and a sophisticated population of 14 million.

The shame, however, was to see them dying in the villages in the knowledge that my own government was to blame for it. One by one a few African governments gave Biafra diplomatic recognition – first Tanzania, then Gabon, the Ivory Coast and Zambia. Eventually, France announced support for Biafran self-determination and admitted it was sending aid to the Biafrans. But it was hard to be proud of Britain's role. The integrity of Nigeria's frontiers and the alleged dangers of balkanization along tribal lines were all very well as ideas, but in truth they were little more than saloon bar opinions in the face of the reality. These Whitehall saloon bar philosophers were sending arms and giving what might well be decisive support to the blockade which was deliberately starving certainly hundreds and probably thousands of Commonwealth citizens to death every day. If the Whitehall mandarins could have seen them starving – children with the unattractive symptoms of *kwashiorkor*, emaciated old men and women, mothers with breasts like dried figs – and if they could have realized that they were responsible for it, I am sure they would have forgotten all their silly saloon bar opinions. Even the politicians – George Thomson and Michael Stewart were the worst offenders – might have had second thoughts.

The Biafrans were not keen for visiting journalists to see the signs of starvation. Instead we were taken to military academies to see the young cadets swaggering round singing patriotic songs, to interviews with the military commander, Philip Effiong, and to meet a mad scientist who had designed a special bomb to ambush federal convoys. The ingenuity of the Biafrans was endless. They refined their own petrol from crude oil, made rockets out of pipes, brewed their own Biafra gin from plantain and cassava. But the starvation was everywhere. Driving away from lunch of stewed goat's head and Biafra gin at an officers' mess one day, I solemnly vowed to myself to do everything in my power to bring the Biafrans' plight to people's attention. Not everyone could go and see for himself. Many tended to discount photographs as propaganda, knowledgeably asserting that they were taken in some famine in the Congo, or that half of Africa is starving half the time anyway. Having seen what was going on, and knowing many of the people responsible, I felt a certain obligation to make a nuisance of myself whenever possible.

The year 1968 also saw the birth of my fourth child and second son, christened Nathaniel Thomas Biafra, as well as the publication of my fourth novel, *Consider the Lilies*. At the time I considered it my best novel, and still think it might have been, but my interest was entirely taken up in the Biafra campaign. I went round most of the universities of Britain, making passionate speeches to their African Societies. The socialist societies and other left-wing groups were not much interested – possibly because the Ibos were Catholics, which was not then a left-wing thing to be, possibly because word had gone out from the Soviet embassies that Biafra should not be seen as a progressive cause. Michael Foot declared his support for the federal Nigerian government on the floor of the House, and few of the hard-line left joined the seventy-odd MPs who expressed concern over the matter.

The role of campaigner did not come easily. We had rallies in Trafalgar Square, demonstrations outside Downing Street. I hastily wrote a book – *Biafra, Britain's Shame* – with Suzanne Cronje, the veteran South African radical, which was well and speedily produced by Michael Joseph. In 1969 I went on a tour of the United States, paid for by Bill Buckley's *National Review* magazine and his *Firing Line* television programme, which he generously put at my disposal for the purposes of Biafran propaganda. I spoke on countless local television stations.

We took time off for a tour of the southern states in a gigantic hired limousine. One of our ports of call was the home of James

Dickey, the poet, later novelist, who had been given some post in the University of South Carolina at Columbia, where he lived in a bungalow on a lake, with a speechless, catatonic wife called Maxine. The visit had been proposed by Bill Buckley, who assured me that Dickey was a great fan of my writings. This seemed unlikely, but I was not going to complain. The trouble was that Buckley had also assured Dickey that I was a great fan of his poetry, and I had never heard of Dickey or his poetry, although we made a half-hearted attempt to buy some at Charlottesville, Virginia, on the journey down from Washington. They had never heard of him in the bookshop, so I assumed he was unknown.

When we arrived in our vast limousine, a couple of hours late, we found that he had invited the entire university to meet us, at a gigantic reception which had been going on for several hours. Four hours later, there were still about twenty guests left and no sign of any food. Mrs Dickey disappeared into the kitchen from which she emerged at one o'clock in the morning with some canned soup which she had spent two hours heating up.

By two o'clock in the morning I had worked out that Dickey had never read anything of mine, although he might have heard of Evelyn Waugh, or possibly Alec Waugh, he was not sure which, in some context or other. Then he started interrogating me about my particular interpretation of his work.

I confessed that I was not a close student, that I had tried to buy a copy of something, anything, he had written in Charlottesville, but they had all been sold out. By then, all the guests had gone, leaving only the speechless Maxine. 'Then why did you come here?' he asked.

A terrible silence fell. Teresa said: 'I think, if you don't mind, it is time we went to bed.' In our bedroom, we discussed climbing out of the window and driving off in our limousine. The window was too small. Next morning we got up at ten, to find Dickey sitting on the stiflingly humid terrace drinking beer. We were waiting for Maxine to bring us a true southern breakfast of grits, he said. Two hours later, she appeared with a sort of semolina. No doubt we would like to watch him practising archery, said our host. We followed him round an assault course of archery targets in a snake-infested swamp. He never suggested that Teresa or I might like to try our skill. After lunch in a restaurant we escaped, sweating with terror. I met Dickey again about ten years later at Muggeridge's house in Robertsbridge, where he had come to do some television programme or other. He seemed to think we had all had a whale of a time.

*   *   *   *

I do not know how much good the Biafran campaign did. A medical charity raised a couple of thousand pounds with Lord Goodman's help. Hugh Fraser, who acted as the Conservative Biafran Whip – the Labour whip was Michael Barnes – eventually persuaded the Conservatives to take an interest. Lord Carrington, a brave man, volunteered to go out, meet Colonel Ojukwu and see for himself what was happening. By then *The Times,* under William Rees-Mogg, was taking our side and so, rather unexpectedly, was the *Sunday Telegraph.* Carrington was duly delivered to Uli airport and inspected the military dispositions. In a letter he sent me on his return he gave the opinion that the cause was lost and the Biafran collapse was imminent.

On this occasion he was quite right, as the Biafran collapse occurred soon afterwards. I was standing in the Bridgewater by-election at the time as 'Save Biafra' candidate, and found myself rather left without a platform. The result would have been farcical in any case. I was backed by a strange group headed by Air Vice-Marshal Donald 'Pathfinder' Bennett, a former liberal with slightly disreputable right-wing connections which my friends in the press were happy to expose. My election meetings, although valiantly reported in *The Times* as major events, had been attended only by a handful of old people with nothing better to do, and some Young Conservatives out for a lark. I resigned my candidature, urging those who would have supported me to support the Liberals instead, as being the only party which had conducted itself with honour through the whole shameful episode. There was no sign of greatly increased support for the Liberal Party in the by-election results.

*   *   *   *

The Biafran episode marked the only occasion in which I have taken up a public cause, with all the pomposity and self-importance which such an activity requires. I think it had a profound effect, convincing me not only of the fatuity of politics – I was already more than half convinced of that – but also of the wickedness of politicians. In their quest for power and self-importance, to compensate for whatever feelings of social inadequacy or sexual insecurity, they are prepared to perpetrate something which is hard to distinguish from mass murder, if they think they can get away with it – in a distant country, in a cause which few people are prepared to follow. It was a salutary lesson, and one which I have never forgotten. Another lesson was how very few people in England cared about such matters.

*   *   *   *

The collapse of Biafra left life on the *Spectator* feeling rather flat. At some point in 1969 Rupert Murdoch invited me to lunch in Boulestin's and asked me to write the weekly leader page article in *News of the World* and another weekly article in the new Murdoch *Sun* for which he paid the princely sum of £80 per week. Merciful oblivion has descended on that episode. I imagine I adopted the necessary right-wing populist tone, but I don't suppose I did it very well as he dropped me after the 1970 election, which unexpectedly returned Edward Heath for his brief but disastrous period in office. Murdoch paid me off generously. At the time, and for a considerable period afterwards, I saw him as a force for good in the country, urging that he be granted a dukedom to celebrate his victory over the printing unions when he moved all his newspapers overnight to Wapping. It was only his frenzied support for Mrs Thatcher, when it was plain to everyone else she had become a fatal liability, which turned him into a national menace. When I met him he was still feeling his way through the London newspaper jungle, and seemed vulnerable and rather likeable.

Perhaps it was some subconscious urge to be sacked by the *Spectator* which led me, one evening when I was feeling bored at the printers, to tamper with the contents page, wittily altering the name of George Gale on the list of contributors to Lunchtime O'Gale. Lunchtime O'Booze, I should explain, was *Private Eye's* name for a drunken hack. George had a slight drink problem at the time, it is true, but the main reason for my intrusion was that his article made some facetious reference to the Waughs which I thought cheeky. The magazine came out on Friday, 13 February 1970, and that morning Lawson sent for me and sacked me on the spot, saying he would make up my wages to the end of the month –

that is two weeks in lieu of the six months' notice our agreement required. I thought that too mean and said rather grandly that I would consult my solicitors, having none. 'And I must make it plain,' said Nigel, 'that the two weeks' wages I have offered is an *ex gratia* payment.'

Somehow, my little prank had caught him on the raw. He may have been right in supposing I had grown bored with the *Spectator*. There had been previous incidents. On one occasion he had rejected my idea for an article and when I wrote it just the same, refused to print it and made me write another, so I gave the original article to my friend Richard Ingrams who printed it in *Private Eye*. On a previous visit to the printers I had been irritated by a leader he had written on Ulster, so I cut it to make it say exactly the opposite of what he intended but he never noticed, or did not say anything if he noticed.

On the day of my sacking I was having lunch with the French Ambassador to meet the Archbishop of Paris, later found dead outside the flat of a prostitute. We all had our problems, but I guessed that news of my sacking would be in the *Evening Standard*, and had to listen to fulsome praise for my *Spectator* political column without saying anything. It was distinctly awkward. Later, having no solicitor, I telephoned my fellow warrior in Biafra's cause, Arnold Goodman, who seemed confident he could bring Nigel to his senses and squeeze some money out of him, but Lawson was adamant. Eventually I took my case to the National Union of Journalists who adopted it as an obvious example of boss-class oppression, but it was over a year before it came to court and in the course of that time Nigel had been sacked as Editor of the *Spectator* and George Gale had been appointed in his place. Gale signified his feelings about the whole squabble by re-hiring me as weekly fiction reviewer. So when we finally assembled in the Marylebone County Court on 15 June 1971 the situation was somewhat confused. I, the plaintiff, suing for wrongful dismissal had been re-hired by the person on whose behalf I had been sacked; the man who had sacked me had been sacked himself and had to justify, on behalf of the company which had sacked him, his decision to sack me. And George Gale, the victim of my malicious prank, who had re-hired me, declined to give evidence for either side on the point of whether or not he had been upset by it.

Under the circumstances, Nigel put on a good show, but he was

on his own. Two previous political correspondents of the magazine, Alan Watkins and Bernard Levin, gave evidence on my
behalf that it was perfectly in the tradition of the *Spectator* for the
political correspondent to make jocular alterations to the Table of
Contents. At the end of the day, rather to my surprise, I was the
winner, with an award of £1,250, being six months' pay, reduced to
£600 after tax and other earnings in the sixth-month period had
been taken into account.

*   *   *   *

On the day of the sacking I walked from Gower Street to Greek
Street where Richard Ingrams hired me as the first political correspondent of *Private Eye*. The pay was not particularly generous
– £50 a fortnight. 'But I imagine that our circulation will increase
so enormously now you have joined us that we will be able to increase your fees accordingly,' said Ingrams.

By odd coincidence, the circulation of *Private Eye* did indeed increase enormously at about that time, although obviously not as a
result of my having joined the team – very few of its readers had
the slightest interest in politics, except possibly of the infantile left.
Although I remained on the *Eye* for sixteen years, and wages just
about crept up in line with inflation, I cannot say that they ever increased much in real terms. But at least the arrangement gave me
an office, a telephone and a home-from-home in London, without
which I felt certain I would have gone mad. Living in the country
has that effect on people. I shared my tiny office with Patrick
Marnham, then a barrister on the run, later to emerge as the great
travel writer. Although he thought I was Jewish, he always treated
me with the greatest of courtesy.

*   *   *   *

A few days after settling in Greek Street, I was asked round by
William Rees-Mogg, editor of *The Times*, whom I had met at the
christening of a shared godson, and invited to contribute a weekly
Saturday column for the handsome sum of £50 a week. This sub-
sidized my work for the *Eye*, as did a weekly column on country
topics which the Editor of the *Evening Standard*, Charles Wintour,
requested. Both columns went rather well, and I thought I had
finally found my *métier*, writing on politics for the *Eye*, current
affairs for *The Times* and lush places for the *Standard*, but provi-

dence was soon to take a hand. The features editor at *The Times* with whom I dealt was a pleasant fellow called James Bishop, who did not mind at all when I printed a violent attack on Sir Alec Douglas-Home, the Foreign Secretary under Heath and an old enemy from Biafra days. Nor did he particularly mind when in the same piece I repeated an old army joke about the curious trousers worn by men in certain parts of the near East, although others' reaction to this second joke was unexpected. In a rehearsal for the Salman Rushdie affair, furious letters were received from half the embassies of Islam, demonstrations were held in Printing House Square and the British Council Library in Rawalpindi was burned to the ground.

I was naturally proud to have caused such devastation, but also rather apprehensive. Fortunately, Rees-Mogg, to his eternal credit, seemed unmoved by it all and James Bishop was as delighted as I had been. The column was going well and I think we were all pleased by it. Unhappily, one of those staff reshuffles then occurred and Bishop was replaced by Charles Douglas-Home, a man I had met several times when he stayed near Chilton Foliat for the hunting, with an unusual and beautiful wife whom I much admired. But he was not someone with whom I ever experienced an instant rapport. He obviously felt that the eyes of his family were upon him to avenge his dim and miserable old uncle. Like many of his sort, he was also something of an Arabist, and expressed dismay at the offence that had been caused throughout Islam by my little joke.

His first action on becoming Features Editor of *The Times* was to summon me to an atrocious Japanese meal in the precincts of St Paul's Cathedral and tell me that although the editor might disagree, he did not personally feel that my column was the sort of thing which should be appearing in *The Times*.

I might have appealed to Rees-Mogg over his head, but it occurred to me that this could very well fail, and would be undignified in any case. It was impossible to work with a features editor who did not want you there, since if ever I wrote a column which was weaker than usual, or questionable on grounds of taste or libel, he could always argue that it should be spiked. So I decided to give in gracefully.

'But do not suppose, Charlie, that I shall bear you no malice,' I said.

'Oh no, Bron,' he said, pulling a public school face. 'I can quite understand that. No doubt I should feel the same in your position. It is a funny thing,' he added, in a whimsical, boyish way, 'but you are the first person I have ever had to, ah, dismiss. It is quite a strange feeling.'

In the final reckoning, I should probably be grateful to him. During my sixteen years on *Private Eye* I had endless opportunity to be rude about people, even a requirement to set up three or four new Aunt Sallys a fortnight in order to knock them down. The great problem was always to find enough people I wished to be rude about. Charlie handed himself to me on the proverbial plate. Every year from then on, at the time of the Miss World competition, I claimed to recognize the familiar features of my old friend Charles Douglas-Home behind the tantalizing bikini of Miss Costa Rica. On countless other occasions throughout the years, he was wheeled on as a comic turn. Whenever we met in the course of the next fifteen years or so, whether in other people's homes or at journalistic events, he would giggle nervously and edge away as fast as he could. It was the perfect relationship, really.

*   *   *   *

I was now fully freelance, without any need to appear in an office more often than once a fortnight. I decided it was time to move further west to the more spacious amenities of Combe Florey, so that was what we did on 28 October 1971 in the thirty-second year of our lives.

Part II
Maturity

CHAPTER
THIRTEEN

Combe Florey 1971-1973

Another reason for the move to Combe Florey was that my mother had been living alone there since her husband's sudden death in April 1966, and although she never complained of loneliness, and was visited quite often by her children, one had the impression that it was quite a burden for a single woman who had allowed herself to be convinced that she was very poor to keep up a huge house with four acres of garden, a further thirty acres of woods, parkland and ornamental water.

It was an over-cautious lawyer who had persuaded her that she was poor, ladling out small amounts of money when she asked for them while he spent several years examining the unfamiliar ramifications of a literary estate. In fact, she was very rich, but she took joyfully to the disciplines of poverty, selling much of the family furniture (and all her husband's books) for a song to Texas University (where, I have been told, they are still to be found in packing cases, or distributed through the offices of the Humanities Center).

In the last years of Evelyn Waugh's life, he discovered that owing to some change in the law he could no longer offset her enormous losses on the farm against his writing income for the purpose of taxation. The farm had to be closed down. She threw herself into market gardening, a change made easier by the devotion of a Combe Florey villager called Walter Coggan – for some reason she never learned his name, and always called him Mr Coggins – who, employed as a part-time gardener, came to talk to her while she laboured in the garden. Evelyn Waugh always referred to him as 'my rival, Mr Coggins', and was being only partly humorous. She actually preferred the gardener's company to that of anyone else. His slightly implausible deference, the embarrassingly apparent sub-text of all advice, the extreme ordinariness of every opinion he advanced, appealed to her deepest sense of social propriety. This was the most natural and acceptable form of human relationship.

'They do say, madam, that if you see a crow with a broken wing, that means 'twill be a good year for raspberries,' he would say in his fine Somerset voice, and she would lap it up.

In the week my father died, Coggins disappeared. My mother got it into her head that I had murdered him (Coggins) and put his corpse in the boot of my car before driving back to Chilton Foliat. I do not know why she should have reached this conclusion, but suppose it must have been the product of stress. In fact he had been out on a blind, something which is well known among Somerset farming folk. But by the time we moved down to Combe Florey in October 1971, Walter Coggan, too, had died, in the way that elderly men have always tended to do. The clergyman, at his funeral, said: 'We have memories of Walter which time can never alter.'

Obviously, he was most missed by his widow and family, but I think it was the loss of Coggins which reconciled my mother to the idea that the little Waughs, as my father used to call us, should move into the main part of the house, and she would move into a more or less disused wing, equipped with its own kitchen and other appointments.

We sold Chilton Foliat rather well to an amiable businessman who has lived in it ever since. The money enabled Teresa to buy Combe Florey from my mother with enough left over to redecorate the main house. It also enabled my mother to refurbish the wing according to her particular requirements, with vast stone sinks which never let the water out and stank. But it was a happy enough arrangement while it lasted.

* * * *

Being a more intensely private person than Evelyn Waugh – who, despite all his protestations to the contrary, was in large part a public figure – Laura Waugh was also, in her own way, more remarkable. As Laura Herbert, she grew up in three households – Pixton in Somerset, a large house in Bruton Street and Portofino – all crowded with guests from every corner of the earth. This gave her a pronounced distaste for social life.

My father had met her first at Portofino, when she was seventeen. A year later, he was in love with her, but his suit did not seem well starred. Laura's family was Catholic. Evelyn, who had become a Catholic in 1930 after the failure of his first marriage, seemed in no position to declare himself a suitor while his annulment was held up, apparently *sine die,* by the Westminster and Vatican bureaucracy. A further complication was that by unhappy coincidence his first wife, Evelyn Gardner, was a niece of Aubrey Herbert and Laura's first cousin. Feeling in the family was strongly against the match. Although Evelyn Waugh was already a successful novelist, and would have been a catch for most teenage brides of the period, the Herberts were not a family to be intimidated by smartness of that sort. Evelyn was thirteen years older than his bride, had already been married to one member of the family and, worst of all, came from a background which was distinctly middle class.

Although, as I have explained, the Waughs came from many generations of professional men – publishers, doctors, clergymen – the gulf between them and the carefree traditions of the aristocracy was as great as if he had been a fishmonger's assistant. Even worse than this, he had already been adopted as a guest, friend, boon companion and private buffoon by families which were even richer and grander than the Herberts. This situation was not improved by the noticeable lack of sympathy between himself and 'the boy Auberon'.

Although Evelyn's affection for the English upper classes and everything they stood for was never in doubt – this was held to be vulgar in itself – their antipathy for each other could easily be explained by the traditional jealousy between privilege and achievement. Although the Herberts were clever and moved in a brilliant circle, Evelyn Waugh was cleverer and noticed too many things to be a comfortable member of any circle.

Under the circumstances, for Laura Herbert to encourage his courtship was an act of most uncharacteristic rebelliousness. She, too, was always displeased by the Brideshead aspect, hating any form of ostentation or grandeur. 'Your dear mother,' Evelyn Waugh would say to his children, 'is the kindest and most hospitable of women, but she has no sense of style.'

Laura's awareness of her social superiority may well have helped to sustain her through a marriage which was not without its trials, nor without its reminders of her husband's success in other fields. Many women (and men) feel depressed and diminished by their spouse's success. Laura Waugh felt no such qualms, being happy enough to be left at home with her cows and children, regarding the whole circus with a profound contempt.

What she found attractive in him, I suspect, was his humour. Laura Waugh, for all her apparent shyness and avoidance of company, was a born satirist. Behind a veil of good manners, she mocked everybody and everything. The strength necessary to support such an attitude came, ultimately, not from any sense of social superiority but from her Catholicism, which grew more devout, and at the same time more sceptical, with age.

Her husband was moody and given to fits of acute depression which left her largely to her own devices. Shunning ordinary human contact, she sought refuge in cows and rejoiced in the company of farming folk. At other times, she retreated into her own private meditations whose direction was not easily to be distinguished from simple misanthropy. She killed time with crosswords, word games and jigsaws. She was at ease with her children and their friends, and with her own family and, of course, with Coggins, but with practically nobody else. She was also haunted by the spectacle of her mother, my once all-powerful grandmother, whom she had to nurse through a last year of distressing debility.

Many thought that she was too self-effacing and let her husband get away with too much, but it suited her as much as it suited him that he should take his meals in the library if he chose, or go away for long periods, seeking warmer climates in the winter, or carousing with smart friends in London. She saw herself primarily as a farmer, her five or six cows the pride and joy of her life. Some interpreted her decision to publish Evelyn Waugh's diaries – they first appeared in a shortened, more lurid serialization in the *Observer* – as an act of revenge, but it was more the product of absent-mindedness. She intended to read the series before publication, but eventually got round to reading only a small part. She hoped that publication of the fuller version, in book form, might undo some of the damage, but never lived to see it. She was not convinced by my arguments, that the diaries were thoroughly enjoyable and interesting and worth publishing. Like many of the upper class, she had a hatred for publicity, but also a passion for selling things. Any crooked timber merchant who came to the door could persuade her to sell him an avenue of mature oak trees at £15 a tree. On this occasion – offered a large sum for her husband's Diaries – it got the better of her once again, but she was protected from severe criticism by meeting only her family, most of whom were quite pleased by it all. It was the only controversial thing she ever did, apart from marrying Evelyn Waugh thirty-six years earlier.

Her politics, in so far as she concerned herself with politics, were those of the populist right. She mistrusted do-goodism, while being profoundly convinced that the working classes were justified in any demands they cared to make. As a woman who had lived all her life in large country mansions, she felt a distinct sympathy for the rumbles of the indigenous urban proletariat against Commonwealth immigration. 'All I mind about these people,' she explained once, looking out of the window at her acres of parkland, 'is that they come over here and take our jobs.' She, who had never had a job in her life, felt instinctive sympathy for those who wanted one, perhaps.

This may seem a slightly sour picture but I am not sure that her life – in the twenty years of her youth, the twenty-nine years of her marriage, or the seven years of her widowhood – was a particularly happy one. When she decided she was poor, she took to an indescribably nasty sherry-type beverage from Cyprus. Only she and one of her sisters were able to drink it. I think it may have contained some toxic substance as it destroyed her sense of balance, while Gabriel, her sister, was similarly affected. During Lent, when she restricted herself to one glass a day, she found a receptacle which others might have identified as an exceptionally large flower vase. But it saw her through.

* * * *

The house at Combe Florey had not prospered under her single occupation of it. She put it on the market, and then decided she did not want to sell it, but rather than withdraw it, which would have involved paying a house agent, she decided to adopt a policy of discouraging would-be purchasers. Broken windows were never mended. She left buckets in the middle of the floor to suggest that the ceilings leaked, and never took them away. My father had left some extravagantly opulent carpets, woven at Wilton on his instructions from original designs for the 1851 Great Exhibition. When her beloved spaniel, Credit, made a mess on one of them in the six years after his death, my mother would leave it there, let it solidify, fossilize, before moving it. Later, she forgot about them.

Credit was famous for the size of his turds, which might easily have been human ones. When Christopher Sykes came to stay soon after we moved into Combe Florey, I found one of them in his bathroom, and assumed he had had an accident.

It may have been the dog, or the old-fashioned sinks that she insisted on installing, but the wing where she lived soon developed an arsenal of smells. None of her family was put off, but I remember friends being mildly appalled. 'Bit of a pong in the widow's pad', complained Richard Ingrams when she had welcomed him there one evening, slightly tipsy.

* * * *

She died quite suddenly of pneumonia on 17 June 1973. My brother James, then a soldier, had been staying with her in the wing. He had to leave early to return to his soldiering, went in to her room early to say goodbye, and found her dead. She had just suffered a spell of pneumonia, but had seemed to be better, spending her last afternoon on earth cutting roses from the front of the house. She was buried on her fifty-seventh birthday, more deeply mourned than her modest nature could ever have understood. Perhaps the rest of the world saw her role as nurturing and protecting the genius of Evelyn Waugh. Her children, obviously enough, saw her role differently. Whereas he regarded them, on the whole, as part of the cross which every Christian must bear, she accepted her children with a peculiar detachment as the people who made up her life.

* * * *

In 1971 I published my fifth and last novel to date, called *Bed of Flowers*. An account of some hippies living in a Somerset commune, it is more contrived and more whimsical than any of its predecessors, and I was unable to convince myself that it marked an improvement. Unlike the others, it even had a theme, almost amounting to something as vulgar as a message, derived from my involvement in the Biafran side in the Nigerian civil war. It failed to find a paperback publisher (until many years later) and failed to find an American publisher at all. The reviews were coy or non-committal for the most part.

Novel-writing is a tedious, self-absorbed business, and the main hope which keeps writers going – that somebody will read their work – is in short supply. When the pot of gold at the end of the rainbow – fame, wealth and the affectionate gratitude of an adoring readership – had been reduced to the faint hope of a literary prize, I decided it was time to seek other opportunities. On top of this there was the fact that I now had a huge house to keep up and four children who were approaching the age when I would have to start worrying about school fees. Add to the 'pram in the hall' syndrome (identified by Connolly as an Enemy of Promise) the particular circumstance that any success which I might enjoy would always be attributed to the fact that my name had already been made famous in literary circles by my father and by my persistent, if bald, Uncle Alec. It was not so much that I objected to cashing in on the name as that I was not going to be allowed to get away with it.

* * * *

The death of my mother, on 17 June 1973, had come as a bad shock. At the time of her death, Christopher Sykes wrote to me that nobody, in his experience, ever got over the death of his mother. I do not know. The death of a second parent also brings with it the certain sense of release, as I described earlier. We are no longer looking over our shoulders for the approval of an older generation. This was small consolation at the time, although it now occurs to me that perhaps one of the kindest things we parents can do for our children is to die reasonably young.

CHAPTER
FOURTEEN

Greek Street 1970-1986

It was on Friday 13 January 1970 that I walked round to 34 Greek Street and offered my services to Richard Ingrams as political correspondent of *Private Eye*. Our very first meeting, many years earlier, was when as an adolescent I was staying in London with the woman who was later to become his mother-in-law – she was some sort of cousin of Gormanston's – and we were taken round to the Ingrams's home in Cheyne Walk. It was full of priests at the time.

My second meeting was scarcely more propitious. When I arrived at Oxford, Ingrams and Paul Foot had already been there a year, both of them at University College, and were established as editors of a magazine called *Parson's Pleasure*. A rumour reached Christ Church that they were planning to give it up and were looking for someone else to take it over, so I went round to Univ with my army friend Sheridan Dufferin, whose role was to be the Mr Moneybags. We both, I think, wore British Warm overcoats, although I do not know how Sheridan acquired one, as he ended his National Service as a trooper.

We were received by Ingrams and Foot, and a third person, a quite attractive young woman who said nothing but spent the whole interview rolling on the floor laughing for some reason I can no longer remember. I had not met Foot before, although it was his mother, Lady Foot, wife of the Governor, who had sat by my bedside in Cyprus through the stifling hot afternoons, reading me extracts from Laurence Durrell. She had told me many times how much she hoped I would get together with her son at Oxford. If only I had, perhaps I could have persuaded him to take an interest in something other than politics. Such a shame, such a shame. But on this occasion it was not to be. After explaining politely that they had no intention of giving up the magazine just yet, Footie asked me what would have been my plans for its future.

I reflected a moment, not having given any thought to the matter, and then said: 'I would want it to be the organ of the bloodies.'

A satirical account of this meeting appeared in the next issue of *Parson's Pleasure*. The incident marked the end of my journalistic ambitions at Oxford, apart from a few pieces in *Isis*, then edited by David Dimbleby. Ten years on, Foot was to become a close friend – witty, wise and possibly the only true romantic of my acquaintance which might explain his strange affinity with the poet Shelley, whom he imagines to have been a socialist. Such a shame. And poor old Dimbleby appears to have sunk without trace into the hellish world of television folk. Unless you happen to watch television, you might not be aware that he exists.

When I next met Ingrams he was already settled in as Editor of *Private Eye* – and already, alas, a teetotaller. I missed all the dramas of *Private Eye*'s first seven years – the libel actions from Lord Liver of Cesspool (which almost closed it), and from Randolph Churchill, the coup against Christopher Booker and his expulsion from the editorship. All these events have been chronicled several times, most notably by Patrick Marnham in his excellent *The Private Eye Story* (London, Deutsch, 1982). By the time I joined, in January 1970, the magazine was well established, with a circulation of some 52,000 (against the *Spectator*'s at this time of some 20,000) and Booker had already trickled back, as a verbal contributor to the 'funnies' section, although he was not allowed at the luncheons.

The atmosphere at *Private Eye* in those days was friendlier and more relaxed than it later became – possibly because we were all public schoolboys, with the exception of Barry Fantoni, the token proletarian, and had nearly all been to Oxford, except for Booker, who went to Cambridge, and always seemed the most serious of the team. John Wells had social ambitions, it is true, and was telephoned from time to time in the office by the drawling voice of

Princess Margaret – hence his nickname of 'Jawn'. Later, he contrived to marry the aunt of my daughter-in-law, Eliza Chancellor,
so he did not do too badly for himself. I marked the occasion with
my traditional advice to take things slowly. Booker later made
himself ridiculous, being filmed on television talking seriously
about architecture with the Prince of Wales, but I never watched
the programme and saw this seriousness as a product of his circumstances: he was terribly poor. Whenever politicians or fellow
journalists inveighed against the suffering of the poor, I thought of
Booker and shivered.

But no sanctity attached to Booker or to his state of poverty. The
truth about the poor, I suspect, is that although we must all
approve of them whole-heartedly, we also find them irritating.
Sanctity attached to Paul Foot, as the only left-winger on the staff.
He was the moral justification for all our confusion of unharmo-
nious responses to the modern world. We all sought his approval,
as if he had been a beautiful girl. But he bore the burden lightly.
Neither he nor Ingrams seems to have changed at all over the
years. For those who find it hard to understand how anyone can
claim to believe in workers' power without being a fool or a rogue,
I produce Footie as my first exhibit. He is clever and funny and
kind. Obviously, there is a screw loose somewhere, but we all have
our oddities. Ingrams doesn't drink, Rushton* can't wear a tie. I
would myself own up to a slight weakness for orientals.

Peter Cook did not share Ingrams's problem with drink. He was
the proprietor of *Private Eye*, but his powers were never fully explained, possibly never understood, certainly never exercised. Ingrams seemed to treat him warily. He was the member of the band
most clearly touched by genius, and it was the genius of pure
anarchy, Edward Lear on super-boost, but without any touch of
the poignancy (or sentimentality) which will always make Lear
immortal. Ingrams, too, is undoubtedly brilliant within the more
cerebral disciplines of instant parody, and Rushton also, as I came
to discover, through the rare idiosyncrasy of his humour wedded
to exceptional draughtsmanship. Whether the work of Ingrams
and Rushton will survive to feed the imagination of future generations remains to be seen. My own small gift – for making the

* All these references refer to William Rushton, not to A.P. Rushton, also
known as Tone, *Private Eye*'s designer and make-up artist.

comment, at any given time, which people least wish to hear – is more ephemeral than any of theirs. Perhaps we should all cultivate our immortal souls.

My political column, called 'HP Sauce' after the then Prime Minister's favourite condiment, took a certain amount of time to find its feet and was only a moderate success at the end of the day. It was all very well insulting politicians and making up funny nicknames for them, but very few people were interested in politicians, and if ever I got a fact wrong, there was the danger of a writ. More litigious even than the politicians were the other political journalists, with whom I had a running battle.

As a relatively new magazine, and because it had never had one before, *Private Eye* had no automatic right to a Press Gallery ticket in the House of Commons, nor did its political correspondent have access to the Lobby. Application for such a ticket had to be made to the sergeant-at-arms, Admiral Sir Alexander Gordon-Lennox. He consulted with the Gallery and Lobby who decided, perhaps not surprisingly, that they did not wish to have *Private Eye* on their pitch. An element of personal hatred may also have crept into it. I had been a member of the Gallery for three years, with access to the Lobby, on the *Spectator*'s ticket, and it is quite possible I had not endeared myself to all the toadies, sneaks and walking sausages in that assembly. In any case, the unfortunate sergeant-at-arms faced an appalling campaign of personal abuse. When a small bomb went off in the Palace of Westminster, he was accused of having farted, he became 'Gay' Gordon-Lennox and a notorious homosexual rapist. Meanwhile, any disparaging story I could persuade one Lobby member to tell me about the revolting behaviour or habits of another found instant expression in 'HP Sauce'. A petition from MPs to the sergeant-at-arms attracted nearly forty signatures, including at least one Cabinet minister in James Callaghan, the future Prime Minister (a friend from *Spectator* days). Crossman refused to sign it, of course, and so did Denis Healey, but Michael Foot signed. I have never been anything but abominably rude to Michael Foot in print, dubbing him 'the posturing ninny' and much else besides, but he has never been anything but kind to me. He even writes for my magazine, the *Literary Review,* which must pay worse than *Tribune* ever did. There is surely a sanctity among the Foots.

The trouble with printing journalists' tip-offs about other journalists is that they are so often untrue. And they are not the sort of story you can possibly check on. 'Is it true, McSquirt, that you were seen coming out of the Members' shower rooms in the company of the sergeant-at-arms?' Dear old Gordon-Lennox never sued – he must have been an exceptionally nice man – but the hacks almost invariably did. And they all received their pay-offs – in those days between £500 and £1,000 – before even issuing a writ.

Although only one libel case ever came to court against HP Sauce, there were a number of irritating complaints, two of which had to be settled out of court. Libel actions, generally speaking, are no joke. They are boring, worrying and take up an enormous amount of time. Irritation and an awareness that the column was no longer much good led me to suggest to Richard Ingrams that it should be discontinued. He came up with the alternative suggestion for 'Auberon Waugh's Diary', which ran for the next fourteen years.

Of all the hundreds of thousands of words I have written in a life's scribbling, 'Auberon Waugh's Diary', later collected in two volumes, *Four Crowded Years* (1972-1976) and *A Turbulent Decade* (1976-1986), is the series of which I am most proud. It started as a parody of a diary then appearing in *The Sunday Times* by Alan Brien, a journalist who had annoyed me when I first started writing for *Private Eye* in 1970 by the simple expedient of saying I was not funny. It is a charge against which there is no defence. He wrote it in the *Observer*, I think, or possibly in the *New Statesman* in a week when he could not think of anything else to write about, and at a time when I was feeling a trifle fragile after my sacking by Nigel Lawson. My political column in *Spectator* had been funny, he said, but he could not detect a glimmer of wit in my *Eye* stuff. It is a sad fact of journalism that people only ever tell you your stuff is any good after you have stopped writing it. The same thing happened when I eventually left the *Eye* in 1986. Life will never be the same, they cried, although nobody ever suggested it was much good at the time. When the collected editions came out – my masterpieces, as I like to think – they scored only two or three reviews each in the entire British press.

Nil desperandum. Van Gogh probably felt the same when nobody paid any attention to his scruffy, overrated paintings. My revenge on Brien took two years to get off the ground, but it ran, as I say, for fourteen years, something neither of us can have reckoned on. Brien, at that stage, affected a beard, and his bearded face stared out from the top of 'Alan Brien's Diary' in *The Sunday Times*. So I was photographed in a false beard and stared out from the top of 'Auberon Waugh's Diary', set in the same format. Within a few months, 'Alan Brien's Diary' had disappeared from *The Sunday Times*, as is the habit on that frenetic newspaper. I dare say Brien shaved his beard off in the intervening years – I did not check. He certainly managed to marry the lovely Jill Tweedie of the *Guardian* – a lady I had always fancied – and I cannot believe she would put up for long with such frivolity. But whatever happened to Alan Brien's beard, mine went on and on and on, adorning the top of the page whenever anything had to be cut out of my copy for legal or other reasons. The significance of the joke was completely lost on succeeding generations of *Eye* readers.

Another reason why there were sometimes gaps in my copy was that whenever I attacked Barry Fantoni, Ingrams cut it out. Fantoni had been a contributor to the *Eye* for many years – certainly, he was senior to me. I did not particularly dislike him, although he was said to have been rude to my wife, once, at a cocktail party. He was also said to have goosed A.P. Rushton, the boy who stuck the pages down, mistaking him for a girl in the poor light. But I had no animus against him for that. We all make mistakes. What I desperately needed was someone to attack, and Fantoni seemed as good as anyone else. A few enemies present themselves to you, as Charles Douglas-Home had done, and Alan Brien, the brothers Shrimsley, Roy Hattersley and 'Lord' Maffews of Shoreditch, the then proprietor of *Express* newspapers, but unless people are prepared to declare themselves your enemies you have to hunt around for them.

Perhaps the original intention to insult or abuse Fantoni was no more than a passing fancy, but as soon as I had been prevented from doing so by Ingrams, I began to fret. It was like the often observed phenomenon of a cat held by its tail. It may have been perfectly happy in that spot before, but as soon as somebody holds it by the tail, it will be prepared to wrench its own tail out by the roots in its anxiety to be somewhere else. I burned to be rude to Fantoni. I tried again and again, approaching the matter from a hundred different angles. Every time, Ingrams cut it out. I waited until he was on holiday, and then filled my column with extravagant praise of Fantoni, but Ingrams had posted a sentry over the page in his absence, who cut it all out. This was the final straw. It was time to move on from the *Eye*.

But all this was fourteen years in the future when the 'Diary' was launched as an extended Alan Brien bait. I lived happily at Combe Florey, going up to London only once a fortnight to attend the *Private Eye* lunch and put the 'Diary' to bed. Having no London abode, and being unable to afford a hotel, I generally stayed with a shrinking circle of friends.

*　*　*　*

The only writ the *Eye* ever had to defend in court on my behalf came from Miss Norah Beloff, the veteran political correspondent of the *Observer*. Our lawyers thought it too preposterous to stand a chance in court, but they reckoned once again without the extraordinary workings of the British legal system. I think the judge, Mr Justice (later Lord Justice) O'Connor, may have had a son at Downside with me, which would not have helped.

The background to the Ballsoff affair, as it was known from *Private Eye*'s unfortunate nickname for Beloff, was a curious one. Paul Foot had been investigating the Poulson case, involving a northern architect and developer who had been paying large sums of money to politicians on both sides of the House, and in local government, in exchange for services which were not always entirely clear. One of Poulson's beneficiaries was Reginald Maudling, an intelligent and able man who had occupied most of the main offices of State in various Conservative administrations and was currently Home Secretary and deputy Prime Minister. He had been paid quite a large salary by Poulson as some sort of consultant.

Suddenly, out of the blue, Beloff printed a violent attack on *Private Eye* for questioning the honour and integrity of Maudling. She described the magazine as a political comic and promoted Maudling as the next Prime Minister, the man who would definitely succeed if Heath fell under a bus.

It looked, to the sceptical observer, as if she had fallen head-over-heels in love with him. Foot secured possession of an internal *Observer* memo which she had sent to the editor, who was then David Astor, describing a meeting with Maudling. Foot printed it, and she sued for breach of copyright. The *Observer*, to its eternal shame, backed her in the action, which was thrown out by Mr Justice Ungoed-Thomas, of holy memory, on the technical point that she did not own the copyright.

Unfortunately, I, too, had put my little oar in with a whimsical piece introducing Beloff as 'delicious 78-year-old Nora Balsoff who sometimes wrote under the nom-de-plume Nora Bailiff ... Miss Bailiff, a sister of the late Sir Alec Douglas-Home was frequently to be seen in bed with Mr Harold Wilson and senior members of the previous administration, although it is thought that nothing improper occurred.' This was obviously intended to be humorous because Douglas-Home (always called Baillie Vass by *Private Eye*, for reasons lost in the mists of antiquity) was not, at this stage, officially thought to be dead. Nor was Beloff yet seventy-eight.

One did not need to know, or even to have seen, Beloff, to understand that this suggestion was obviously made in jest. The essence of a libel is that it must lower its victim in the estimation of right-minded or sensible people. No ordinary person, reading the piece, could possibly believe that it accused Beloff of being found in bed with Harold Wilson and other senior members of the previous administration. This did not stop her counsel, Tom Bingham QC (now Lord Justice Bingham), expressing the utmost indignation at this foul aspersion. One QC, Anthony (now Mr Justice) Lincoln had turned down the brief because he happened to come to dinner in my house the day before it was offered him. Bingham was not put off by being a friend of my sister, Margaret, and her husband Giles FitzHerbert. He seemed genuinely appalled that such a wicked accusation could be made against a maiden lady of spotless character. Bernard Levin, writing about the case afterwards, said he was amazed Bingham could keep a straight face throughout, as he quoted an Irish ruling of the 1830s to the effect that those who commit libel in jest, jest at their peril. The judge, who was, of course, Irish, was profoundly impressed. Beloff was awarded £3,000.

Five years later, Beloff finally found her man. She married Clifford Makins, the well-known journalist. I published my little epithalamium in the *Eye* 'Diary':

I hoped I would be asked to be best man at Nora Beloff's wedding today, since I imagine it was I who supplied a large part of the bride's dowry. It makes me very happy to think that the

£3,000 I gave her in libel damages a few years ago might have helped her find such a suitable husband as Clifford Makins, the well-known journalist.

Perhaps I had better explain myself. Like Nora, I had been a political correspondent for some years, when, tantalized by the unavailability of my luscious opposite number on the *Observer* I decided to make a joke about her. At least, that was what I intended to do. As it turned out, whether from incompetence or over-excitement, I made an allegation about her personal life of such a foul and loathsome nature that even now I blush to the roots of my remaining hair when I think about it.

For 56 long summers, Nora has resisted the advances of the coarser sex. Nothing will ever be the same again. Even as I write, I imagine that Clifford Makins is exploring the unimaginable delights of her body, never sweeter than when first sampled.

If I had been best man, I would have given Clifford the advice I always give bridegrooms on these occasions: *take things gently at first: there's no rush.* A new bride should be treated like a new car. Keep her steady on the straight, watch out for warning lights on the ignition and lubrication panels and when you reckon she's run in, give her all you've got.

Now I suppose I had better go and get drunk.

By all accounts, the marriage was blissfully happy.

Just in case there remains any doubt, my little whimsical piece was a joke and was not intended to suggest that Norah had misbehaved with anybody.

*   *   *   *

The essence of the 'Diary', as it emerged, was that it was a work of pure fantasy, except that the characters in it were real. If ever some president or head of state paid an official visit, I was there to greet him. If ever the Queen gave a ball or luncheon party, I was there to dance with her or help her survive the terrible bores who had in fact been invited – their names were often available in the court circular or gossip columns. The technique, whenever possible, was to find someone who had been present and could give an amusing account of what had happened, and then stretch and distort it, inserting myself in whichever role seemed appropriate – the sexual opportunist, the millionaire patron of the arts and learning, the M.I.5 or CIA agent, the drunk, the Thomist theologian, the confidential adviser to princes and presidents. It worked very well indeed, and I began to think I might have created a new art form. However, its success was partly because there was the slight suspicion in the back of people's minds that I might indeed be very rich and grand, and they could never be absolutely sure when I was pulling their legs.

After a time, I began to be a bit muddled on this point myself. The great danger of this new art form, and the reason why nobody had ever tried introducing it before, was the law of libel. If my subsequent column 'Way of the World' in the *Daily Telegraph*, which started in 1990, lacked the insouciance and abandon of the *Private Eye* 'Diary', this was because every word had to be read by libel lawyers. It was not the objections they raised which had a stifling effect on its *joie de vivre* – most of them seemed either fatuous or irrelevant to the laws of libel – as the fact of their presence which cast a blight.

However, they have greater knowledge than I of current legal practice, and the sad truth is that the libel scene has changed immeasurably since the days of 'Auberon Waugh's Diary', which ended in 1986. The 'Diary' seemed to lead a charmed life in this respect. Only three writs were received in its fourteen years – from John Pilger, the Australian heart-throb, from Bernard Shrimsley, then editor of *News of the World*, and, to her shame, from Claire Tomalin, then literary editor of *The Sunday Times* – and none of them, as I have said, went to court. Shrimsley grabbed the derisory £250 which I had paid into court as a hedge against a nominal award and ran for it; Pilger settled for nothing and Tomalin received, I think, £2,500. All were staked by their respective newspapers – *News of the World, Daily Mirror* and *Sunday Times*. It is hard to feel pity for newspapers which pay for their employees to sue other publications when they are themselves landed with astronomical awards against them.

But the truth is that the rules of the game have changed. Since the lower tabloids started pushing their luck with seriously aggressive intrusions into the private and sexual lives of television stars, buying stories from prostitutes and rent boys as well as from sisters, wives and girl friends, word has got around that anyone who finds himself the subject of adverse or disparaging comment has only to sue, and the courts will almost always reward him handsomely. The laws of libel, requiring a mendacious statement to someone's detriment, have nothing to do with it. Disparagement is enough. As a result, newspapers will almost always try to settle. Any adverse comment is made at the writer's peril, while vulgar abuse, which was once specifically excluded from libel by common practice and case history, if not by statute, is tantamount to a tax-free gift.

* * * *

The *Eye*, of course, always thrived on vulgar abuse. But vulgar abuse cannot be indiscriminate. It is irritating to those who have spent time and trouble cultivating the vituperative arts to see what passes for vulgar abuse in the proletarian newspapers. It is even more irritating to be treated by humourless, sycophantic people like the wretched Clive James as some sort of public hangman. Vituperation is not a philosophy of life nor an answer to all life's ills. It is merely a tool, a device, part of life's rich pageant, and in the right hands, a happy part of life's pageant, a salutary tool. It redresses some of the forces of deference which bolster the conceit of the second-rate; it also prevents the first-rate from going mad with conceit. It was Clive James who first put forward the danger of children crying on the way home from school as a good reason for not abusing the famous and powerful – I think he was showing his concern for Harold Evans at the time. The answer is, of course: let them cry. Anybody who has had anything to do with children knows perfectly well that they cry and then they stop crying. It is an incident of no importance. Convicts in prison may be excused such nauseating sentimentality about children as we read every day in the gutter press, but the suggestion that nobody in public life may be criticized or tormented for fear of his children being upset is an absurdity.

* * * *

Occasionally, nevertheless, one has doubts. My long persecution of Cyril Connolly is a case in point. Friends of my father and members of his circle divided sharply into those who were prepared to take a friendly interest in Waugh's bright-eyed young son – like

Graham Greene, John Betjeman, Harold Acton, John Sutroe, David Cecil, Ann Fleming, Christopher Sykes – and those who conspicuously weren't, like Anthony Powell, Maurice Bowra and Cyril Connolly. I met Connolly on numerous occasions – with the Goldsmids at Somerhill, in the Beefsteak Club and with my bald Uncle Alec – and started making friendly overtures, but Connolly was interested only in himself.

The persecution started when, on re-reading *Enemies of Promise* one day, I came upon the passage where he claims never to have masturbated at the age of eighteen and a half. Was this a record, I asked, and wrote off to the Editor of the Guinness Book of Records suggesting that an acknowledgement be made. Norris McWhirter answered privately what his researches suggested: that Connolly's achievement, although admirable, was no world record. But letters continued to appear for months on the point of whether Connolly should be congratulated for his self-control or warned against its dangers, whether he was setting a good example or not, whether masturbation was healthy or otherwise.

Further evidence was adduced from a review Connolly wrote about Jan Morris's *Conundrum*, describing how she underwent a sex-change operation in Casablanca. Connolly went off into a long maunder about his own private parts:

> It's bad luck on her that the reviewer chosen for this book should have a castration complex, for there is nothing I dread more than injury to those parts whose activities are still in the private sector and which I regard as the source of so much intellectual authority, lucidity, judgement and visual pleasure.

Poor Connolly! I commented:

> Visual pleasure indeed. If this horrible old man can't keep his eyes off himself at the age of 70, he might have been better advised to experiment a little earlier like everyone else.

When he died six months later I was sad to lose another character from my private gallery, and resolved to write a book about him which may not have supported the point made by Alisdair Clayre that he was the Greatest Living Englishman (an inappropriate accolade, alas, already), but would try to establish him as a supreme comic literary archetype: greedy, vain, idle, petulant, yet with a sublime wit and high intelligence to see he was all those things. There was a furious reaction to this, and even Ann Fleming refused to help me, all of which gave me further incentive. I became obsessed with Connolly, reckoning that my little book would vindicate his career and turn out to be the Missing Masterpiece which had always eluded him.

Spending Christmas of 1974 with my brother-in-law, Michael Onslow (as he had become since our first meeting so many years ago in Combermere Barracks, Windsor), we were served with a dish which consisted of a roast goose with a roast pheasant inside it, a roast duck inside the pheasant and a roast woodcock inside the duck. It was an exquisite dish. Reflecting on how much Connolly would have enjoyed it – how it might have been invented specially for him – I felt a terrible remorse and decided not to write the book after all.

* * * *

The Shrimsley libel action was a spin-off from the much greater Goldsmith crusade, which has already been chronicled several times, most particularly in Richard Ingrams's *Goldenballs* (London, Private Eye/Deutsch, 1979). It starts with the nasty spectacle of the diarist being caught with his trousers down. A journalist Patrick Hutber, whom I knew slightly and who had been to at least one *Private Eye* luncheon, joined Goldsmith's ill-fated newsmagazine *NOW!* (usually called *TALBOT!* in *Private Eye* for some long-lost reason, but always *TOADY!* in the 'Diary', after its ill-fated editor, Tony 'Toady' Shrimsley, who used to say that he was 'enthused' by the thoughts of its proprietor, Sir James Goldsmith). The *Eye*, which was conducting a campaign against *NOW!* saw this as something of a betrayal, although I am not sure why. Returning from a Christmas party at the *Sunday Telegraph*, where he had been city editor, Hutber was involved in a car crash. My information was that he was only slightly injured, but I decided to ham it up and announce that he was hovering between life and death. In my 'Diary' entry, I put the blame for this sorry turn of events on his quest for grocerish gold (Goldsmith, in those days, was best known as a grocer) and ended my piece with a few verses from Chesterton's *Songs Against Grocers*. In fact Hutber had been grievously injured and died a few days after *Private Eye* appeared, leaving a widow and young family.

Such catastrophes are an occupational hazard for the vituperative artist. I was nearly caught the same way when the journalist Kenneth Alsop died, having just composed a horrendous attack on him. Luckily the news reached me in time. By judicious cutting, with the addition of a few 'nots' and 'scarcelys', I was able to turn it into an idiosyncratic tribute of sorts. On other occasions which I do not propose to mention, I have not been so lucky. The only thing to do under these circumstances is to keep your head down and tell everybody you have gone to live in New Zealand.

In response to my ill-considered piece, Anthony Shrimsley devoted a whole page of *NOW!* to denouncing me and Ingrams (who had nothing to do with it) as being worse than vermin – sadists, liars, not fit to be received in the company of decent people. He challenged me to sue if any of these statements was untrue. In fact, as he must have known perfectly well, there was nothing remotely libellous in them. They were statements of honest opinion. Next his brother, Bernard (nicknamed 'Slimy' for reasons which I have now forgotten) Shrimsley, who was Editor of the *News of the World*, printed an attack in his New Year leader page in the John Field column, denouncing me to the seven million-odd masturbating readers of his disgusting newspaper as 'Rat of the Year'.

During my days on the *News of the World* this column had always been written by the Editor, Mr Stafford Somerfield, a fine upstanding west country Liberal. Inquiries suggested that nowadays it was normally written by a hack whose name I have forgotten but whose various sackings and other misadventures had been chronicled in the *Eye*. In the course of denouncing the hack, I presumed that the present Editor (Bernard 'Slimy' Shrimsley) was too idle or illiterate to write it himself.

It was this presumption that led to Bernard Shrimsley's writ because, in fact, he had written this particular item himself. Even so, his case was a weak one. He had denounced me as 'Rat of the Year', and he did not normally write the John Field column. His motive in bringing the action was presumably to throw as much dirt as possible over the Hutber episode, as a simple act of revenge. But a certain amount of dirt inevitably accumulates around the ears of any editor of the *News of the World*, and I set myself the task of digging it up in the months while we awaited trial, and printing it in my *Spectator* column.

Eventually, Bernard Shrimsley grabbed the £250 we had paid into court and ran for it. Once again I seem to have been stricken by remorse. On 1 October 1980, while judging the great *Private Eye* Newsagent of the Year competition (for the newsagent who had most reduced his order for *NOW!*), I wrote in my 'Diary':

> Poor Toady. I feel I may have been beastly to him in the past, and to his dear brother Bernard ('Slimy'), the former editor of the *News of the World* whose pathetic climbdown over his libel action should be seen as a cause for commiseration rather than glee.
>
> Alas, I fear there is no truth in the rumour that the two brothers are thinking of joining the Roman Catholic Church. At any rate it seems unlikely that there is any truth in the rumour as I have just this moment invented it. But history is often moulded by poetic visions of this sort, and I think I will send Lord Longford round to see them. For myself, I propose to make a pilgrimage along the path of the old Crusades, lighting candles in all the churches on the way to advance this pleasant idea.

For once I was as good as my word. Next day Teresa and I set off on a Swann Hellenic cruise.

* * * *

October 2nd 1980

FIRST to St Mark's in Venice where two huge candles burn side by side in honour of those unfortunate brothers, one for Toady, one for Slimy. Then to Ravenna where I light another two in the Church of S. Apollinara in Classe under the wonderful Byzantine mosaics of sheep on a green background.

Soon candles will be burning all over the Adriatic and eastern Mediterranean, that God may see fit to lighten their sad lives and fill their poor shrivelled hearts with His love, giving them the fortitude to face the misfortunes and personal tragedies still in store for them.

October 4, 1980

IN THE cathedrals of Corcula and Dubrovnik Croatian peasants cross themselves and pray before miraculous statues – in the hope that one day God will remove the curse of socialism from their unhappy land, but four candles burn in the gloom with another purpose, for the salvation of the brothers Shrimsley, no less – two for Slimy, two for Toady....

The litany continued from Crete, Istanbul and all over the Eastern Mediterranean. Candles burned at the Crusaders' Hospital in Rhodes and at the shrine of the Apocalypse in Patmos where St John dictated his incomprehensible Book of Revelation. They do not appear to have had any effect. Anthony Shrimsley died tragically young soon after the closure of *NOW*, while his brother Bernard, having been sacked from *News of the World*, was made first editor of the *Mail on Sunday* but lasted only ten issues before moving on again. Their motives were honourable, if vindictive. The only moral to be drawn is that honourable causes are seldom advanced by the employment of lawyers.

* * * *

The long-running Goldsmith fight, when the millionaire Sir James Goldsmith made a serious effort to close down the magazine by launching sixty writs simultaneously as well as a private prosecution for criminal libel, hoping to send Ingrams to prison, was not really my squabble, although I appointed myself Director of the Goldenballs Appeal and wrote various letters to *The Times* etc. in that capacity. The appeal eventually raised over £30,000. I was called into court only once, when Goldsmith sought an injunction preventing me and a gang of others – Ingrams, Marnham, Dempster, etc. – from making any adverse comment about him or his solicitor, Mr Eric Levene, while the case was pending. It was my first (and so far only) experience of a witness box in the High Court – my action against *Spectator* for wrongful dismissal had been heard in the Marylebone and Bloomsbury County Court. I was surprised by the summons, since I had never met or written about Goldsmith, so far as I knew. But the summons made me determined to shoot off some adverse comment about him before the injunction could be granted. My trouble was I knew nothing about him, so I confined myself, in my *Spectator* column, to suggesting that from photographs he had a repulsively ugly face. I also speculated at some length (*sic*–ho-ho) about his virile member. To my great pleasure, this article was read aloud in court by Mr Justice Donaldson (later Master of the Rolls). He read it very well.

Mr Lewis Hawser QC (later Mr Justice Hawser), for Goldsmith, did not dispute my comment about his client's face and had nothing to add to my tentative speculation about his other parts, but insisted that I had indeed written about him in *Private Eye* a month previously when, discussing the famous libel action Dering *v.* Uris of 1964, I wrote: 'Obviously, Dering was ill-advised to bring such a libel action, even in England where libel laws make it a haven for every sort of crook and pervert in public life.'

Although nobody was named, Mr Hawser felt that the description of 'pervert' must, in the circumstances, be taken to apply to a well-known politician, and the description of 'crook' must be taken to apply to his client. I denied this, pointing out there was no reason to suppose Sir James was a criminal. Even if he had been a criminal, he was by no means the *only* one around. There were also the Kray brothers, the Richardson gang, Mr Poulson, the Cambridge rapist, all of whom were protected at some time by the libel laws.

In the course of his cross-examination, Hawser persuaded me that I might easily have been thinking of his client when I wrote the sentence, but I still had no reason to suppose that he was a criminal. It was a question of whether the cap fitted. Thinking it about him was not the same thing as writing about him.

Anyway, Hawser lost the application and Goldsmith did not get his injunction.

*   *   *   *

At the end of the day, both sides spent an enormous amount of money to no very good effect. Goldsmith received a knighthood on Lady Falkender's famous 'lavender list' section of Harold Wilson's resignation honours. This was thought by some to be his reward for taking on *Private Eye* which was not in her ladyship's favour in those days. I may have annoyed her by debating at some length the tactless but to me absorbing question of whether her two illegitimate children, born before her elevation to the peerage, but unquestionably out of her body, were entitled to call themselves 'The Honourable'. This question has never been resolved to my satisfaction. I consulted Garter, but he was non-committal, hinting that research into the matter would involve enormous fees. Against Goldsmith's knighthood was the fact that he was prevented from buying the *Observer*, which many attributed to his action against *Private Eye*, and had to start his own news magazine, *NOW!*, which failed to secure enough readers. It is this public association with a failed enterprise which may rankle most, I suspect – certainly more than having the size of his virile member discussed in a low-circulation weekly.

I have met Goldsmith on a couple of occasions since – once, to my terror, finding I had drawn him as partner for bridge in the Portland Club, where I had been taken as a guest. On both occasions, he has treated me with the greatest affability, as if all were forgiven and forgotten, but I am not sure I would be happy to find myself alone with him out of doors after dark.

Looking back over my career, and at all the people I have insulted, I am mildly surprised that I am still allowed to exist. It all makes the old nursery point that 'sticks and stones may break my bones but words will never hurt me'. There is scarcely a politician in business whom I have not abused at one time or another, yet most of the senior politicians (Hattersley is an exception) greet me as if I were an old friend, on the rare occasions we meet. Nor is this amiability confined to the politicians themselves. I was almost invariably rude about Anthony Crosland, pretending to confuse him with Richard Crossman, or sending love-messages to his wife, as in this typical example:

May 1st 1973
A telephone call today from Pauline Peters of *The Sunday Times*, asking if she could interview me for a profile in the Colour Mag. Somebody obviously wants a knocking-job done, which might be quite fun. But then I think of Mr Eldon Griffiths's sensible speech at Margate over the weekend on the subject of knockers:

'There is too great a readiness to knock and snipe and smear,' he said, 'particularly among opinion formers in the communications industry.'

Of course, I know nothing about this Pauline Peters, but I

didn't particularly like the sound of her voice, which seemed a little highly-strung for my taste, so I decided to take Eldon's advice. If only they had sent round the delightful Susan Barnes – preferably without her deplorable husband, the boorish and conceited Anthony Crosland. It would be a real privilege and pleasure to be knocked by her.

Elsewhere, whenever I mention this 'serious, peachlike, rather conceited Labour politician' he is liable to be given a footnote: *noted for having a pretty, gifted wife.* Perhaps this is why, thirteen years after her husband's death, I am still a good friend of Susan Crosland, whose devotion to her husband and to his memory, is unquestionable. Crosland himself never bore malice, and rather enjoyed a totally mendacious account I gave of his lunching with the Queen Mother who also mistook him for Crossman and asked after the asparagus in his native Germany....

*　*　*　*

The well-known politician to whom Mr Lewis Hawser referred as being the obvious subject of my reference to perverts in public life who sheltered behind the libel laws was named in court as Jeremy Thorpe, then leader of the Liberal Party. The hearing was held, technically, in chambers, which meant the judge did not wear a wig and no reporters were present.

It was two years before the allegations against Thorpe came to a head with his arrest in August 1978 on charges of having attempted and conspired to murder a male model, Norman Scott, with whom he was acquainted, four years earlier. My own first mention of the matter came on 15 December 1975, when I describe how west Somerset was buzzing with rumours after Scott, 'who claims to have been a great friend of Jeremy Thorpe, the Liberal statesman, was found by an AA patrolman weeping beside the body of Rinka, his Great Dane bitch, which had been shot in the head.' I ended my piece on a friendly, encouraging note:

My only hope is that sorrow over his friend's dog will not cause Mr Thorpe's premature retirement from public life. Jeremy is not only a very wonderful person in his own right, he is also a gifted impersonator of London celebrities like

Lady Dartmouth* and Mr Heath. Indeed, in the whole of fashionable London, I can think only of John Wells as possibly being his equal in this field and Wells, of course, has other disadvantages.

The 'other disadvantages' in John Wells were a tendency to sniff, which I had spotted at an early stage in our acquaintance. But this friendly, encouraging attitude towards Thorpe did not represent my true feelings at that time. Other journalists, like the Cambridge-educated Christopher Booker and the previously mentioned John Pilger, seem to live in a perpetual state of indignation, but practically nothing made me genuinely indignant, at any rate since the Biafran war five years earlier. Rather to my surprise, I found myself genuinely indignant at the suggestion that murder was to be reintroduced as a means of political advancement for the first time since the Tudors, and even more indignant that the legal and political establishments in all their forms – which included, at that stage, the police – were going to cover up the whole episode. In the event, it turned out that my anxieties were unfounded, as Thorpe was totally innocent of all charges brought against him. But it was this anxiety that sustained me through four years of what may have seemed to be no more than another routine persecution of a politician. It led me to accept Ingrams's satirical suggestion that I should stand against Thorpe in the General Election of 1979 on behalf of the Dog Lovers' party of Great Britain, and even after Mr Justice Cantley's extraordinary summing up at the Old Bailey trial and Thorpe's subsequent acquittal on all charges, it led me to write a book about the trial, making whatever points remained to be made. The book, called *The Last Word: an Eyewitness Account of the Thorpe Trial* (London, Michael Joseph, 1980) still strikes me as quite good. I urge anyone who has a copy to give it another try. It is certainly much better than my previous *cri-de-coeur, Biafra, Britain's Shame* (London, Michael Joseph, 1969).

* * * *

Meanwhile, my pursuit or hounding of Thorpe followed its usual oblique, crablike course. On the day before the trial of the dog

* Later Countess Spencer.

shooter, Andrew Gino Newton, in Exeter, *The Sunday Times*
allowed Thorpe to print a violent attack on the defendant including the information that he (Thorpe) was not and never had been
a homosexual. On the day the trial opened, Wilson announced his
resignation and the Snowdons announced their impending
divorce, so the event was rather eclipsed, but the fact that nobody
ever mentioned the laws of contempt in relation to *The Sunday
Times* article and the trial of Newton made me wonder what was
happening.

In November 1977, when Newton was released from prison and
offering his story round the newspapers, Thorpe called a press
conference in New Scotland Yard, of all places, to announce his innocence in the face of persistent rumours. I wrote in my 'Diary' for
5 November 1977:

TO NEW Scotland Yard where Jeremy Thorpe has called a
press conference to discuss various allegations that have
been made about his sex life. I have many interesting new
allegations to make, but they throw me out at the door.

When all the weeping toadies are assembled, only one of
them dares to ask him whether he has ever done it. Mr Keith
Graves, of BBC TV, who is hereby given the Gnome Award for
News Reporter of the Year, has been vilified by every prig and
pharisee in Fleet Street for asking the only worthwhile
question.

Poor Jeremy. He is his own worst enemy, but with friends
like these he really has no need of himself. The only remaining mystery is why the Liberal Party policy committee
decided to murder Scott rather than Jeremy.

In an affectionate moment, Thorpe had written to Scott that
'bunnies can and will go to France'. When the glorious moment of
Thorpe's arrest came in August 1978, I was in France, staying at La
Pesegado, with Ferdinand and Julia Mount and their children as
guests. By sheer good luck a previous tenant had left a television
set behind, and as Ferdie was interested in politics we watched the
French news.

*   *   *   *

August 5th 1978

NEWS of Jeremy Thorpe's arrest breaks like a thunderclap over the Languedoc countryside. There is dancing in the streets, ceremonial rabbits are cooked and groups of peasants with lanterns are to be found wandering the lanes far into the night, singing at the tops of their voices and beating the hedges with staves.

   ... Over here, where people were understandably alarmed by Thorpe's assertion that 'bunnies can and will go to France', a collection is being made to provide some token of their gratitude and relief over the new development.

   I suggest that this take the form of a monument to Rinka, the unfortunate [Great Dane]. Contrary to general belief, the French are even more obsessed by dogs than the English are, and a monument subscribed by Languedoc farmers to stand at the lonely, windswept spot on Porlock Hill, Exmoor, where Rinka was so foully done to death would be poignant testimony to the neighbourly way in which Europeans share each other's sufferings and joys.

A picture of the monument was supplied by William Rushton for my 'Diary' of 30 October 1978, when I describe myself as leading a deputation to the lay-by on Porlock Hill – just fifteen miles from Combe Florey – which 'stands in silence for a while in memory of the dead Great Dane, Rinka, who gave her life to create a better world'.

All those present pledge themselves anew to the struggle. Rinka's sacrifice will not be forgotten. She *will* be avenged, and a cleaner, healthier society will arise. Rinka lives on in our hearts.

I sat throughout the week of magistrates' court hearings in Minehead, taking notes. The atmosphere was less formal than at the Old Bailey. Thorpe wandered up to me one morning and said: 'Scribble, scribble, scribble, Mr Waugh', with a sickly grin. It was the last exchange I ever had with him. I did not go down to North Devon to canvass support as Dog Lovers' Party candidate in the General Election, as I had been banned by the courts from publishing my election manifesto or giving any account of why I was standing. Mr Carman, Thorpe's barrister, applied to the Divisional Court to have me committed to prison and my manifesto banned, but the Lord Chief Justice threw it out. On appeal, Lord Denning reinstated the ban, dismissing my counsel's arguments with contumely, and saying he had been reading *Private Eye* and was in no doubt of my intention to pervert the course of justice.

Even so, seventy-nine people voted for me. Thorpe lost his seat, but the most interesting feature of the result was how few Liberals switched their votes. Despite Thorpe's name being dragged through the press every day for a week, with lurid accounts of buggery, financial crookery and attempted murder, fewer then 5000 voters out of an electorate of 77,000 actually switched their votes away from him at an election which produced a bigger Conservative swing elsewhere. He still received 23,338 votes, having received 28,209 in October 1974. One wondered how much harm was really done to anybody by the written word, and how our savage laws of libel can really be justified except as a convenience for the rich and powerful to save themselves from criticism.

* * * *

My last libel threat was rather a sad one, and contributed as much as anything else to my decision to leave *Private Eye*, if only because it showed the way the wind was blowing in matters of libel. Its origins were farcical enough. A friend, Henry Porter, who was walking out with the *Eye's* lovely secretary, Liz Elliott, and was quite a good friend of the *Eye*, was writing the Atticus column in *The Sunday Times* and thought it would be a good joke to send me a spoof letter on *Sunday Times* notepaper purporting to come from Claire Tomalin, *The Sunday Times* literary editor at that time. The letter asked me to review an anthology of homosexual writing edited by Adam Mars-Jones, adding a hope that I would review the book favourably, knowing that I was especially well disposed toward homosexuals.

It did not occur to me that the letter was not genuine, although I was puzzled that it started 'Dear Auberon Waugh', rather than 'Dear Bron'. I did not know Claire well, and she belonged to a different literary tradition, but we had always enjoyed cordial relations. I liked and admired her husband, the journalist Nicholas Tomalin, who had been killed on the Golan Heights by a Syrian sniper. There were various tragedies in Claire's life, not least, in my view, an attachment to Michael Frayn, the dreaded Cambridge humorist. But I had nothing against her and rather admired her in several ways.

In the normal course of events I receive quite a number of letters every day, like many other people in my business, and it would surely be a sign of incipient madness to start suspecting that a letter from an acquaintance was, in fact, a forgery. Still, it was an odd letter. Claire had never asked me to review before, which was scarcely strange as I had been holding up *The Sunday Times*'s books pages as a general hate focus for as long as I could remember, and the proposal was not an entirely serious one.

I decided that Claire was making a rare excursion into the fun-and-games department, and instead of answering the letter to say that most unfortunately I was too busy to review her homosexual anthology, I write in the 'Diary' as follows:

JOURNALISTS cannot afford to be too choosy about the newspapers they work for. I think I have written for nearly every newspaper in Fleet Street, drawing the line only at *The Sunday Times* and the *Sunday People*. To be fair, I must admit that the *Sunday People* has never asked me.

Today a strange letter arrives from the Literary Editor of *The Sunday Times,* Ms Claire Tomalin, enclosing a smutty paperback with a picture of two Lesbians on the cover. It describes itself as an anthology of recent Lesbian and Gay fiction.

She wonders if I would like to review it for her. I seldom look at the books page of *The Sunday Times,* but I suppose this is the sort of book its ghastly readers enjoy. But the oddest thing about Ms Tomalin's request is contained in her last two sentences:

'Before starting please phone me to let me know what sort of line you are going to take', she writes, 'I would expect a generous review.'

As I say, I have written for some pretty odd publications in my time, but I do not think I've ever received instructions from a Literary Editor about what sort of review I was to write. It makes one wonder about all those crazy Somerset majors who say there is a left-wing homosexual conspiracy in the media.

This sally must have caught her at a bad moment. Knowing nothing of Henry Porter's practical joke, she saw it as a gratuitous and undeserved attack on her good name. Upset and angry, and supported by sympathetic friends, she took the matter to my traditional enemies in the legal department of *The Sunday Times*, who immediately swaddled her in comfort, assuring her that she had a cast-iron case. The article meant that she was a lesbian of such left-wing views as influenced her judgement and made her unsuitable for employment by *The Sunday Times*; furthermore, she was guilty of the unethical practice of bringing improper influence to bear on reviewers in an attempt to slant their reviews.

In fact nearly all literary editors give a certain amount of guidance to reviewers (although I am sure Tomalin never did) but seldom as baldly as in the spoof letter.

As soon as I learned I had been the victim of a practical joke, I printed a craven, although unagreed, apology – the first and only one which ever appeared in the 'Diary'. It is the custom of libel solicitors on these occasions to demand an apology which destroys any possible defence in the subsequent libel action, and then plead aggravation when you refuse to print it. This is the apology I wrote:

Claire Tomalin

Claire Tomalin, Literary Editor of *The Sunday Times*, wishes me to state that the letter bearing her name from which I quoted in the last issue was a forgery, written without her knowledge or consent. In the circumstances I am happy to withdraw and apologize for everything I said about her.

Technically, an unagreed apology is valueless either in satisfaction or in mitigation of damages, but a jury might not accept that. I hoped it might mollify Tomalin, and it seemed to show common sense, not to say common decency, to explain myself. But once lawyers have been brought in (and *The Sunday Times* had agreed to take over the case) nothing is quite so easy as that. My enemies on *The Sunday Times* plainly reckoned they had caught me with my trousers down, although the newspaper was going to look rather odd explaining the activities of its employee, my friend

Henry Porter.

The barrister chosen to conduct the case for *Private Eye* in the Shrimsley case was Patrick Milmo, but I had a vague memory of having beaten him in a competition for the Abingdon Prize for Oratory at Downside (although it might have been his brother) and, after a first conference in chambers, I decided to present my own case in court, leaving Milmo to wave the flag for *Private Eye*, Pressdram and Ingrams. On the present occasion, Milmo was acting for Tomalin and I made the same decision.

This is always a tremendously unpopular thing to do. It brings an element of anarchy into the smooth process of the law, dedicated to fleecing the public according to its own sacrosanct procedures. Ingrams decided (quite rightly) that there was an element of exhibitionism in my decision, which he deplored, but agreed to go along with. The decision had been taken to defend the action. We would probably lose, since defendants always lost, but the *Eye* could not go on paying out money without ever defending a case. The elements of absurdity in the case, and the curious picture which would emerge of the plaintiff, should discourage other plaintiffs, and damages, in the context of a genuine misunderstanding immediately acknowledged, should be small.

My defence was that I had not accused Tomalin of being a left-winger or a lesbian, and that even if I had it was no disgraceful or shameful thing to be a left-winger nor, in the current climate of opinion, was it considered a disgraceful or shameful thing by right-minded and sensible people to be a lesbian. This last point may have seemed a dicey one to take before a London jury, but I had a long queue of witnesses lined up to testify to that effect, and it would have left Tomalin in the curious position of arguing that it was indeed a disgraceful and shameful thing to be left-wing or lesbian. Claire Tomalin is not, and never has been, lesbian, nor is she particularly left-wing, but she belongs to a liberal tradition which would vehemently defend both proclivities.

Looking at the huge file on this case, which went on for two years, I see the enormous amount of work I put into it, writing the equivalent of a book in letters to solicitors, letters to potential witnesses and articles in the *Spectator* taunting the plaintiff and her backers. These last might well have been used in aggravation of damages if the case had gone to court, but I had decided that the only way to deal with this libel was to go for bust. We paid £251

into court to cover a token or nominal award in respect of the
point about the literary editor giving instructions to reviewers,
which was immediately withdrawn and apologized for. But the
only tactic, as I saw it, was to have the case laughed out of court
with an award of derisory or contemptuous damages.

Unfortunately, as the time for the court action drew near, both
Ingrams and Tomalin began to get cold feet. Tomalin's QC, John
Wilmers, dropped dead, as often seems to happen, and *The Sunday Times* had to find another one. Ingrams and Geoffrey Bind-
man, the *Eye*'s solicitor, had a quarrel and Ingrams moved the
case to Oscar Beuselinck at Syrett, Webb. Our counsel, Desmond
Browne, had said all along that we would lose. If we lost, it could
well be that Tomalin, who is a comely, intelligent and trans-
parently honest person, as well as being a widow and mother of a
handicapped child, would win the sort of astronomical damages
which have since become almost routine, although the alleged
libel was a tiny one, the result of a joke perpetrated by a *Sunday
Times* employee, and instantly retracted.

At any rate, Tomalin offered to settle for £2,500 plus £5,000
towards costs. It was very tempting to settle an action so cheaply,
and Ingrams eventually decided to settle – I am not sure of the
final terms – despite his earlier assurances to me that he would
not do so. I made several attempts to sabotage the settlement by
writing inflammatory articles about the case in *Spectator*, but
Theodore Goddard, Murdoch's solicitors who have acted in
numerous cases against me on behalf of Murdoch employees,
would not rise to the bait. At the beginning of the case, they re-
acted to any mention of Tomalin's name with dire hints of six-
figure damages. Claire behaved honourably, giving the money to
charity. I behaved rather less so, publishing '*In Tomalinam*' (all
the speeches I would have made in court had I been called to do
so) in the next edition of the *Spectator*.

No doubt Ingrams's decision was the right one. My first reaction
was one of immense relief, despite all my bravado. It was like a
boxer who is told that his championship match has been cancelled
two minutes before it is due to start. I had lived and breathed
Claire Tomalin for two years. The fact that the whole battle was
due to be fought on a note of farce by myself, and of awesome
solemnity, self-righteousness and indignation by counsel for
Tomalin, made it all the more of a challenge.

My second emotion was one of severe depression, rather like post-natal (or more accurately post-abortion) depression in a woman. If all libels were to be settled with large sums of money out of court, what joy was there in writing them? I had always urged that the *Eye* should choose its cases more carefully, fighting only those which referred to jokes and settling those which involved serious allegations of misconduct, however correct the allegations might be. This had not worked in the case of Beloff, it is true, but I reckoned to have studied the form since then. Instead, it always did the opposite.

The Tomalin settlement was in November 1985. In January 1986 I accepted Naim Attallah's offer to take over the editorship of *Literary Review* from Emma Soames, who was moving to become editor of the *Tatler*. There were other reasons for deciding to move on. Footie had left the *Eye*, and so had Marnham – in Marnham's case, after a quarrel with Ingrams which seems to have left them permanently estranged. Dempster had quarrelled and left. McKay was in a strange limbo, still attending *Eye* functions as a sort of official enemy. The magazine had moved from Greek Street to new offices in Carlisle Street just when the atmosphere was beginning to deteriorate. Ingrams seemed to be taking less interest in the magazine. A new employee, O'Hanrahan, made rude noises and insolent faces every time any of the public school-educated contributors walked in or walked out. It was plainly time to move on.

At a farewell lunch party at the Escargot, Greek Street, I was presented with a handsome silver-plated wine funnel in token of my sixteen years' service, but Ingrams rather stole the show by announcing his resignation as Editor on the same occasion. He had decided it was time to move on, too. The announcement came as a thunderbolt. Emotional scenes broke out. Beautiful Liz Elliott and Sheila Molnar wept. The editor-elect, a rather small young man called Ian Hislop, sat tight-lipped while I pleaded with Ingrams to remain, offering to sack the *Literary Review*; Hislop then walked out in a huff, saying I had insulted the young. Only William Rushton growled: 'High time, too!'

Everything settled down. I had always assumed that when I left the *Eye* it would attack me mercilessly, but this has not yet happened. Hislop, less sensitive than he at first appeared, emerged as quite a genial fellow. The magazine is much the same as it always was, sometimes better, sometimes less good, certainly no nastier. With so much nastiness coming out of the *Sun, Daily Star, Today* and the rest of them, this is probably no bad thing. My affection and admiration for Richard will always carry, in addition, a heavy burden of gratitude. Nobody else would have published Auberon Waugh's 'Diary', let alone kept it going for fourteen years. However ephemeral it is bound to prove, I suspect it will remain my proudest achievement. The enemies we made were worth making, the battles we fought together were worth fighting. I am happy and proud to have been given the chance to serve beside him.

CHAPTER
FIFTEEN

Here and There 1973-1990

At the age of thirty-four, I found myself in the disconcerting position of someone who had already done all he had set out to do. I had married and fathered four children. Dearly as I loved them all, I did not want to have any more. I had written five novels, and decided that that particular seam was exhausted. I enjoyed all my work – it then consisted of a weekly column in the *New Statesman*, a weekly novel review in the *Standard*, a fortnightly Diary in the *Eye*, and a monthly book review in *Books and Bookmen* – and could think of no jobs I wanted to do more, or could do any better. Above all, I had somehow managed to secure occupation, if not possession (it belonged to my wife) of Combe Florey, which was something I had scarcely hoped to achieve. True, it was somewhat denuded of its grandeur, since most of the furniture and the pictures which belonged to a trust set up by my father, had to be divided between the children, and my mother had sold much of the rest. But it was still a much grander house than most of my contemporaries lived in, and quite grand enough. After my mother's death in 1973, when we inherited a certain amount of junk furniture which nobody else wanted, I suddenly lost the acquisitive urge.

The trouble with living in a beautiful house set in beautiful countryside is that once you have seen it and appreciated it all, that experience is over and it is time to move to the next thing.

This may sound spoiled, but it is obviously true. My trouble was that I could think of nothing I particularly wanted to move to. I sat around eating too much and drinking too much, enjoying my work but little else. Was this all that life held?

I had made a few trips at the end of the sixties – to Israel, for the Six Day War in 1967, for American *Cosmopolitan*, to Biafra for the *Spectator* in 1968, a month touring the United States for *National Review* in 1969, but throughout the early seventies our horizons were limited to family holidays at La Pesegado and occasional dashes to Rome, where one or another of my sisters always seemed to be living. Then in 1975 I attended a strange literary conference at Lahti, in northern Finland, which happened to coincide with the celebration of Midsummer Day, when all the Finns go mad and prance around in the burning sun at midnight, collapsing under trees out of drink and exhaustion. It was most unlike life in Somerset, and for the first time I began to develop a taste for the company of foreigners such as had been my poor Uncle Auberon's ruin. Auberon died the year before, sitting at his desk in the sitting-room at Pixton reading the *Sunday Telegraph* and wondering whom to telephone next. I was at La Pesegado at the time and missed his funeral, but it is possible that something of his unquiet spirit settled on me that year.

However, it was not until the New Year of 1978, when I was sitting in a jacuzzi at Champneys Health Resort, near Tring, with three enormous Arabs discussing the delights of Bangkok – with special reference to the famous Thai massage – that I really decided there was more to life than contemplating the Somerset countryside. Everything the fat Arabs had told me turned out to be true, but they had not prepared me for the charm of the Buddhist culture nor the delights of that cheerful, clever race. On my first visit Christian Carit, sister of David Carit, the Christie's picture expert and a friend from London days, was living there married to a husband attached to the American embassy. She took me to lunch with a famous character on the Bangkok scene, Princess Chumpot, who lived in a palace surrounded by a huge and beautiful garden. We ate a meal made up entirely of different flowers from her garden, all cooked in different ways yet somehow more or less preserved in their pristine state. European visitors also took off their shoes, and were expected to know how not to point their toes or show the soles of their feet. It was my first experience

of the Thai *haute politesse* which is also, somehow, combined with
a highly irreverent and racy wit. Meeting other Thais on subsequent visits, at the beautiful home of Nick and Kai Spencer, I
learned to love everything about this beautiful country. On the
way back from that first visit to Bangkok I returned via Athens,
where my cousin Polly Grant was living, and, on a whim, skipped
over to Cyprus.

It was strange to revisit Cyprus twenty years after my major débâcle with a machine gun on the Kyrenia road. My brother-in-law,
Giles FitzHerbert, was deputy high commissioner there in 1978,
which meant that we were privileged to move between the Greek
and Turkish sectors with a jaunty wave. The Ledra Palace Hotel
was full of Canadian United Nations' soldiers blubbing over photographs of their loved ones back in Winnipeg, and the whole place
seemed dingy and commonplace compared to my memories of it.
But then a hijacked airliner full of hostages landed at Larnaca airport. It was surrounded by Cypriot police and troops. A plane load
of Egyptian commandos landed, planning to execute some daring
SAS-style raid to release the hostages. The Cypriots objected and a
shoot-out developed between the Egyptians and the Cypriots. In
the middle of it, I telephoned the airport to inquire about my luggage, which was supposed to follow me from Athens once KLM
had traced it.

'Please, sir, can you get off the line, we have an emergency
here.'

'No, I wish to find out what has happened to my luggage.'

'But, sir, they are shooting. Bullets are flying everywhere. People
are being killed.'

'That's all very well, but I have to go out to dinner this evening
and I do not even have a change of shirt. Have you heard from
KLM?'

My nephew, Harry FitzHerbert, who must then have been about
five, was obsessed by the idea that if we revisited the scene of my
machine gun accident, we might find the finger I had lost as a result of it. In fact the finger had been removed in Westminster Hospital six months later, but it seemed a shame to disappoint the lad.
I took a small cutlet bone from the table at lunch in a nearby
taverna and when we reached the spot, hid it by the side of the

road. He was overjoyed, and brought the trophy home in triumph.
We held a great debate about what to do with it – whether we
should bury it in the garden and build a little chapel over it, like
the monument to Lord Anglesey's leg at Waterloo. In the middle of
the debate, Harry was found to be nibbling the sacred relic. His
mother took it from him and threw it away.

* * * *

A Senegal invitation came from *Private Eye*'s sister publication in
Dakar, *Le Politicien*, which was celebrating its second anniver-
sary. The message came through – transmitted, needless to say, by
Marnham – that I was to make a speech in French on breast-
feeding. This seemed odd but by no means impossible, as I was
writing a regular column in a medical magazine – *British Medicine*
– at the time and had been conducting a campaign against compulsory breast-feeding in National Health hospitals. So I composed
a speech on this subject in French, with considerable labour, only
to find when I landed in Dakar that the subject chosen was not
breast-feeding but press freedom. There was no way even to
describe the misunderstanding, since '*la liberté de la Presse*' bears
no resemblance to '*le nourrisson naturel des bébés*'.

Press freedom was rather a tender subject in Senegal because it
had existed for only a few years and there were alarming signs
that the philosopher-President, Leopold Senghor, was beginning
to have second thoughts. I did not meet Senghor but the Senega-
lese Minister for Culture, who was present at the lavish banquet in
the Hotel Vichy, took it all in good part, nearly rolling off his chair
as I launched into my passionate argument against the inconvenient, disfiguring and cruel practice of breast-feeding. Later, we
all went to a night club and made fools of ourselves in the traditional African manner.

A trip to Mauritius was an ordinary press freebie for a party of
journalists who were guests of the chain of hotels there. I was
delighted to find Claudie Worsthorne, wife of the great Conservative thinker, among the party. We danced into the small hours to
the strains of Boney M. She told me that her husband wore a hair-
net in bed. From that moment I started my long campaign to have
Peregrine Worsthorne knighted, which reached fruition only at
the end of 1990.

In May 1980 I went to Japan. I claimed to be researching the disputed point whether or not the Japanese had pubic hair, on behalf of *Private Eye* readers. The question had been raised by Francis King in a novel, and produced a lively correspondence. If asked what I was really doing in Japan I would have to say I was not sure. I asked myself this question one morning when I woke up in a town in the far north of Japan where not a single person spoke English, where there was not a single building more than thirty years old and nothing whatever in the way of scenic beauty except a freak mountain at which I was invited to look by telescope on the hotel terrace.

Further south, the Japanese were more communicative. At Saga, in Fukuoka province, on my way to Nagasaki, the hotel manager kindly asked me out to inspect his crabs. These turned out to mean his drinking clubs or hostess bars – a major feature of the Japanese scene. In one of them I was given thin slices of raw horse to eat in a gingery sauce. It was better than steak tartare or Carpaccio, and set me on a quest for bizarre and exotic foods which was to embrace snake in Thailand, dog in Manila and crocodile in Cuba, although I never found anyone to serve me raw monkey's brains in China.

Next year saw me back in Thailand for a determined effort to find an opium den. These had been dangled before my eyes as one of the great delights of the Far East for many years – by Graham Greene, by my Uncle Alec Waugh, and by our neighbour in France, the Marquis de Laurens Le Castelet, who claimed that they existed in Bangkok. The general rule in Thailand is that if you want anything you ask a taxi-driver – my father had the same theory about the porter at White's – but although I had many strange adventures in Bangkok in my search for an opium den, I never found one and came to the reluctant conclusion that they no longer exist.

Eventually I found one in northern Thailand, in a hill village in a forest outside Chiang Mai where I was taken by a youth on a motorbike. It was not at all as I had imagined, all plush and sloe-eyed maidens to prepare the pipes, but a very rough and ready affair in a house on stilts with an old man to prepare the pipes and the village headman to talk to me and prevent me going to sleep. I lost count of how many pipes I smoked – they claimed it was twelve when I came to pay, but I dare say it was six. I was taken, scarcely able to walk except in a curious gliding motion, back to the Ringcome Hotel in Chiang Mai, full of Drug Enforcement Agency Americans who swarm over these parts like a German army of occupation. It was an exceptionally pleasant experience, but I could not urinate for two days afterwards – quite a hardship in a hot climate where you tend to drink a lot of liquid – and I am not sure that I would care to repeat it.

*   *   *   *

Cuba was in a poor shape to receive tourists. I was assigned a Cubatour guide of my own, with whom I struck up a friendly relationship. As well as feeding me on crocodile steaks at a crocodile farm – it tastes rather good, halfway between lobster and pork – he took me to a sort of voodoo ceremony which was also attended by a group of cooing blue-haired American tourists. A black man came into the clearing carrying a white chicken. 'How sweet,' cooed the Americans, 'don't you think that's just divine?' Then the black man bit off the chicken's head, poured the blood into a glass and offered it around, laughing hysterically. There were no takers.

On the way back, my Cubatour guide said:

'You write your report for the newspaper. Now I must write my report on you.'

'What will you say?' I asked.

'I will say that you like mulatto women and you like rum,' he said.

*   *   *   *

The great wonder through all this period was that I managed to keep up my regular weekly commitments – to the *New Statesman*, later *Spectator*, and a regular weekly review for the *Evening Standard*.

My reviewing stint on the *Evening Standard* ran for seven years until the end of 1980, during which time I read practically every novel of note which came out with one or two notable exceptions. In the course of my stint, Express Newspapers, which owned the *Evening Standard*, was bought by an East End businessman called Victor Mathews, a man of no intellectual pretensions and what seemed to me crass, proletarian views on most subjects. It was plainly my duty to persecute him in *Private Eye*, which I did with a series of Victor Mathews jokes. The source for these jokes was always given as my friend William Hickey – Peter Tory or Peter McKay – the gossip columnist of the *Daily Express,* who must have annoyed me in some way at this time. Rushton created a wonderful portrait of 'Lord' Fingers Maffews, the elephant-man lookalike, with Mathew's face and an elephant's trunk, which reappeared in many different situations.

All this caused a certain amount of friction between my blameless editor, Charles Wintour, and his proprietor, Lord Mathews, as he had become. Most editors nowadays would have sacked me without hesitation, but Charles was an excellent editor of the old school. Only once did he ask me, as a personal favour, if I could lay off Lord Mathews for a bit, as I was making his position very difficult. I said I would do my best. Then he announced his own retirement, and I realized that my days on the *Standard* were numbered, so I approached the *Mail* and secured the post of lead reviewer there before starting up again:

October 29 1980

WITH THE sad news of Sir Charles Wintour's retirement as Editor of the *Evening Standard* after sixty years, I reluctantly decide it is time to move on from the newspaper where I have been writing regular columns for nine years and reviewing novels every week for the last seven.

Wintour was one of the few civilized and effective journalists in Fleet Street . . . . I think I will move my books column to the *Daily Mail* in the New Year. People will laugh at me for this, remembering that I once swore never to write for the *Mail* again while its editor (who likes to be known as 'Mr English') was suing the *Spectator* for alleged libel. Such people ignore the influence of Christian forgiveness and ordinary compassion in human affairs.

I have never met Mr English and I hope I never have to do so, but I saw a photograph of him once and received the strong impression that he was wearing a wig. It is impossible to be angry for very long with a man who wears a wig.

I met English (who nowadays likes to be known as 'Sir David

English') only once during my five years as chief book reviewer for the *Daily Mail*, which ended when I moved to the *Independent* in 1986. He gave me luncheon in the White Tower and assured me that he did not wear a wig.

Next day, I wrote of an imaginary farewell lunch party which Lord Mathews had given in my honour. In fact Lord Mathews had given exactly such a lunch party, but it was not in my honour and I was not invited. He had been heard by someone present to black-guard my good name and that of my father, offering the opinion that we were both sexual perverts:

October 30, 1980

TO THE Black Lubayanka, in Fleet Street, where Lord Fingers Mathews has organized a small lunch party to mark my departure from Express Newspapers at the end of the year after nine years of faithful service. He has asked the Archbishop of Canterbury, Dr Runcie, Sir Iain Moncreiffe of That Ilk, Sir John Junor (of some other Ilk), Sir Melvyn Bragg, the delicious, 23-year-old Lady Olga Maitland, mouth-water-ing Prue Leith and a bevy of beautiful women including Edna Healey, no less.

I must say, Lord Maffews is a jolly good host. He doesn't like the look of our *escalope de veau à la crème* so has a special dish brought to him, no doubt containing jellied eels, stewed whelks, parsnips, tripe 'n' elephant trunk pie and other homely delicacies. He says how very much he enjoys nearly everything I and other members of my family have ever written, and how sad he is that his own humble class origins make it impossible for me to go on working for him.

The other great sadness is that the lovely Lady Maffews is Not Ible to be Wiv Us. I hope all is well. If I thought there was any estrangement between them I might have to sell the story to my old friend Peter Tory, whose excellent William Hickey column in the *Daily Express* is the only thing worth reading in that doomed newspaper.

As the time drew close for my move to the *Mail*, I began to feel sad about leaving the *Standard*, which was a decent, small paper with an honourable, old-fashioned editor. On 12 December 1980, I wrote in the 'Diary':

> As my time to leave the *Standard* draws near after seven
> years as its fiction reviewer, I wish some kind person would
> buy the paper from its present owner, Elephant Man look-
> alike 'Lord' Maffews (as my friend William Hickey wittily
> describes him). Such a philanthropist could send this whelk-
> guzzling oaf back to Bermondsey where he belongs, reinstate
> Sir Charles Wintour as editor and let me resume my novel
> reviewing.

* * * *

Between 1973 and 1980 I also wrote a regular, monthly, long review for *Books and Bookmen.* This was run by an extraordinary
man called Philip Dossé, who also owned a stable of other magazines, *Plays and Players, Films and Filming, Music and Musicians*
.... He was a bachelor, son of an army chef, about whose early life
little is known. He wrote to me from out of the blue smothering me
with extravagant and unconvincing praise, asking me to review
for his magazine, to which I was already well disposed as it had
chosen my second novel, *Path of Dalliance*, as its novel of the year
in 1963.

When I agreed, he deluged me with letters and kept it up for six
years, sometimes sending me two or three in a day, written in a
terrible, neurotic scrawl, and letting me into every detail of his life
and his office. A homosexual, he lived with his mother in Notting
Hill and cooked elaborate meals for her. He came to Combe Florey
once bringing two large suitcases, both stamped with a coronet
over the letter 'B'. They belonged to Lord Boothby, a friend of his
with whom he sometimes stayed in Eaton Square. One suitcase
was immensely heavy when he arrived, extraordinarily light when
he left. We discovered that it had held dozens and dozens of small
bottles of barley wine, which he had been drinking in his bedroom. When offered drinks, he refused all except champagne, saying he never touched alcohol.

His genius was to get the great and good to write for him –
generally retired, but by no means always – presumably by the
same methods he employed on me. The list of reviewers was most
impressive, running from Oswald Mosley and Enoch Powell to
Michael Foot, Cecil King and the Prince of Wales. A banquet to

mark the magazine's twenty-fifth birthday was attended by the Bishop of London, Sir Arthur Bryant and a score of luminaries.

But then his mother died, and he discovered that she had not been married to his father. The intelligence completely destroyed him. At the same time, the financial situation of his magazines grew worse. His letters grew more and more desperate and then dried up for a space of weeks. Finally, there came a stricken letter apologizing for having let me and everyone else down. He had committed suicide. I often think of his fate when I contemplate my own position on *Literary Review*.

*　*　*　*

When Anthony Howard invited me to contribute a column to the *New Statesman* in 1973, I accepted with some misgivings. It was a brave decision on his part, because although readership of the *New Statesman* in those days undoubtedly included all that was brightest and best in the country, it also included a solid mass of deeply serious, deeply committed Labour supporters with very little sense of humour, who might well be deeply shocked by his choice of a frivolous, deeply uncommitted columnist of pronounced anti-socialist views. What made his choice even braver was that the circulation was already falling fast and continued to fall during my two and a half years association – as, indeed, it has done pretty well ever since.

Tony never tried to influence what I wrote, never meddled with the copy and only once turned down a piece, and that was because it was no good rather than because he did not approve of it. Luckily, I managed to write another piece in time for the copy deadline: hastily knocked out within the hour, it was one of my more successful pieces, and earned inclusion in the collected volume, *In the Lion's Den*, which Michael Joseph brought out in 1978.

He was mean with the money, but since becoming Editor of *Literary Review* I see his point of view and am certainly in no position to throw stones at him.

I had very little to do with the rest of the *New Statesman* crowd after attending the magazine's 60th birthday party, just before I joined on April 12, 1973. In those two and a half years, I think I visited the offices in Great Turnstile only once.

*　*　*　*

It was to the sixtieth birthday party of the *New Statesman* that I happened to take Tina Brown, as a nineteen-year-old undergraduate from St Anne's College, Oxford. I had met Tina a few weeks before when she came to Combe Florey to interview me for *Isis*, bringing a young man in tow – Stephen Glover – who later became Editor of the *Independent on Sunday*. She expressed a desire to attend a *Private Eye* lunch, and I naturally complied. It was plain that this extremely attractive young woman was going to go a long way. Tina was later to say that these two events – the *Private Eye* lunch and the *New Statesman* party – altered the whole course of her life. She happened upon the famous *Private Eye* lunch at which Richard Crossman announced that he, Aneurin Bevan and Morgan Phillips, General Secretary of the Labour Party, had all perjured themselves in their famous libel action against *Spectator* which had jocularly suggested that they had been drunk at a socialist conference in Venice: Phillips at least had been drunk as a skunk throughout it. This point had not particularly impressed itself on Tina, but she wrote an extremely witty account of the lunch party in *Isis* which so pleased all the journalists mentioned in it that in no time at all she was the toast of London. The *New Statesman* party marked her first appearance in the world she was soon to conquer so effortlessly.

In those days she would sit beady-eyed and rather silent at table, and then retire for a long visit to the lavatory where she would write down everything she had seen and heard on lavatory paper and put it in her bag for later transcription to her diary. I believe that the famous, unseen Tina Brown diaries were later burned by her brother in the course of a family squabble. If so, it was an act of literary vandalism comparable to anything perpetrated by the House of Windsor, and perhaps comparable to the destruction of the great library of Alexandria.

She was to alter the path of my life when she appointed me Wine Correspondent of *Tatler* whose editor she had become in the intervening years. My first essay in this new career of wine-writer which Tina offered me had unfortunate consequences. I had decided to write my column under the pseudonym Crispin de St Crispian. I thought this a good Tatlerish name, but my real reason for adopting a pseudonym was that I thought wine so important that I wanted freedom to be able to insult even my closest friends and relations in the search for Truth. Foolishly, in my over-excitement I blew my cover by announcing it in the *Eye* 'Diary' for 25 January 1982:

> WONDERFUL NEWS that in the teeth of fierce competition I have been appointed Wine Correspondent of *Tatler* magazine. I must not let success go to my head. There will be many embittered losers and jealous hacks who will now be my enemies. They will have to be dealt with.
>
> All my life, as I now realize, I have wanted nothing more than to be *Tatler*'s Wine Correspondent ... As I pen my first column for April – about a terrible *faux pas* by Alan Watkins, the Islington gormandizer – I realize I've discovered a new art-form. I can't make up my mind whether to write it under my own name or pseudonymously as Crispin de St Crispian, which should be a pretty impenetrable disguise. I wouldn't like to upset my old friend Alan.

In my first piece, I also decided to complain about some wine served by a cousin, who lived in Devon. He has the eccentricity that he actually prefers bad wine to good. This is most depressing for someone like me who has striven to raise the standard of wine served in the country houses of Somerset and Devon. On this occasion I chose to compare his wine, in its presentation and appeal, with 'a dead chrysanthemum on the grave of a still-born West Indian baby'.

I thought this summed up what I felt about the wine rather neatly, but a young midwife in Lambeth – who was also, as I discovered later, pregnant – took grave offence at it, and reported me to the Press Council, with the assistance of the Lambeth Race Relations Officer, who declared that the association of 'West Indian' with bad wine was clearly contemptuous and inflammatory.

On 1 March 1983 Tina and I were hauled before the Press Council to answer these charges. The Race Relations industry had dredged up a senior West Indian to testify that he had found it offensive, and the Race Relations man gave evidence in support of the midwife, who struck me as rather charming as well as being heavily pregnant. We were allowed to cross-examine, which was great fun – a realization of all my Walter Mitty fantasies. I suggested that 'West Indian', as applied to wine, might suggest a spicy flavour, redolent of guavas and mangoes, excellent in themselves but alien to the true taste of grape. It was all deadly serious. After many months' deliberation on the part of the council, the complaint was not upheld.

Tina stood beside me throughout the ordeal, keeping a beautifully straight face. She is a most remarkable person, warm, affectionate and loyal. It was a great sorrow when she chose to marry Harold Evans, the midget north-country journalist, twenty-five years her senior, who was an arch-enemy of the *Eye* at that time. But the marriage appears to have been a happy one. They have a handsome son, George, of whom she is very proud, and more recently a delightful looking daughter, Isabel. I have not seen her often since her marriage to Evans, but it is always a great joy when I do.

* * * *

After leaving *Tatler* in fury over a new editor, who lasted only a few months, I went to write the wine column in *Harpers/Queen* which paid better although I had the impression that nobody was reading it. As I learned more and more about wine, I was amazed at my audacity in accepting the *Tatler* job. Having drunk it all my life, and bluffed my way through any conversation which threatened to become knowledgeable, I reckoned myself qualified.

In fact, wine is a vast subject, as I soon began to learn. Even if you confine your interest to France, or to one region in France – Bordeaux, Burgundy, the Rhône, Alsace, the Loire – there are books and books to be written on it without covering all the ground or necessarily getting it right. More is involved in the enjoyment of wine than the taste. There is also snobbery and avarice – the pleasure of the hoarder and the bargain-seeker. At the time I started writing my column, the best French wines were becoming too expensive for English pockets, shrunk by the growing indolence, incompetence and indiscipline of our island race, but excellent new wines, much cheaper and almost as good, were beginning to make their appearance from all over the world: Australia, New Zealand, South Africa, California, Chile, as well as wonderfully cheap 'dumped' wine from behind the Iron Curtain; traditional wine-making countries like Spain and Italy were making giant strides to improve their products. One of my best personal discoveries was of a brilliant wine from the Lebanon, Château

Musar, made by the indomitable Serge Hochar under conditions
that would win him the DSO with every harvest if he were carrying weapons rather than grapes across the Bekaa Valley.

Wine trips took me all over Europe, three times to Australia and
once to the Cape in time that had to be fitted in between other
journalistic engagements. Some of the most enjoyable were to the
Douro Valley, as a guest either of the Robertsons at Vargellas,
where the best of Taylor's port is made, or of the Symingtons at
Bomfin, the home of Dow. By happy coincidence, I was at Bomfin
on the night of the 1987 General Election. Tim Stanley-Clarke,
Dow's inspired publicity manager, was offering us the 1970 Dow
that evening, but as the results of the election started to come
through he decided to switch to the 1963 and sent down to the village for musicians to enliven the party. The guests became an *ad
hoc* skiffle group, with me using the two bottles which had held
the Dow '63 to clink together as harmoniously as might be. This
worked very well until the news came through of Shirley
Williams's defeat. In my joy and excitement I banged the two
bottles together and both broke, spilling twenty-four years-worth
of slimy blood-coloured dregs over my trousers and the white carpet. My trousers were easily thrown away, but I believe the stain
on the carpet has never been completely removed. It remains as a
poignant memorial to that glorious occasion in British political
history.

My second Australian visit was to Sydney, to act as a super-
numerary wine judge in the January 1988 Sydney Wine Show. It
opened two days after the Australia Day bicentenary celebrations,
which I had celebrated with a mammoth Australian wine tasting
at Lords. Everyone had a hangover. Chairman of judges was Len
Evans, a magnificent giant on the international wine scene, as
witty and as warmhearted and as generous as any man on earth.

My third visit was to launch the Penfold Grange 1983, the flag-
ship of Australian reds which, although made from the Shiraz
grape, is better in its best years than any Hermitage I have ever
tasted, and comparable only, perhaps, to a Cheval Blanc 1947 or a
Latour 1928.

I have tasted the Latour only once, staying at Chateau Latour
with the Alan Hares when Alan was appointed manager of the
Pearson family interest. My first sublime experience in wine was
staying with George Clive in Herefordshire when he produced a

bottle of Cheval Blanc 1966. I have tasted that wine quite often since then, and while finding it excellent, have never had quite the same experience. In any case, it paled into insignificance beside my first encounter with the Cheval Blanc 1947, which was at a dinner given by Mark Birley in Mark's Club for the eightieth birthday of my cousin Harry Waugh, the great claret man, formerly of Harvey's. At least we have decided we are cousins. No formal link has been established. That experienced convinced me for once and all that the very best wine merits all the pseudish and far-fetched hyperbole for which the wine-writer's trade is notorious. My second encounter with the Cheval Blanc 1947 was when Naim Attallah discovered some bottles of it in his cellars, and gave me one for a Christmas present. That confirmed me in the certainty that there *is* a pot of gold at the end of the rainbow. The only real question is how much time one should spend searching for it.

Australian wines could probably have swept the world – certainly the United Kingdom – if only they could have kept their prices down for a year or two. Among the white wines, their chardonnays are incomparable and their form of riesling is richer and naturally fruitier than anything obtainable in the same price bracket from Germany or Alsace. Among the reds, their shiraz (*semble* syrah) is incomparable and their cabernet sauvignon, although more problematic, is capable of great things when blended with shiraz or merlot or malbec – and even, occasionally, on its own. Their problem was to overcome the snobbery of the traditional wine drinker, who will always return to France until Australian wines have the same cachet. All fashions in Britain start with the relatively impecunious young intelligentsia. It was they who made Chelsea smart before it became expensive, then Islington and Notting Hill, now Fulham and Hammersmith and Battersea. If Australia could have established itself in their drinking pattern before becoming expensive, there would have been no looking back. Unfortunately, a combination of high interest rates, greedy growers and a silly tax system levied at point of production rather than point of sale combined to prevent Australia conquering the world, at any rate for a year or two.

My only disappointment in the first Australian experience was that although my hostess, Senator Amanda Vanstone arranged a great kangaroo banquet for me in Adelaide, she was unable – in fact refused to try – to produce a koala for me to eat. I don't think I want to try a dingo or a wombat, although a platypus might be more interesting, I never saw one and rather doubt whether they exist.

CHAPTER
SIXTEEN

Doughty Street 1976-

Towards the end of 1975 I had been writing my *New Statesman* column for two and a half years – at first fortnightly, in tandem with Francis Hope, a brilliantly clever Oxford contemporary, then, after he was killed in 1974 in the Turkish Airlines disaster outside Paris, weekly. I began to feel my position on the *New Statesman* was getting a little shaky as I became less and less sympathetic to Mr Wilson's third and fourth administrations which had been elected on a promise of abject surrender to the unions. My hatred of socialism, like some facial wart which can be concealed by make-up for only a time, was beginning to show, and this was bound to create friction eventually.

At about this time Harold Creighton sold the *Spectator* to Henry Keswick who had been with me at Dix's school a quarter of a century earlier, where we had been in the Woodpeckers' patrol of Trappes-Lomax's scout troop together. I had seen him once or twice after Oxford, usually with a falcon perched on his wrist and looking rather lost, but in the meantime he had gone off to join the family firm of Jardine Matheson in Hong Kong, made several million pounds and come back to England wondering what to do with himself.

Henry, who was always lampooned by *Private Eye* as 'Fatty' Keswick and credited with an insatiable appetite for Scotch eggs, appointed Alexander Chancellor as his editor. It was an inspired choice. Alexander, a collateral descendant of Richard Surtees, the great sporting novelist, had been working for Reuters, where he was correspondent in Rome for many years, and was almost unknown in Fleet Street at that time. I knew him slightly through the Somerset connection – his brother John had married the daughter of our Lord Lieutenant – but chiefly through Rome where he was a great friend of my sister Margaret. He lifted the *Spectator* from the really rather dim and dingy depths to which it seemed to me it had sunk under Creighton to make it into something original and unexpected on the scene of 1976. Although a Labour voter – I suppose out of some vague concern for the lower classes, and dislike of the pompous rich – he was uncontaminated by any connection with the Labour *apparat*, and without any affectation or side in his nature.

When he asked me to move my *New Statesman* column called 'First Person' to the *Spectator* I accepted with some alacrity. I started back with the *Spectator* on 1 January 1976, my *New Statesman* column renamed 'Another Voice', in uninterrupted continuation.

* * * *

I landed Chancellor in two libel scrapes of interest. The more serious libel case dragged on for two years, the plaintiff being staked by the *Daily Mirror*.

John Pilger first came to my attention when I was hired to present a three-part television series by Central Television called the *Class Waugh*, or something of the sort. The reason they hired me, it transpired, was to balance a similar three-programme series by that veteran left-winger, John Pilger. Both series were accompanied by announcements that they represented only the presenter's views.

In 1974 my bullet wounds from Cyprus started giving trouble again. An abscess formed deep inside my chest, in the collapsed cavity where a lung had been removed, and became what is called a chronic empyema. But it was not properly diagnosed until 1976, when I spent four weeks in hospital undergoing surgery. This visit to Westminster Hospital where, over the years, I became a regular part of the landscape, was one of the pleasantest experiences of my life, attended by beautiful, smiling nurses, deft and self-effacing surgeons and a ward sister I still dream about. It was extraordinary how the place deteriorated in the next five years. However, returning to the *Eye* in October 1976, I explained my absence:

> The crisis resulted from my foolish and intemperate laughter at one of Pilger's programmes on television, described by the grotesque Philip Norman in *The Sunday Times* as 'three hard news reports on world affairs'. Something about the bottomless stupidity and deviousness of Pilger's face had me in stitches even before IBA's extraordinary announcement at the end, that the views expressed had been Mr Pilger's own.
>
> This idea, that Pilger himself thought up all those *kindergarten* left-wing opinions and attitudes, had me in such paroxysms as might easily have been mistaken for the last stages of rabies. It was at this stage that someone wisely telephoned for an ambulance.

My next visit to hospital, in June 1977, was uncelebrated in the *Eye*, but I observe that after this I made a habit of explaining hospital visits as having been occasioned by excessive indulgence of this sort – usually laughing at enemies or people who were suing me.

The plaint of Pilger *v.* Waugh, Chancellor and the *Spectator* was eventually withdrawn, with both sides paying their own costs, on the basis of an agreed statement and an undertaking which originally read, as demanded by Pilger:

> Each of your three clients undertake not to refer to Mr Pilger directly or indirectly (save for the statement above-mentioned) in connection with the 'Sunee' story and it is clearly understood between the parties that this undertaking is to be honoured in the spirit as well as in the letter.

After objections, this undertaking was amended as follows:

> Mr Waugh, Mr Chancellor and the *Spectator* undertake not to libel Mr Pilger in any subsequent references to the 'Sunee' story – this undertaking to be honoured both in the spirit and in the letter.

So far as this undertaking has any weight – since libel is already recoverable in law – I think it must mean that I undertook not to mock him in any account I gave of my own version of events. It is this undertaking which has prevented my writing to correct the various versions he has given. But if I am not to mock him, I must keep it very short.

John Pilger wished to write a story exposing the exploitation of child labour in Thailand. This abuse is rampant throughout South East Asia, most of the Far East, Africa, and, for all I know, South America. However, he chose Thailand as his target. For this purpose he arranged to 'buy' a five-year-old girl called Sunee in Bangkok, and then wrote in the *Daily Mirror* of 22 March 1982 an emotional account of how he had restored her to her mother, from whom she had presumably been kidnapped, in Phitsanulok province.

When I first read the story in the *Mirror* I did not initially doubt that something of the sort had occurred, although I was suspicious of Pilger's motives for choosing Thailand to blackguard in this way. By chance, I was going to Hong Kong a few days later to give a talk to the International Press Club. There I met various journalists including Derek Davies, Editor of the *Far Eastern Economic Review,* whose suspicions seemed to coincide with my own.

A month later, it emerged that Pilger had been hoaxed. The girl 'Sunee' was in fact a Bangkok schoolgirl, who had been attending her school in Bangkok for four years, and had been living there with her mother throughout this period. I wrote a piece in the *Spectator* on 12 June 1982 announcing this discovery. Pilger claimed to find words in my piece which accused him of having been party to the hoax, of having knowingly set it up himself. At the time of writing, I had no idea whether he had set it up or not, although this was plainly a matter to be investigated. In fact, he hadn't. He had merely been hoaxed. The motives of the hoaxers would appear to have been as much to please Mr Pilger and his companion, Mr Tim Bond, whom they liked, as to gain the money involved, which was small.

Initially, the editor of the *Mirror* decided that there had been no hoax, and that it was all an elaborate cover-up by the Thai government. To this day, Pilger appears to believe the hoax was an elaborate conspiracy to discredit him and his journalistic methods. I have no comment whatever to make on any of this.

*　*　*　*

Chancellor was extremely brave and robust throughout the Pilger affair, writing leaders and publishing articles every time we received more damning evidence that Pilger had, indeed, been hoaxed. On an earlier occasion, I am sorry to say, he lost his nerve. Just before the General Election of 1979 he had printed my Election Address to the voters of North Devon on behalf of the Dog Lovers' Party, and turned up in the Law Courts to hear the Master of the Rolls, Lord Denning, reverse the decision of the Lord Chief Justice, Lord Widgery, in the Divisional Court, on Jeremy Thorpe's application to have it barred. Chancellor had to go through the farce of trying to recall all copies of a magazine that had gone out a week earlier. But the experience seriously frightened him.

Then, during the Thorpe trial, I took a day off to attend the libel action of Gillard *v.* Goldsmith in which Michael Gillard, *Private Eye*'s city editor, unsuccessfully sued Sir James Goldsmith for having written to various Fleet Street editors calling him a blackmailer. I wrote an account of the trial – which was conducted, as it happens, by Mr Justice Neill, whom I believe to be some sort of uncle of Alexander's – and handed it in as my weekly *Spectator* article.

Alexander turned white and started shaking. He believed that he had had a narrow escape from being sent to prison for contempt over my election manifesto. The severity with which Lord Denning had treated my counsel, Desmond Browne, had impressed him. He was not going to risk being sued by Goldsmith.

I had been asked to drinks that evening by Sybille Bedford, a writer for whom I had great admiration and who had been sitting next to me throughout the Thorpe trial. I did not want to waste time over Alexander's pusillanimous scruples. We met in a pub in Soho and went over the piece line by line. I agreed to some changes. Still, he went on and on, saying Goldsmith was a most dangerous man, he had heard from Taki Theodorakopoulos that Goldsmith was looking for an opportunity to sue the *Spectator*. By now it was too late for me to join Mrs Bedford who, I feel sure, had prepared the most delicious canapés and opened a bottle of some wonderful German wine – the invitation was never repeated. But all the whey-faced poltroon would promise was that he would think about publishing the article, as amended.

That week, the *Spectator* arrived and there was no 'Another Voice' in it. I sent Alexander a nine-page letter of abuse, closely written in narrow lines, ending with the announcement that I was leaving the *Spectator* for three months to write my book about the Thorpe trial. If he kept paying my retainer on a sabbatical basis while I was away, I would return to *Spectator* at the end of the three months. If he didn't, I wouldn't.

I don't know whether I was right or wrong about the article, which has long since been thrown away. I reckoned to know rather more about the law of libel at that stage than he did and had written it very carefully. But of course in one sense he was absolutely right, that libel law, as taught in Gatley and even in Carter Ruck has nothing whatever to do with libel practice, where the plaintiff always wins, however absurd or feeble his case, unless he happens to be called Michael Gillard (or Michael Meacher). At any rate, Alexander agreed cheerfully enough to my terms, and said he had enjoyed my letter of abuse.

* * * *

And still Alexander remained my friend. In fact, I love him like a brother and would happily die for him. But then the horrible moment arrived and Alexander Chancellor was sacked.

Fatty Keswick decided after a very short time that he didn't really like owning the *Spectator* after all, so he sold it to a friend of his called Algy Cluff. In fact it was passed from hand to hand for the next ten years like a bad penny. Algy is a tall, very thin, heterosexual bachelor millionaire who was once an officer in the SAS. He inherited a million or so from his father, but has made many millions since, mostly by discovering oil. He drives a Rolls-Royce and dresses in the natty gents' suiting of the 1950s, but does not really look as if he belongs anywhere, except possibly in a novel by Sapper or by Denis Wheatley. Alexander, whom he had inherited from Fatty Keswick, would not let him have the slightest say in the running of the magazine, and treated him in a very lordly fashion. It was hard to see what possible joy he would get from the £100,000 or so it was losing every year.

I know the drama of Alexander's sacking only at second-hand. I was not a participant. But the generally accepted version of the story is that Alexander had hired A.N. Wilson, the novelist, as his literary editor, and then wished he hadn't. An opportunity arose to sack him when a reviewer sent in an article which praised the appalling Clive James, so Andrew (Wilson) altered it to say the opposite. The reviewer complained and Clive James complained, so Alexander was able to sack A.N. Wilson, saying this was unethical behaviour.

Next thing – or so the story goes – the sacked Andrew Wilson makes friends with Cluff and starts whispering into his ear that Chancellor is no good, Chancellor drinks too much, Chancellor is never in the office.

This was exactly what Algy wanted to hear, so he sacked Alexander, and appointed Charles Moore.

I wrote a short, bitter note in my *Private Eye* 'Diary':

January 19, 1984

My friend Alexander Chancellor telephones that he has given up editing the *Spectator* after a difference of opinion with the magazine's exciting young proprietor, Archy Clough or 'Cluff'. When I ask my friends if I should resign, too, they all say 'Yes'.

Shit. There goes another £8000 a year.

I was in some doubt about whether honour required me to resign in sympathy. Johnny McEwen, the art critic (and younger brother of my best friend at Dix's school, David McEwen), had resigned, and so had Simon Courtauld ('Lavish MacTavish'), the business manager and deputy editor. I was Alexander's appointment and friend, and scarcely knew the new editor at all. Charles Moore was rumoured to be twenty-three years old, and a growing middle-aged mistrust of the young weighed in the balance. Alexander said I shouldn't resign, he didn't want me to resign, he wanted me *not* to resign, but I couldn't help feeling he would secretly be rather pleased if I did. Then Alexander advised Charles Moore that if he wanted me to stay he should waste no time talking about loyalty to the *Spectator* or anything like that, he should simply offer me more money. I am ashamed to say it worked.

* * * *

Despite my misgivings, there was no particular friction in my relations with Charles Moore. He turned out to be highly intelligent, and quite perceptive, although rather thin and lacking the apparent substance of such predecessors as Chancellor, Gale and Lawson. Charles was tolerant of my idiosyncrasies, but I could not help feeling he rather disapproved of me. He tolerated 'Another Voice' because, after eight years, it had become an expected part of the *Spectator* mix, but I never received the impression that he enjoyed it much. His arrival brought with it a host of young men in pin-striped suits with loud voices and double-barrelled names which I never learned. I went to Doughty Street less and less, and was seldom recognized when I did, always having to explain myself to the receptionist. On the last occasion I went to one of the *Spectator*'s summer parties – in 1989 – I was asked to dinner afterwards, but found myself sitting next to some young persons on the business and advertising side who not only did not recognize me but had no idea, when I told them who I was, that I was a journalist or a contributor to the magazine. They were perfectly polite, and we had a long discussion about their career prospects, which was the only thing that appeared to interest them. People will say this was good for my character, and a suitable punishment for thinking of myself as a fairly big fish in a small pond, but after twenty-two years of writing regular weekly articles for the magazine – with only two, shortish, intermissions – it had an unsettling effect.

Charles moved on in early 1990, having apparently grown bored with the job after six years, to reappear before very long as Deputy Editor of the *Daily Telegraph*. His place was taken by Dominic Lawson, whom I had last seen as a child of ten in Nigel's house in Hyde Park Gate. He seems an intelligent, lively, engagingly reckless sort of person. I do not know him well, but I should guess he will make an excellent editor. Although no radical, he seems to have a certain hatred of the rich. My father brought me up to believe that if one had to be bored, it was better to be bored by a rich bore than by a poor bore. My children's generation, to which Dominic belongs, seems to take the opposite view.

CHAPTER
SEVENTEEN

Beak Street 1986-

I mentioned in Chapter Fourteen how Naim Attallah approached me in January 1986 and asked me to be editor of the *Literary Review* to replace Emma Soames, who was moving to Hanover Square to edit the *Tatler*. I had first heard of *Literary Review* from my sister, Margaret, three or four years earlier, who had just discovered it and swore it was better than *Books and Bookmen*, which rather annoyed me. It had been founded only in 1979 by Anne Smith, the Edinburgh academic, as a counterblast to the academic approach to literary criticism. She made it respectable. The next editor, Gillian Greenwood (from the *Books and Bookmen* stable, as it happened), made it lively. The third, Emma Soames, made it smart. The idea was, I think, that I should make it successful, but sadly enough, five years later, it continues to lose money hand over fist. Sales have doubled to the mighty figure of 10,500 a month, but advertisements are slow to come in. All hopes at present reside in a newly appointed advertising manager, the strangely named Jonathan Dewlap. Only Naim's enthusiasm has kept it going – and the devotion of its staff, contributors and subscribers.

I first met Naim when he was kind enough to employ my elder daughter, Sophia, in his publishing firm, Quartet Books. Sophia had come down from Durham University with a good degree in English, wanting to find employment in publishing. Although badly paid, it is a crowded profession. Naim makes a point of employing bright young women down from the universities, paying them even less than is normal in their first jobs. It helps, too, if they are pretty, cheerful and well born. Sophia was extremely pretty and cheerful, and if I was not noticeably well born, at least I had appeared on the *Terry Wogan Show*. They got on like a house on fire and are still friends six years later. Through Sophia I met Naim and his delightful seraglio of pretty, cheerful, well-born young women, who use him as their springboard into London life. He is happy to be so used, and the system seems to work, as Quartet, although outside the mainstream of London's dismal, introspective publishing scene, produces some excellent books.

On first impression, Naim appears as a bubbling pixie, full of strange and wild enthusiasms. Articulate and outgoing, he seldom wastes a sentence, although he speaks a lot. His favourite word is 'wonderful'. On the few occasions when things are not wonderful, he scowls and goes into an angry speech until the matter is cleared up, and then he finds something new which is wonderful to laugh about. When he is upset – and although he does not seem to mind being lampooned in *Private Eye*, he is surprisingly sensitive to signs of hostility from any other publication, and particularly upset by any display of ingratitude – he has to be comforted by sympathetic friends and pretty women. But behind the little boy façade he has a quick, shrewd mind which is never at rest, whether thinking of how to make someone happy or advance a friend, or of some commercial opportunity for one or another of his myriad enterprises. Even these are mere playthings compared to his main employment as financial director of Asprey's to which, in 1991, he added Mappin and Webb.

A Christian Palestinian from Haifa, he made his millions, it is thought, by playing the exchange rates, and invested them shrewdly – in, among other things, the bricks and mortar of his Poland Street headquarters, and 51 Beak Street, where *Literary Review*'s offices are situated, as well as the group design department, the Academy Club, the group's accountant and various other enterprises. Nobody looking for a small literary magazine to edit could have hoped for a pleasanter office.

There I found Kathy O'Shaughnessy who had served as Deputy Editor under two previous editors and was slightly miffed to have been passed over for the editorship a second time, attributing it perhaps accurately to the fact that she was not nobly born and did not have grand connections. I had admired her from afar for several years and was overjoyed to be working in such close proximity. She greeted me with all the warmth of her generous nature, and did not make me feel an intruder at all as she took me over the most elementary first steps in magazine production. She had rather strict views on things like politics and feminism, the greatest contempt for those who relied on parental help or influence, and was in many ways a model of young womanhood, but was too intelligent and too nice, as well as having too much sense of humour to let any of these interfere with the normal enjoyment of life. Unfortunately, the missed promotion and the lack of prospects had blighted her enjoyment of the job, and I was heartbroken when, after four months, she allowed herself to be lured away by Emma into a better paid but scarcely more worthwhile job in Hanover Square, as literary editor of *Vogue*. Many of my friends assumed she had left because she hated me, but I do not think that was the reason.

Next came Kate Kellaway, straight from running the English department of a school for 1200 black children in Harare. By then we had been joined by Grub Smith, a boxer from Cambridge who turned out to be the grandson of the GP in Dulverton who had delivered me as a baby and, indeed, circumcised me with great cruelty three years later. A Downside boy, with down-to-earth views and a sense of humour which is best described as Rabelaisian, Grub was a strange part of the mix, but a successful one. I knew that Kate, who, like Kathy, had won a brilliant First at Oxford, was the right person for the job when, in her first issue of the magazine, she printed a review by David Profumo of a book called 'The Dictionary of Disgusting Facts'. It was so disgusting that I felt my few remaining hairs stand on end, but Kate rocked with laughter and hero-worshipped Profumo as a result. She is a person of limitless warmth, generosity and sense of fun, as well as of high intelligence and with a fatal organizing ability which, unless she is careful, will always keep her in dull jobs. Unfortunately, her life's ambition was to work for the *Observer* and when a job came up she was off, remaining only as our esteemed theatre reviewer, like a lingering fragrance.

Next came Laura Cumming, also from Oxford, with valuable experience in the publishing world which brought a host of bright, left-wing reviewers into the magazine. Laura, a blonde bombshell in every sense, stayed two and a half years, and effectively shaped the *Literary Review* as it eventually emerged under my editorship. She invented the "Oppression" section, into which we tended to dump any books dealing with South Africa, South America, domestic politics, religion, marriage, education. A very strong character, given, like Grub, to occasional alarming mood-swings, she endowed the magazine with all the intense loyalty of her passionate nature, and while she was not holding secret meetings to aid the Polisario rebels in Morocco, made it her entire life.

It was during Laura's tenure that Robert Posner arrived to take over the business management of the magazine, and a whole new dimension of zaniness descended upon the magazine. Robert had spent many years – we were never quite sure how many – as a fish farmer on an Israeli kibbutz and another long spell – we were not sure how long – in Afghanistan, no doubt studying the flora and fauna, between selling computers for Canon. When we met him, he was living in a squat and working as a motorbike delivery boy. He was the obvious man to rescue the subscription, advertising and office management of *Literary Review*, all of which he did (except, perhaps, the advertising) with a breath-taking panache.

Since we could offer him little in the way of money, we decided to award him an honorary doctorate, and it was as Dr Posner that he sat over his humming computer. Later, when we founded the Academy Club in the basement, he became a key figure in that. Appointed Secretary, he became Captain Posner, as I felt strongly that all Club secretaries should have a military title, and anything above the rank of Captain seemed rather to be chancing our luck. I liked to think that at weekends he stood in Oxford Street in a tall hat and frock-coat, offering to perform the three-card trick for the edification of tourists and visitors to London. In that role, he would have been known as Professor Posner. On his 40th birthday, the Academy Committee – myself, Victoria Glendinning, Attallah, Cumming and Sophia Sackville-West – promoted him to Major.

After Laura had gone to seek her fortune as Literary Editor of *Listener*, Lola Bubbosh eventually emerged; still Deputy Editor at the time of going to press.

She had arrived from Washington as an intern, or unpaid slave. We had several of these, among whom Elizabeth Daniels, from Tennessee shone out in glory. There is a quality of benevolence and simple goodness among some young American women which their counterparts in the Old World seem to have lost. Lola, a Catholic of Armenian extraction, developed a devotion to the magazine which became almost alarming in its intensity. At other times, when nothing challenges her beloved chick, she is the gentlest, kindest person imaginable, radiating a sweetness and joy which spread throughout the entire building. If the magazine had an essential quality of niceness, as against the nastiness which people claimed to perceive in *Private Eye*, it came from her. By nature left-wing (like Laura) and vegetarian by adoption, reluctant to say a bad word for anyone, she shows her claws only when she sees the magazine threatened.

*   *   *   *

My move to *Literary Review* was overshadowed by the tragedy of my sister Margaret's death, run over by a car in north London when visiting an art gallery with some friends on 28 January 1986. I had hoped she would be a bulwark of support on the magazine – in fact, she would have made a better editor. It was a desolate moment in my life. A speech I was to have made two evenings later at a dinner of the Folio Society was read for me by Patrick Marnham who, by coincidence, was to have dined with me and Meg the night after her death. A huge party, planned by Naim to say farewell to Emma Soames as editor and welcome me, had to be postponed.

It was held some weeks later in the Travellers' Club, Pall Mall, the first of many parties Naim gave for *Literary Review*. They included the *Review*'s 10th birthday party, a very grand affair in the Reform Club. The library at the Reform Club has often struck me as one of the loveliest rooms in London, and certainly one of the best to give a party in. If only the members were less dim, it would be a wonderful club to join.

I had to leave for China next day and was away for a full month, thereby missing the later developments. Apparently one of our guests – the daughter, as it happened, of a great friend – was caught short and could not find a ladies' lavatory, so she availed herself of the gentlemen's, where a member was so shocked to find her that he reported the matter to the committee. There are other, more lurid versions of the same story, but that is the one which seems most likely. At any rate, I returned from a month abroad to find a letter banning me and Naim from ever giving another party in the Reform Club, with no reasons given. I do not suppose I would ever have had occasion to give another party in the Reform Club (although Naim might well have wanted to), but it was the old problem of holding a cat by the tail. Suddenly, it seemed an appalling shame that such a beautiful building designed by Sir Charles Barry should be controlled by such bores.

Every club, I suppose, has its quota of bores and pompous oafs. It is only when they manage to take it over that the dimness really sets in, becoming eventually its dominant characteristic. I played with the idea of mounting a massive ten-year campaign, using initially the very few acquaintances I had among the members, to topple the committee, fill the club with Our Sort of People and establish unisex lavatories, such as you have in nearly all private homes. But then I decided there were too many things to do in life, and I simply did not have the time to do them all. Perhaps this decision was the first real acknowledgement of middle age. I simply did not have the energy to declare another great war and wage it to the bitter end.

Instead, we decided to found a much smaller club of our own, a club where God willing, there would be no pompous bores, or where, at least, they would never gain the upper hand. The actual inspiration for the Academy Club, or more properly the Academy, now a thriving concern in the basement of 51 Beak Street, came from a weekend at Combe Florey when Victoria Glendinning and I were lamenting the old French Club, in St James's Place, to which we had both belonged. It had an informality, a friendliness and a lack of pretension which had passed by the Groucho. So Victoria and I decided to go it alone.

Naim was delighted when we told him that we had decided to use the basement of his premises in Beak Street for a private members' club for writers and their friends, to which other professionals would be admitted, even publishers and agents, provided they were Our Sort of People. In fact, we never used this expression, but it was the great unspoken thought. 'Wonderful, wonderful', said Naim, reaching for his cheque book.

The end-product is not exactly as it was conceived. In effect, it has become a smaller, slightly bohemian version of Pratt's, somewhere between an ordinary luncheon and dinner club, a Viennese café, a wine bar with spirits and a Soho drinking dive. A bevy of beautiful, out-of-work actresses comes to wait at table. The membership list is an extraordinary document, kept secret except to members. Apart from friends and relations of the committee, it is made up of many people who were on Naim's invitation list for parties, stars of stage and screen, (even a few pop stars, although the grandest ones use it seldom), with a strong preponderance of the better sort of journalists. It seems to work very well, and may well survive as a monument to my occupation of Beak Street long after *Literary Review* has disappeared. But at the moment the magazine basks in Naim's benevolence.

CHAPTER
EIGHTEEN

Combe Florey 1973-

Throughout the second half of the 1970s and into the early 1980s, I had to spend large parts of the year more or less confined to Combe Florey, with occasional day trips to London for the *Eye*, as a result of the distressing surgical condition of my chest. My surgeon at Westminster Hospital, Mr Charles Drew, who had been a junior consultant under Sir Clement Price-Thomas when Sir Clement collapsed the left side of my chest by thorocoplasty in 1959, discovered that the only treatment for the persistent empyema, which returned again and again and did not respond to antibiotics, was to insert a tube deep into an old bullet wound in the back. This drained into dressings strapped to my back with sticking plaster. My poor wife had to change the dressings and clean the wound every day. Once a week, the tube was shortened by half an inch until, after about seven weeks, it could be thrown away, the wound would heal and I could resume normal life until the next infection set in. If the original wounds were disfiguring, they became quite terrifying under this treatment, and I hid myself away like a Monster of Glamis.

In addition to caring for a sick husband, Teresa had to look after four children and a large house, entertain guests and run a huge garden which had, in itself, occupied my mother full time. In 1975 she added to these burdens by enrolling at Exeter University for a degree course in French and Italian literature, which involved driving the hour's journey into Exeter four or five times a week, and making up the time, somehow, to read her books, absorb the commentaries and write her essays.

At the end of the day, she won a First Class Honours degree and basked in the admiration of the west country, being the first person in my family or hers to achieve such a distinction. Thereafter she set herself to translate books from the French and Italian for various publishers before acknowledging her fate to be a novelist, publishing her first novel, *Painting Water*, in 1983.

My attitude to her novels was not, I hope, patronizing, but it might have been a trifle world-weary. I had been through all the same hopes, joys, disappointments twenty-two years earlier; it was twelve years since I had published my fifth novel and decided to call it a day. Reliving the same experiences was rather like starting a second family at the age of fifty: back to all the monthly nurses, the buckets of Milton, the smell of nappies . . . .

But as novel followed novel, she began to build up a steadily growing army of devoted followers. The publishers never increased their print order, but the books always sold out. *Painting Water*, about the wife of an estate agent in Surrey, was followed in 1985 by *Waterloo Waterloo*, about a retired major in Devon; next came *Intolerable Burden* (1987) about a social worker in London, followed by *Song at Twilight* (1989) about a retired schoolteacher in Somerset. They are quite unlike any other novels being written; although irritating, class-conscious reviewers of the D.J. Taylor school often compare her to Barbara Pym, I imagine this is entirely on class grounds, as there is not the smallest resemblance in the writing. Other reviewers have compared her to Proust, which is scarcely more accurate, as it seems to me, if more flattering. However, my pose as the senior, world-weary novelist of the team is beginning to wear a little thin. As I write this, she is engaged on her fifth novel, which will bring her score up to my own. Evidently, it is time for me to write another.

* * * *

In 1980, in addition to all the medical problems, I was beginning to work quite hard with four children being educated. I had regular columns in *Spectator, Standard, Private Eye, British Medicine* and a monthly long review in *Books and Bookmen*. In the course of the year, I swapped the *Standard* for the *Mail*, as already mentioned, and, with the death of Philip Dossé, moved my monthly review to the *Sunday Telegraph*, where Nicholas Bagnall was literary editor. He seemed to delight in sending me the most boring books he had received, but there was method in this. I have noticed that the most boring books often produce the best reviews. It may be harder to be convincingly enthusiastic about a book than it is to have fun kicking it around a bit, but negative reviews become boring after a time. Some of the best reviews are where you are given a really dull subject and then proceed to make jokes about it.

In 1981, John Thompson, who had become Editor of the *Sunday Telegraph*, offered me a weekly column on the newspaper's leader page. He had been Deputy Editor of the *Spectator* under Nigel Lawson, and was an old friend, but I was a little bit nervous of taking too much money from the *Telegraph* at that stage. Its Editor-in-Chief, Lord Hartwell (as Michael Berry had become) was an unknown quantity, not only after my questionable behaviour over the U Thant affair between my father and Lady Pamela, but also because I had fallen into the habit from time to time of describing his wife in the *Private Eye* 'Diary' as sporting a famous Gunner moustache and being called Lady Fartwell. Moreover John, although a good man and a friend, had not played a particularly heroic role over my sacking from the *Spectator* in January 1970 when – at any rate according to Lawson in court – he had supported this bestial behaviour on the part of his editor. So it seemed unwise to put too many eggs in that particular basket, and I agreed to write a column only fortnightly.

In fact this soon emerged as a general policy, never to have too many eggs in one basket, nor to receive more money from any one employer than I could afford to lose, or easily replace. It was not only a question of survival in a hard world – freelance contributors can be sacked at a moment's notice, and have no rights beyond what they can secure for themselves – it was also a question of keeping editors in their place. Like so many human beings, they like exercising power, and it is the business of writers to frustrate them, or newspapers would read as if they were written entirely by the same person.

John Thompson was the least power-hungry editor imaginable, and my column stayed at the same place, at the top of the leader page, all the time he was there. When the Berry family sold the newspapers to Conrad Black, and he appointed Peregrine Worsthorne as editor, things did not go quite so smoothly. Perry is not, of course, a vain man, but I had the impression that he rather resented the expression of opinions other than his own on the page which now belonged to him. His first action on becoming editor was to announce that he was moving the column off the leader page. I resigned. Perry would probably not have minded in the least to lose me, but other counsels prevailed, and I agreed to write a weekly column subject to an understanding that any attempt to move it to another page would constitute dismissal by terms of the agreement. What in fact had happened was that his dear wife, Claudie, had told him that if he lost my column, she was going to cancel the *Sunday Telegraph.*

Next he put his own column on top of mine, striding the entire page as a signed leader like some sort of proclamation from an occupying general. After a struggle, I let him get away with this, suspecting that I would have done exactly the same if I had been in his place. He spent the rest of his editorship trying to demote the column into a box at the bottom of the page, precipitating an instant resignation every time. Then some of his friends thought of a new joke to play on him. Whenever he went away for the weekend and, in an agony of suspense, watched people reading the *Sunday Telegraph* at breakfast, the joke was to read it in absolute silence and then burst out: 'I say, Waugh's got rather a point here, don't you think, Perry?' or 'Ho! ho! ho! A very good joke by Waugh here, I must say.'

*   *   *   *

In 1982 I had bought a large, four-bedroomed flat in Hammersmith, partly to give us both a *pied-à-terre* in London when life in the country became too excruciatingly boring, but chiefly as a place for the children to live as, one by one, they finished their education.

The investment in the London flat paid off, as it was from that flat that my elder daughter, Sophia, found herself a husband, Julian Watson, an admiral's son who was then employed in publishing. They were married at Combe Florey on 28 June 1986 at prodigious expense, but seem to have lived happily ever since. I had to abandon the writing of this chapter for a day to visit my first grandchild, Constance Watson, born on 24 July 1990. She is a sublimely beautiful child. Perhaps my last faltering steps will be taken hand-in-hand with my granddaughter, towards the kissing gate at Combe Florey, to inspect some rare and mysterious butterfly, or to put a daisy chain on her great-grandparents' graves....

*   *   *   *

In 1986 I also decided it was time to leave the *Daily Mail* after five years. My old friend Gordon Mackenzie had retired from the literary editorship and John Bryant had just left the newspaper, the books page had been moved from its position on page seven facing the leader page to the back regions, David English had been knighted and there was a sour, Thatcherite, down-market smell emanating from its pages.

I thought of moving my review column to the *Telegraph*, but at the last minute switched to the new *Independent* instead. This rather annoyed Max Hastings, who had become editor of the *Telegraph*. One result of this was that when Michael Wharton, who had been writing the Peter Simple column for twenty-six years and was now approaching his seventies, announced that he wished to write less often, nobody approached me to fill the gap – in fact I only learned the job was going when told that Christopher Booker had got it.

This might have seemed a minor set-back to my Life Plan which was quite simple. At Combe Florey, there are nine cellars stretching underneath the whole of the house except the old kitchen, now the games room, and the wing where my mother lived, now inhabited by my secretary, Amanda Cameron, and her husband. Of those nine cellars, one is occupied by the central heating plant and is unsuitable for storing wine, and another is too damp. My Plan was to go on working flat out until all seven remaining cellars were full of wine, and then retire from the tumult and strife of London to Combe Florey to write drivelling novels which nobody wanted to read, and drink it all.

The thirty-five acres around the house should provide enough food for the simple tastes of a poor literary man, but my tastes in this respect have never been very simple, and it never occurred to me to doubt that I could fill out the vegetable soups and course-ground wholemeal bread with rare sauces supplied by writing the Peter Simple column in the *Daily Telegraph*, which would also pay for the Poll Tax, electricity bills, the running of a motor car and other necessary adjuncts to the simple, inebriate life. If it seems presumptuous to have supposed that I could inherit the Peter Simple column, I knew that the great Michael Wharton himself had announced to our shared friend, Richard West, that he had left a letter, to be opened on his death, bequeathing me the column and all its inhabitants, with their lands and flocks, electronic gadgets and their Boggs Oafmobile motor cars. I was ready to take up the burden whenever necessary. My only anxiety was whether I was sufficiently mellow for the task. I would look at myself anxiously in the mirror: was I ripe enough yet? Was I sufficiently decayed?

Meanwhile, I had to watch Booker grimacing and gibbering on the sacred ground. He wrote under the name of Peter Simple II, alternating with Wharton as Peter Simple. I cannot believe I was alone in finding his contributions an acute embarrassment: now shrill and hysterically indignant, like some redbrick creature of the 1970s complaining about South Africa, Vietnam and student grants in a long, cacophonous wail, now painfully maudlin and twee, writing about cricket or the flora and fauna of the countryside in pious, goody-goody Cambridge tones.

But I did not see how I could be expected to do anything about it. I was hopelessly busy, writing in the *Spectator, Independent* and *Sunday Telegraph* weekly, editing *Literary Review* on three days of the week, running the *Spectator* Wine Club and preparing to open the Beak Street Academy. On top of this, Booker was a friend of sorts, although I had deeply offended his wife by a joke in the *Spectator* about his polygamistic tendencies – the offence was made worse by failing to recognize her at a party. Perhaps it was some sort of troubadour's revenge which explains the next episode, although I put it down myself to ordinary battiness.

On my return from China at the end of May 1989, I had filled only three and a half of my seven cellars. I wrote an affable account in the *Spectator* of what I had seen, concluding with the observation that it was hard to take the student demonstrations too seriously, because they were obviously taking place, at that stage, with official blessing. When we were there all the students wore goody-goody faces and were being shepherded along by smiling policemen. Then, a week later, came the massacre of Tienanmen Square, which I had visited weeks earlier to pull faces at the wax effigy of Mao Tse-Tung, posing as his corpse, in the mausoleum devoted to him. Obviously, the mood changed later, or possibly the balance of power in the Politburo.

Then, on 6 June 1989, Booker wrote a piece in the *Daily Telegraph* called '**An End To Waugh**'.

> ... Mr Waugh admitted that he had arrived in China 'as a tourist on holiday, determined not to interest myself in politics, even less to try to understand the Chinese character'. But fortunately the 'demonstrators' were only 'a minor distraction, their dislocating effect much exaggerated by the wishful thinking of the world's press'.
>
> 'The only serious inconvenience they caused,' Mr Waugh reports, 'was to one member of our group – a marquess of recent inheritance' who was bitten by a dog and was then 'denied access to anti-rabies serum for several hours by students demonstrating outside the hospital'.
>
> It is just as well that Mr Waugh did not prolong his holiday until last weekend, or these tiresome people who were clogging the streets with 'official approval' might have caused his distinguished party even more 'serious inconvenience' as they tried to get back to their hotel for dinner after an agreeable day's sightseeing. ... At least in this respect the current *Spectator* redeems itself with a trenchant report by Mr William Shawcross on our treatment of the Vietnamese refugees, which displays all the journalistic and human qualities so signally lacking in his fellow-contributor Mr Waugh.

PETER SIMPLE II

I do not think I am particularly thin-skinned, but this high-minded lecture struck me as an unmistakable declaration of war. All hesitations about whether or not I was sufficiently decayed were forgotten, the Life Plan was scrapped. On that day I started on a necessarily oblique and tortuous, sometimes crablike campaign to take over the column, the details of which I do not propose to reveal. By the end of the year, six months later, it had all been settled. On Monday, 7 May 1990 I wrote my first piece under Peter Simple's old banner: Way of the World.

On 17 November 1989, I celebrated my fiftieth birthday. Others shrink from that particular milestone, but I felt immensely proud to have got there, for some reason or other. Alexander Chancellor, who celebrated his own fiftieth birthday a few weeks later, seemed to have the same feelings about it, so we gave a joint party at the Polish Hearth, in Hyde Park Gate between the two dates. Alexander hired a wonderful 22-piece 1930s dance band, but I found myself too fat to dance.

On the day itself, Teresa planned a huge dinner party at Combe Florey. That part of it she could not keep secret, since it involved sitting twenty-nine people down to table, getting out all the silver, hiring attendants, etc. She told me that it was for neighbours and local people, and I wondered anxiously who on earth she could have asked. It turned out that she had asked all the people whom she judged I liked most in the world, from all over the country and from foreign parts, and arranged to put them all up either in the house (which is almost infinitely expandable) or in the neighbourhood. As the guests arrived one by one or two by two, I grew happier and happier.

I could never remember a happier evening, nor one where Combe Florey looked more resplendent. Perhaps the only moral to be learned from this drawn-out narrative, and the only real wisdom I have acquired in fifty years of living, is the banal, frequently-made point that happiness requires no more than good food, good wine, laughter and the presence of friends. I shall not embarrass people by describing the food. The wine, which was excellent, was one of Avery's wonderful old *renommés* burgundies, a Vosne Romanée Les Suchots 1976 posing as something else. One could hope for no more. Even friends may not be altogether necessary. The problem with friends is that once one has assembled them, one is not quite sure what to do with them next. We ended the night singing in a maudlin fashion around the piano, music by the two Alexanders, Waugh and Chancellor. Alexandra Ward booked Alan Watkins to sing 'Abide with Me' at her elderly mother's funeral, whenever that event should occur. Nine months later, my son Alexander announced his engagement to Eliza Chancellor, beautiful, clever, warm-natured elder daughter of our friends Suzy and Alexander. For the moment, at any rate, the cup of happiness seemed to be full.

* * * *

My father described Combe Florey as 'a plain, square house on a hill' in a letter to my mother-in-law in 1961. In fact it is a large, extremely grand and handsome house, not square at all, finished in red sandstone in the 1740s, with an imposing great portico on an elevated perron, the doorway being noted (like the window surrounds) for Gibb rustications. The only things which spoiled it were some heavy plate-glass lattice windows put in by the previous owners at the turn of the century. Evelyn Waugh replaced two of these with their original thick-timbered sash windows, but then ran out of money and enthusiasm. My mother replaced another two when she moved into the wing, which had previously been derelict. We replaced another two and thus completed all the twelve windows on the east elevation at a moment when I found I had some money to spare.

This leaves nine lattice windows on the south elevation and another four on the west. I hope to replace them all with the money from the publisher's advance on delivery of the manuscript of this autobiography. When I say 'I hope' the order has already been given, and the windows are being made as I write. I merely hope that the publisher does not go bankrupt, or rat on the deal, so that I cannot pay for them. Whether I can or can't, they should be in place before the year is out.

They will be my monument. Having written five novels which give me little or no pleasure to re-read, ten other books of varying degrees of topicality – the only one which I would claim as my masterpiece, the second volume of *Eye* Diaries with illustrations by William Rushton, will so far fail Connolly's thirty-year test as to be incomprehensible within a decade – and millions of words of ephemeral journalism, I am happy to have restored the windows of a minor country house to their former glory. There they will remain until the house is burned down, or taken over by the local authority as a hostel for unmarried mothers, who will no doubt wish to restore plate glass throughout.

Which brings me to the end of my labours. Now I have written it down, I can forget it all again, and go back to eating. I have lost 10½ pounds, at a cost of considerably over £100 a pound. Will this do?

Shrubland Hall,
Suffolk.
27 July, 1990.

INDEX